THE FIERY BROOK

THE FIERY BROOK:
Selected Writings

LUDWIG FEUERBACH

Translated and introduced
by Zawar Hanfi

VERSO
London • New York

Published by Verso 2012
© Verso 2012
First published in English by Anchor Books 1972
Translation and introduction © Zawar Hanfi 1972

3 5 7 9 10 8 6 4 2

Verso
UK: 6 Meard Street, London W1F 0EG
US: 20 Jay Street, Suite 1010, Brooklyn, NY 11201
www.versobooks.com

Verso is the imprint of New Left Books

ISBN-13: 978-1-78168-021-6

British Library Cataloguing in Publication Data
A catalogue record for this book is available from the British Library

Library of Congress Cataloging-in-Publication Data
A catalog record for this book is available from the Library of Congress

Printed in the US by Maple Vail

Contents

Preface

With the exception of the Introduction to the *Essence of Christianity*, the Preface to its second edition, and the *Principles of the Philosophy of the Future*, all other writings of Feuerbach included in this volume are first translations. The Introduction and the Preface to the second edition of the *Essence of Christianity* have been available in English since 1854 in the excellent translation by George Eliot (Mary Ann Evans). In retranslating them, I have been led by a desire to achieve an overall uniformity of style and terminology, rather than by any false hope of improving upon the inimitable prose of George Eliot. In the case of the *Principles of the Philosophy of the Future*, a new translation can be more easily justified. Manfred Vogel's translation, otherwise quite readable, contains some serious mistranslations. To take one example: By losing sight of the anti-idealist context of Feuerbach's philosophy and by sticking literally to the German expression *sich entleiben* (literally, to commit suicide), Vogel gives the following rendering: "Just as when a man commits suicide he negates the body, this rational limit of subjectivity, so when he lapses into fantastic and transcendental practice he associates himself with embodied divine and ghostly appearances; namely, he negates in practice the difference between imagination and perception." Feuerbach is referring to the neo-Platonic contempt of the body and the senses that carry for the neo-Platonic sage the imperative to detach himself from the body and to regard all corporeality as negative. The German *sich entleiben* here does not have the sense of "committing suicide," but of "decorporealizing oneself." A more appropriate rendering would be as follows: "Just as by decorporealizing himself or by negating the body—the rational limit of subjectivity—man lapses into a fantastic and transcendent practice, surrounding himself with corporealized appearances of spirits and gods, that is, practically eliminating the distinction between imagination and sense perception. . . ."

The Introduction to the volume consists of three sections. In the first section, I have briefly discussed the relevance of Feuerbach to contemporary thought and society. The second section is devoted to an exposition of Feuerbach's philosophy. Its main themes and motives are developed through a discussion of the selected texts in their order of succession. This unfortunately involves some repetition, for which I can only request the indulgence of the reader. In the third section, I have discussed the relationship between Feuerbach and Marx, which, I believe, is demanded by the logic of the historical significance of Feuerbach's philosophy.

I am grateful for the help which Dr. David Roberts so generously extended in reading parts of the manuscript. Dr. John Playford and John Love let themselves be used most amicably as "guinea pigs." I am indebted to both of them for their creative listening. I am thankful to Miss Bronwyn Newbold for typing the manuscript.

Melbourne
November 1971   Zawar Hanfi

THE FIERY BROOK
Selected Writings of Ludwig Feuerbach

Introduction

I FEUERBACH TODAY

Feuerbach's philosophy reached the pinnacle of its fame and historical significance in the forties of the nineteenth century and declined sharply in the same decade. He was one of the earliest of those nineteenth-century thinkers who turned their back on the great metaphysical tradition of the West. Although dwarfed by the towering figures of Kierkegaard, Marx, and Nietzsche, Feuerbach in his own modest way is one of the founders of contemporary philosophical sensibility. The basic motives and elements of his thought—his opposition to idealism, metaphysics, philosophical system building, his humanism and naturalism —have been absorbed by the pathos of contemporary European philosophy. At one time experienced as explosive and electrifying, these elements and motives seem to have lost their thrust. Feuerbach's thought, seen from the vantage point of today, contains only "embryos capable of development."[1]

Feuerbach's philosophy has been discussed almost exclusively within the context of the development of historical materialism; it has been read only as a chapter in the book called *Karl Marx*. The Feuerbachian phase of Marx had become an accepted fact long before the publication of Marx's early works in 1927 and 1932. Marx in his—and

2 THE FIERY BROOK

Engels'—*Holy Family* had celebrated Feuerbach as one in whom "the destructive criticism in Germany" had gone over "to a perception of real man" and as one who had "unveiled real secrets."[2] Contrasting with this acclamation, there came, in the *Theses on Feuerbach,* Marx's rejection of Feuerbachian materialism as contemplative. It was natural to see his Feuerbachian period in the time that intervened between Marx's differing assessments. This assumption was reinforced by the following two passages from Engels' *Ludwig Feuerbach and the End of Classical German Philosophy:* "Then came Feuerbach's *Essence of Christianity.* With one blow it pulverized the contradiction, in that without circumlocution it placed materialism on the throne again. . . . The spell was broken; the system [of Hegel] was exploded and cast aside. . . . One must himself have experienced the liberating effect of this book to get an idea of it. Enthusiasm was general; we all became at once Feuerbachians." The *Theses on Feuerbach,* which were published for the first time in 1888 as an appendix to the work just quoted, are described by Engels as "the first document in which is deposited the brilliant germ of the new world outlook."[3] Only after the publication of Marx's early writings has it become possible to resolve the question as to the nature and extent of Feuerbach's influence on Marx. Accordingly, the philosophy of Feuerbach has once again come into the limelight. But again, the interest it commands is determined not so much by its own independent significance as by its relevance to the question about the specificity of Marx's theory.

The assumption that Marx went through a Feuerbachian phase has not gone unquestioned. The *Parisian Manuscripts,* in which the influence of Feuerbach on Marx's critique of political economy and on his theory of man is decisive, have also been interpreted as determined more by Marx's critical appropriation of Hegel's *Phenomenology* than by the contemplative anthropology of Feuerbach. In an article on the *Parisian Manuscripts,* also published in 1932, Herbert Marcuse observed: "We know from the *Theses on Feuerbach* that Marx draws a line of demarcation between himself and Feuerbach through the concept of human practice. On the other hand, he thereby (more precisely through the concept of labor) turns back to Hegel over across Feuerbach. . . . The matter is therefore more complex than simply a straight line development from Feuerbach to Marx subsequent upon a renunciation of Hegel. What happens is rather that Marx at the origins of his revolutionary theory once again appropriates, on a transformed basis, the decisive achievements of Hegel."[4] According to Heinrich Popitz, the actual extent of Feuerbach's influence on Marx has been overrated, because Marx, "notwithstanding his high estimation of Feuerbach [in the *Parisian Manuscripts*], had already drifted away from Feuerbach and had resumed a direct discourse with Hegel. But even for the earlier period, the influence of Feuerbach is limited."[5]

In recent years, Louis Althusser has advanced the thesis that there is no continuity from the young Marx to the mature Marx. The works of the former are supposed to be determined by what Althusser calls the problematic of Feuerbach, whereas only those of the latter are to be taken as providing the textual basis whereupon the specificity of Marx's theory rests. Althusser draws an absolute line of demarcation between the problematic of Feuerbach and that of the mature Marx. In substantiation of this thesis, Althusser refers to an "epistemological break"[6] in Marx's writings occurring in 1845; that is, in the *Theses on Feuerbach* and the *German Ideology*. There is undoubtedly a preponderance of Feuerbachian concepts in the early works of Marx, as in *On the Jewish Question, Hegel's Philosophy of the State*, and the *Economic and Philosophic Manuscripts*. According to Althusser, Marx in these works "is no more than an *avant-garde* Feuerbachian applying *an ethical problematic to the understanding of human history*."[7] The term "problematic" is used by Althusser in the sense of a total context or structure which, possessing an autonomy of its own together with an inner relational and organizational coherence, constitutes the sustaining ground of an interrelated constellation of concepts. Thus understood, a problematic is supraindividual; it is a horizon encircling the individual, within which he articulates his thought. Individual thought is therefore always situated within a problematic from which it derives its perception of problems and its sense of direction. And any substantial transformation of thought must presuppose its transition from one problematic to another. In its application to the young Marx, the concept of problematic comes up against certain difficulties. Even if it is true that Marx moves, in the *Parisian Manuscripts,* for example, within the framework of Feuerbachian anthropology, there is sufficient evidence to show that Marx, while using the concepts characteristic of that framework, puts a different content into them. For example, the way Marx interprets species-being can be grasped only with reference to Hegel's *Phenomenology;* his concept of labor as the process of man's self-creation completely transcends the scope of Feuerbachian anthropology. At least in the *Parisian Manuscripts,* Marx is epistemologically much more attuned to the moving principle of Hegel's dialectic of negativity.

In view of what has just been said (this question is further discussed in Section III of this Introduction), Althusser is completely wrong in saying that "the young Marx *was never strictly speaking a Hegelian.*" It seems that it is primarily due to the idea of exclusivity contained in his concept of problematic that he is driven to the untenable position of having to insist on the nonexistence of Hegel's influence on Marx. Moreover, Althusser has yet to establish the truth of his claim. So far, his position is only assertive: "So the thesis that the young Marx was a Hegelian, though widely believed today, is in general a myth."[8] But Althusser's theoretical project of working out the specificity of Marx's theory by extricating it from its anthropological and theological distortions centering largely around a watered down concept of alienation must be looked upon as a fruitful contribution to Marxist scholarship. It is in this context that his concern to pinpoint the conceptual and theoretical distinctions setting Marx apart from his predecessors must be acknowledged as timely and valuable. It was this concern that motivated him to translate the writings of Feuerbach between 1839 and 1845,[9] for a "comparative study of Feuerbach's writings and Marx's early works makes possible a *historical* reading of Marx's writings, and a better understanding of his development."[10]

Quite apart from its being bound up with the history of Marx's thought, the philosophy of Feuerbach shares a common ground with contemporary European philosophy with respect to the latter's rejection of traditional epistemology. Ever since metaphysics was founded by Plato and Aristotle, it has looked upon given reality not as self-subsisting and self-explanatory, but as dependent upon a transcendental realm of being revealed only to a reason that has purged itself of sensuousness. It has posited an intelligible world over against the sensible world. This dualization of reality had the epistemological consequence of thinking that mind and body, reason and existence, being and becoming are opposed to one another—the rational subject confronting the sensuous object. How is an interaction between two entirely different orders of being possible? How does the subject know the object? The answers given to these questions, from Plato to Hegel, are enormously different, but common to all of them is the assumption of a world-less subject counterposed to a thought-less object. The situation is certainly different in the philosophy of Hegel, but even there the Idea and Nature are opposed to one another, and there is no satisfactory explanation of how the Idea goes forth from itself as Nature. In Martin Heidegger's *Daseinsanalytik* the traditional subject-object dichotomy is overcome through his understanding of man (Dasein) as "being-in-the-world."[11] The question of traditional epistemology—how does the knowing subject move out of its inner "sphere" into another and external sphere of the object—is a secondary question, because it must presuppose the fact that the subject *is* there (exists). In this presupposition the being of the subject remains unquestioned, unexplained, opaque. The analysis of the being of the subject reveals that it is *in* the world. This being-in is the mode of being of Dasein. The world is not something that is given to Dasein externally and hence discovered by it through its cognitive acts. Rather, the world belongs to its ontological constitution: It is always in the world and has its world within it. Feuerbach, too, rejects traditional epistemology in so far as his species-being is a being that is always and from the very outset objectified. It is what it is only through its object. But the object does not exist in the form in which it is the object of the species-being independently of it, or as "it-self-ness," so that it is only subsequently known, experienced, or appropriated. According to Feuerbach, the mode of man's being is such that he is always with his objects which are his manifest being.[12]

Notwithstanding the historical distance separating us from Feuerbach, his philosophy has a ring of contemporaneity about it. This is especially true if we look at it in relation to the present-day movement of radical dissent. It may appear that in its actual practice the advanced industrial society has rendered the critical-emancipatory significance of Feuerbach obsolete. Feuerbach's life was a prolonged victimization by a politically reinforced religious orthodoxy and a religiously reinforced political regime. The society he lived in was in many ways despotic, authoritarian, and puritanically ascetic; it lagged far behind the achievements of the Enlightenment and the French Revolution. The advanced industrial society with its sensual paradise of affluent consumption, its constant accentuation of pleasure, its fusion of sexuality and business, its "permissiveness," is worlds removed from the constricting society of Feuerbach's day. Yet with all its "acceptance" of the body and the senses, of pleasure and sensuality, the advanced industrial society has in no way superseded the image and the role of the senses, the concept of the whole unalienated man underlying Feuerbach's anthropological materialism.

II THE PHILOSOPHY OF FEUERBACH

Every new philosophy derives its transcending principles out of a critical appropriation of the dominant positions into which philosophical tradition has concentrated itself. The "New Philosophy" of Feuerbach cannot be adequately grasped unless it is seen as taking its point of departure from a criticism of the idealist-speculative philosophy of Hegel. The all-pervasive Hegelianism constituted the philosophical horizon in which Feuerbach's thought was born. From the very beginning he was irresistibly drawn towards the system of Hegel, the greatest feat of philosophical architecture since Aristotle.

But Feuerbach was at no time an orthodox Hegelian and never unconditionally devoted to Hegelianism. There is sufficient evidence to show that his philosophical perception was never completely determined by the principles of Hegel's philosophy. Even when Feuerbach declares himself to be a disciple of Hegel, he is not unreservedly so. On no other philosopher does Feuerbach lavish so much praise as on Hegel, and yet to no other philosopher is his relationship as ambivalent. From the earliest stages of his assimilation of Hegel's philosophy, there is in him a core of resistant independence.

When Feuerbach began as a student at the University of Heidelberg in 1823—Hegel had taught there from 1816 to 1818—anyone entering upon a study of theology was more than likely to come under the influence of the then philosophy *par excellence* of Germany—Hegelianism. The lectures of Carl Daub, a follower of Hegel, introduced the young student of theology not only to the subject of his choice, but also to the philosophy of Hegel. But "after having absorbed the best from the great Daub,"[13] Feuerbach was soon craving for an initiation into philosophical mysteries at the hands of the master himself. He moved to Berlin in 1824 to spend the two most decisive years of his philosophical life.

Soon after he had started attending the lectures of Hegel, Feuerbach was writing to his father: "What was still obscure and incomprehensible while I was studying under Daub, I have now understood clearly and grasped in its necessity through the few lectures of Hegel which I have attended so far; what only smoldered in me like tinder, I see now burst into bright flames."[14] By 1826, Feuerbach had "gone through the whole of Hegel. With the exception of Aesthetics, I have heard all his lectures, and those on Logic even twice."[15] Feuerbach's interest in Hegel's Logic must be particularly noted since, as we shall see later, his final break with the sovereign of German philosophy—documented in 1839 through his *Towards a Critique of Hegel's Philosophy*—would derive its justification from a criticism of the Hegelian Logic. Meanwhile, Feuerbach most perceptively characterizes the Logic as "the *corpus iuris,* the *pandects* of philosophy," as containing "the whole of philosophy according to its principles of thought—both ancient and modern;" and as "the presentation of his [Hegel's] method."[16]

Long before Feuerbach had evolved a philosophical position of his own, he had occasionally expressed certain doubts concerning the relation in Hegel's system between Logic and the Philosophy of Nature. These doubts also foreshadow the characteristic view of nature in his fully developed philosophy. Even before his Doctoral Dissertation, *De ratione una, universali, infinita,* he was being assailed by a fundamental doubt concerning the feasibility of the transition of the Hegelian Idea into Nature: "How is thought related to being, and the Logic to Nature? Is the transition from the Logic to Nature legitimate? Wherein lies the necessity or the reason for this transition?"[17] These doubts are directed against Section 244 of Hegel's *Encyclopaedia* which reads as follows: "The Idea which is independent or for itself, when viewed on the point of this its unity with itself, is perception, or intuition, and the Idea to be perceived is nature. But as intuition the Idea is invested with the one-sided characteristic of immediacy, or of negation, by means of an external reflection. But the

Idea is absolutely free; and its freedom means that it does not merely pass over into life, or as finite cognition allow life to show itself in it, but in its own absolute truth resolves to let the element of its particularity, or of the first characterization and other-being, the immediate Idea, as its reflection, go forth freely itself from itself as Nature."[18] Later, in his *Preliminary Theses on the Reform of Philosophy*, Feuerbach would unceremoniously dismiss this as cryptic theology: "At the end of the *Logic*, the absolute Idea even comes to take a nebulous decision to document with its own hands its descent from theological heaven."[19] But already at this stage, Feuerbach retorts in his characteristically incisive and blunt fashion: "If nature did not exist, the Logic, this immaculate virgin, would never be able to produce it out of itself."[20] In his letter to Hegel, written in 1828 and sent together with a copy of his Doctoral Dissertation, Feuerbach speaks of himself as a direct pupil of Hegel. The young disciple assures the master that his Dissertation "lives and has its being in the speculative spirit;" that it was "the product . . . of a study which was sustained by a free . . . living, and essential (as opposed to formal) appropriation and absorption of those ideas and concepts which form the content of both your works and oral discourse," that it "bears the traces of the kind of philosophizing which could be termed as the realization and worldly-becoming of the Idea, the ensarkosis or incarnation of pure Logos." And yet he emphasizes here the principle of "sensuousness"—later a key concept of his philosophy—when he says that he would like to see the Idea not as suspended above the sensuous and the phenomenal, but rather descend from "the heaven of its colorless purity" down to the particular. Also, Feuerbach's anti-Christian pathos finds its expression in his remark that Christianity was no longer an absolute religion, that it was only "the antithesis of the old world in so far as it had reduced nature to an existence devoid of spirit."[21]

Feuerbach's sporadically expressed dissatisfaction with the philosophy of Hegel assumes the form of a systematic and self-confident criticism in his *Towards a Critique of*

Hegel's Philosophy which, appearing in 1839 in Arnold
Ruge's *Jahrbucher,* announces his rejection of Hegelianism. Feuerbach proceeds by showing that the two most
characteristic qualities of Hegelianism are also the two of
its most questionable aspects—its reliance on speculation
and its drive towards system. In order to appreciate the
thrust of Feuerbach's criticism, it is essential to acquaint
ourselves with what Hegel understands by speculation and
system. This is unfortunately by no means an easy task,
especially in view of Hegel's own methodological principle
that philosophical knowledge could not be stated in the
form of a naked result "as if shot from a pistol," but had
to be presented as the process of its becoming, for "the
tendency is a mere drift which still lacks actuality; and
the naked result is the corpse which has left the tendency
behind."[22]

From the point of view of contemporary philosophical
sensibility, speculation is a pejorative term. Speculative is
all thinking that is cut off from empirical reality and hence
purely subjective, all that is unrelated to objective facts.
And because it is wildly neglectful of the facts of reality,
it is empty and arbitrary. Hegel's philosophy is far from
being speculative in this sense: It is neither arbitrary, nor
subjective, nor unrelated to empirical reality. On the contrary, it is rigorously oriented to concrete reality; it is as-
tonishingly empirical because of the staggering wealth of
concrete historical-experiential material which has gone
into its formation, accounting for its tremendous conceptual penetration and sweep. Speculation in Hegel is the
theory of reality and, as such, identical with the power of
reason to transcend all that presents itself to ordinary understanding as fixed, isolated, and limited by its own individuality. In transcending the fixity of the individual,
speculative thought lays bare those totalities that lend
meaning and definition to the individual phenomenon. In
this sense, all theoretical activity is speculative.

Perhaps the best way to understand what Hegel means
by speculation would be to recall his characterization of
philosophy. In a definite sense, the Hegelian philosophy is

the conceptual self-articulation of reason. "That philosophy is one and can only be one rests on the fact that reason itself is one."[23] The one reason expresses itself in the one philosophy. But it can be easily shown that there is not one philosophy, but rather many and different philosophies. However, according to Hegel, this is true only from the standpoint of the intellect which remains confined to fixed determinations of concepts and to their distinction from others. Intellect is the thought that produces only finite determinations and moves within them.[24] Hegel's philosophical system, as understood by its architect, contained within itself—of course in a sublated form—all past philosophies in so far as they constitute the self-movement of the Notion, the medium of philosophy as such, and hence also of reason. This self-movement of the Notion is the inner unity binding all philosophies together. "Each philosophy," says Hegel, "is complete in itself, and contains, like a genuine work of art, its totality within itself."[25]

Thus, a particular philosophy, existing as it does in the form of historical specificity, is nothing but philosophy as such—the one, self-identical philosophy presenting itself at a certain stage of its conceptual self-articulation. Hegel says: "But if the Absolute—like reason as the form in which it appears—is eternally one and the same, as it undoubtedly is, then every historically particular reason which looks at and cognizes itself, produces a true philosophy and resolves a task which like its resolution, is the same at all times. Because the self-cognizing reason has in philosophy to do with itself alone, the whole of its work, like its activity, lies within itself; and with regard to the inner essence of philosophy there are neither predecessors nor successors."[26] Philosophy springs from what Hegel calls the living originality of the Spirit in so far as the Spirit redeems the essence of philosophy from the historical specificity of its form of appearance. This historical specificity is, so to say, its body in which it is imprisoned. In the process of its formation, philosophy, that is, the form in which the Absolute appears, is severed from the

Absolute precisely because it has taken a fixed phenomenal form. The "exertion of the Notion" consists in lique-
fying the congealed form of the system whereby the living
movement of the Absolute and of the Notion is restored.
The hiatus between the historically congealed form of a
system and the life of the Absolute is designated by Hegel
as the dichotomy,[27] from whence the need for philosophy
arises. Only by stepping out from its phenomenal form,
that is, from a particular system of philosophy, does reason re-establish its rapport with the Absolute. The only
interest of reason is to overcome the dichotomy between
the Absolute and the totality of limitations; that is, a specific system of philosophy. "For reason," says Hegel,
"which finds consciousness imprisoned in the particular,
becomes philosophical speculation only in so far as it elevates itself to itself and entrusts itself to itself and to the
Absolute, its object."[28] The Hegelian speculation is thus
the theoretical activity of reason in terms of which the
Absolute realizes its self-identity in the multiplicity of its
phenomenal manifestations.

The Absolute is the subject par excellence of Hegel's
philosophy. It is the principle of identity underlying all
phenomenal-historical multiplicity, and philosophy is the
comprehension of its movement of self-realizing self-
presentation. The Hegelian philosophy is essentially a system in so far as the categories of the Absolute (Logic),
its self-alienation into nature (Philosophy of Nature), the
overcoming of its alienation in self-consciousness (Philosophy of Subjective Spirit), and the objectifications of
the subjective spirit again into culture and state (Philosophy of Objective Spirit) constitute a dynamic totality or a
system in which all its moments are mediated with the
self-identical Absolute—identity in difference. The movement of the Absolute is not linear, but circular. It is already in the beginning what it becomes in the end: Its
end is contained in its beginning. The difference between
the beginning and the end is only that between immediacy
and mediatedness. Resting initially in the concentrated
tension of its unfolded, undifferentiated generality, it

passes through the moments of its becoming—nature, self-consciousness, reason, and spirit—to return to itself as Idea, the absolute unity of Notion and objectivity; as the Absolute Spirit which is in and for itself, namely, the Absolute having comprehended itself in the unfolded richness of its own inner content.

The Hegelian concept of system thus depends on the assumption that all the different forms in which natural and spiritual reality exist are the objectifications of a self-identical subject. If all objectifications—and no matter at what level of articulation—are related to the same subject, they must ultimately belong to an organic unity, must be woven into an order of inner coherence. The concept of system as the conceptual unity of contradictions is necessitated by the concept of identity which is mediated with itself in the opposite and the contradictory. The Hegelian system is the comprehensive totality of the moments of the Absolute in its progressive self-realization. The Absolute is teleological in the sense that it is its own goal which, although already given at the beginning, is realized only in the end after it has passed through the necessary stages of its actualizations, stages which constitute an ascending order from the lowest forms of inorganic nature to the highest form of the Absolute Spirit. The Hegelian philosophy is the Odyssey of the Absolute. It is the presentation of the process of the Absolute's self-realization. All reality—natural, human, and intellectual—is seen by Hegel in relation to the Absolute: It is for the sake of the Absolute.

According to Feuerbach, Hegel's "system knows only *subordination* and *succession;* co-ordination and coexistence are unknown to it."[29] The process of the self-unfolding of the Absolute goes through a series of successive stages where the earlier stage is incorporated into the following one, thus losing its independence and autonomy; its intrinsic reality becomes subordinated to the higher reality of the succeeding stage. The forms of reality are integrated into the hierarchy of the manifestations of the Absolute, so that their own existence acquires the

character of "for-the-sake-of." It is in this sense that Feuerbach criticizes Hegel's method as having its basis in "exclusive time," that is, in an exclusively onward movement
that never returns to the moments it has passed through.
The Hegelian method is therefore a stranger to what Feuerbach calls "the tolerance of space," because space allows
all things to coexist without the right of one thing to exist
infringed upon by another; the relation of things to one
another in space is that of co-ordination rather than that
of subordination. It is precisely the right of the phenomena
of reality to maintain their intrinsic autonomy which
Feuerbach is most concerned to establish, and which goes
by the board in the Hegelian Totality. "To be sure," says
Feuerbach, "the last stage of development is always the
totality that includes in itself the other stages, but since it
itself is a definite temporal existence and hence bears the
character of particularity, it cannot incorporate into itself
other existences without sucking out the very marrow of
their independent life and without robbing them of the
meaning which they can only have in complete freedom."

In contrast to the philosophy of Hegel, nature accords
a different treatment to things in so far as it "combines
the monarchical tendency of time with the liberalism of
space." There is certainly succession in nature because
there is development in it. But in nature, the truth of the
plant is not just the flower; the leaf equally belongs to
its truth. Hence the observation of Feuerbach: "The stages
in the development of nature have therefore by no means
only a *historical* meaning. They are indeed moments, but
moments of a simultaneous totality of nature and not of a
particular and individual totality which itself would only
be a moment of the universe, that is, of the totality of
nature."

The Hegelian philosophy, Feuerbach argues, is itself a
phenomenon belonging to the world and must therefore
reconcile itself to the modest status of being just one particular, "empirical"—that is, empirically given—philosophy.
This is not to belittle its overwhelming greatness and significance. Feuerbach is only too willing to acknowledge

that the philosophy of Hegel "is distinguished from all previous philosophies by its rigorous scientific character, universality, and incontestable richness of thought." Or: "Hegel is the most accomplished philosophical artist, and his presentations, at least in part, are *unsurpassed models of scientific art sense* and, due to their rigor, *veritable means for the education and discipline of the spirit.*" But it cannot be "the absolute reality of the idea of philosophy." As a particular expression of human mind, it cannot be its absolute expression; being a phenomenon of this world, it is limited by the laws of this world: "Whatever enters into time and space must also subordinate itself to the laws of time and space. The god of limitation stands guard at the entrance to the world. Self-limitation is the condition of entry. Whatever becomes real, becomes so only as something determined. The incarnation of the species with all its plenitude into one individuality would be an absolute miracle, a violent suspension of all the laws and principles of reality; it would indeed be the end of the world."

But apart from the general principle applied above, there are, Feuerbach argues, other considerations that make it impossible for Hegelianism to claim the status of absolute philosophy. For one thing, it came into being at a particular point of time; that is, in a particular historical context defined by the tradition of philosophy or by the definite level of thought at which mankind then stood. As Feuerbach says: "Every philosophy originates . . . as a manifestation of its time; its origin presupposes its historical time." Anything that must presuppose something else for its existence cannot claim to be absolute. But there is another sense in which the Hegelian philosophy claims to begin without any presupposition whatsoever—it proceeds from pure Being. In other words, it claims to start from the beginning, as such, because Being is no particular point of departure, but absolute beginning in so far as it is the condition of all particular starting points. Thus, Hegelian philosophy "starts from that which is itself the beginning." Feuerbach seeks to demolish this claim by

first showing that the notion of making an absolute beginning in philosophy is itself determined by the tradition
of metaphysical philosophy which, since Plato and Aristotle, has always sought to establish a first principle as the
point of departure to cognize reality in its truth. It is,
therefore, easy to see that in claiming to begin with no
presuppositions whatsoever, that is, to make an absolute
beginning, Hegel is in fact bound to "the old question as to
the first principle of philosophy," thus documenting the
limitedness of his philosophy by the tradition of philosophy.
Even the necessity in Hegel that self-presenting thought
essentially constitutes a system, is determined by the need
in philosophical tradition to systematize knowledge and
reality, a tradition "essentially interested in . . . formal
system rather than in reality." Secondly, Feuerbach argues that Hegelian Logic does not begin with *real* being,
but only with the notion of being. Instead of making a
real beginning, Hegel is only documenting the extent to
which he is determined by the metaphysical notion of the
first principle. Feuerbach asks: "Is the notion of beginning
not itself subject to criticism? Is it immediately true and
universally valid? Why should it not be possible for me to
abandon at the start the notion of beginning and, instead,
turn directly to that which is real? Hegel starts from being;
that is, from the notion of being or abstract being. Why
should I not be able to start from being itself, i.e., from
real being?" This distinction between the notion of being
or abstract being, and real being is the Archimedian point
from whence Feuerbach undertakes to unhinge the Hegelian philosophy.

Hegel's *Phenomenology*, "the science of manifested
spirit,"[30] proceeds from empirical, sensuous consciousness, regarded as "immediate knowledge in the strict sense
of the word."[31] The result of "the phenomenological consideration" is "the Idea as pure knowledge" and it "has
determined itself to be the certainty which has become
truth, the certainty which, on the one hand, no longer has
the object over against it but has internalized it—knows
it as its own self—and, on the other hand, has given up

the knowledge of itself as of something confronting the object, of which it is only the annihilation; it has divested itself of this subjectivity and is at one with its self-alienation."[32] The *Logic* on the other hand begins not from immediate knowledge, but from the "simple immediacy" of pure being. The result of *Logic*, the pure science, i.e., "pure knowledge in the entire range of its development,"[33] is also the Idea; "the science concludes in this way with the comprehension of its own Notion as pure Idea which is what the Idea is."[34] Feuerbach's quarrel with Hegel is that the idea of an absolute beginning, both in the *Phenomenology* and the *Logic*, is not at all so; the beginning is by no means without presuppositions. The Idea is there right at the beginning of Hegel's philosophy as its unquestionable assumption. In beginning either from immediate knowledge, or from pure Being, Hegel actually begins from the Idea: "That the starting-point is Being is only a formalism, for Being is here not the true starting point, nor the truly primary. The starting point could just as well be the Absolute Idea because it was already a certainty, an immediate truth for Hegel before he wrote the *Logic*; i.e., before he gave a scientific form of expression to his logical ideas. The Absolute Idea—the Idea of the Absolute—is its own indubitable certainty as the absolute truth. It posits itself in advance as true; that which the Idea posits as the other, presupposes according to its essence the Idea again. In this way, the proof remains only a formal one."[35] The unquestioned and "uncritical" assumption of the truth of the Idea is the Hegelian *fait accompli* which is tarnished only by the idea of a beginning without presuppositions at the beginning of the *Logic*. Thus, the method of Hegel, in terms of which he presents the process of the absolute Idea, is nothing but an attempt to release the Idea "from the confines of a subjective intellectual conception" in order to demonstrate that "it also existed for *others*." Hence, the Hegelian method is "the expression of this superfluous necessity, of this dispensable indispensability or indispensable dispensability." The Hegelian Being is not the antithesis of the Idea, be-

cause it is already the certainty of the Idea, "nothing other
than the Idea in its immediacy." The Idea does not demonstrate its truth through a *real other*. If Being is itself the
Idea, the antithesis is only a formal one. Being in the sense
of Hegel's *Logic* directly contradicts being in the sense of
"the intellect's empirical and concrete perception." According to Feuerbach the logical being is arrived at only in
terms of an immediate break with real perception. This
involves not only a criticism of Hegel, but of the whole
of modern philosophy from Descartes and Spinoza onward which is accused by Feuerbach of making an "unmediated break with sensuous perception" and of its "immediate taking itself for granted." To make use of a later
formulation of Feuerbach, philosophy must begin not
with itself but with non-philosophy.

According to Feuerbach, thought must take into account its Other: The Other of thought is sensuous reality
existing as "this-being," as *haeceitas*. For example, in the
first chapter of his *Phenomenology,* Hegel "does not refute the 'here' that forms the object of sensuous consciousness, that is, an object for us as distinct from pure thought;
he only refutes the logical 'here,' the logical 'now.' He refutes the *idea* of 'this-being.'" The *Phenomenology* and
the *Logic* begin "not with the 'other-being' of thought,
but with the idea of the 'other-being' of thought."

In so far as Hegel takes the object of his philosophy—
the Absolute—for granted, his philosophy is concerned only
with the form in which the Absolute presents itself. Hegel
does not establish the content of his philosophy in a critical
and genetical way. Feuerbach advances his genetico-
critical method as against the speculative method of Hegel
for which all contradiction belongs only to the form of
the Absolute which is posited—according to Feuerbach
"uncritically"—as identical with itself. The genetico-critical
method does not "dogmatically demonstrate" or dogmatically assume an object, "but examines its origin"—"questions whether an object is a real object, only an idea, or
just a psychological phenomenon." The Absolute philosophy, according to the analogy taken by Feuerbach, is

comparable to the theological view of nature which regards comets or other strange phenomena as immediately the workings of God, whereas the genetico-critical method is akin to that of the natural scientific view of the nature and behavior of phenomena, for example, that the gall-nut is produced by the sting of an insect rather than by a devil. To further illustrate the genetico-critical method, Feuerbach takes the concept of nothingness as an example, a concept that arises only where this method is lacking. Feuerbach says that "thought can never go beyond being, because it cannot go beyond itself, because reason consists only in positing being, because only this or that being can be thought, but not the genesis of Being itself." Being has no beginning; it is just simply there. To posit nothingness is an act of "absolute arbitrariness and thoughtlessness." The concept of nothingness is only a product of thought which is incapsulated in itself, which is unable to justify itself in the teeth of an antithetical reality, the real source of thought and its content. Reality does not allow for the concept of nothingness to emerge. In this sense, nothingness is the limit of reason, because nothingness is the absence of all reason. The function of the genetico-critical method is to apply the acid test of reality to the content of thought, to scrutinize whether a concept has its genesis in reality; i.e., in concrete, sensuous reality or not.

In contrast to the whole of modern philosophy, but in particular to the idealist-speculative philosophy of Hegel which proceeds from thought and reduces sensuous reality to a secondary, derivative status, Feuerbach advances the idea of a genetico-critical philosophy that finds its fundamental principles in "the *natural* grounds and causes of things." His deep concern is to show that thought has its genesis in real Being, that real Being cannot be derived from or dissolved in thought. The critical function of philosophy consists in ensuring that thought is not divorced from its real, natural basis: "Philosophy is the science of reality in its truth and totality. However, the all-inclusive and all-encompassing reality is nature (taken in the most universal sense of the word)." In one of those formulations that Marx made his own and later used against "the conqueror of the old philosophy" himself, Feuerbach says: "The deepest secrets are to be found in the simplest natural things, but, pining away for the Beyond, the speculative phantast treads them under his feet." What Feuerbach sets out to achieve in *Towards a Critique of Hegel's Philosophy* is the emancipation of nature from its idealist-transcendent subjugation, and together with this its restoration to an autonomous, primary reality. A primary, autonomous, immanentized, and anti-metaphysical nature is the fundamental principle of Feuerbach's philosophy upon which he bases his anthropology, that is, his theory of the nature and essence of man.

Feuerbach gives a systematic exposition of his anthropology in the Introduction to the *Essence of Christianity,* the work which, appearing in 1841, established Feuerbach as the liberator from the tyranny of the system of Hegel. In the oft-quoted words of Engels: "The spell was broken; the 'system' was exploded and cast aside. . . . One must himself have experienced the liberating effect of this book to get an idea of it. Enthusiasm was general; we all became at once Feuerbachians."[36] The reason behind this conversion to Feuerbach's philosophy is, of course, the reunion it proclaimed of a nature released from its confinement to a dark, inferior, truthless order of reality to be overcome and transcended by an antithetical reason, and man as a being of plenitude capable of pouring himself into the infinite richness of religion, art, and philosophy. The *Essence of Christianity* showed that the plenitude of God is the plenitude of man, because the object of man "is his manifest being, his true, objective ego."

In order to arrive at the specificity of man's being, Feuerbach proceeds from the distinction between man and the animal. That which sets man apart from the animal—his *differentium specificum*—is consciousness. After what we have learned of Feuerbach's anti-idealist stance, this ascertainment comes as an anti-climax. It may be argued in defense of Feuerbach that he is not hypostatizing consciousness as a metaphysical entity in its own right, but referring to human consciousness, that is, to something that is anchored in the being of man. In the language of Heidegger, the consciousness of Feuerbach is not a metaphysical category, but an existential characteristic belonging to the ontological constitution of man.[37] Be that as it may, there is an innate difficulty in the materialist philosophy of Feuerbach which keeps him imprisoned in the realm of self-consciousness, his criticism of Hegel notwithstanding. Marx's later rejection of Feuerbach is motivated precisely by the necessity to abandon the realm of consciousness, should the reality of man and his world be salvaged from its mystifying explanations; with Feuerbach in the foreground of his mind, Marx says: "Man can be distinguished from the animal by consciousness, religion, or anything else you please. He begins to distinguish himself from the animal the moment he begins to *produce* his means of subsistence, a step required by his physical organization."[38]

According to Feuerbach, the animal does not possess consciousness, for "consciousness is given only in the case of a being to whom his *species,* his *mode of being,* is necessarily linked with knowledge. This makes consciousness again into something specifically human, because the animal is not capable of knowing. In being conscious, man knows himself as this conscious being: He is to himself an object of thought. But a being who is an object of thought to himself can also make other things the object of his thought; a self-knowing being is also an other-knowing being. Because of this span, knowledge has the character of science: "Science is the consciousness of species."

The consciousness of man, that is, consciousness in the strict sense of the word, is not finite or limited. A caterpillar, for example, is confined to the world of a caterpillar; it is a limited being, because given its biological constitution, its instinctual pattern, it cannot transcend the boundaries of its limited world. It cannot make objects

foreign to its world—and its world is its manifest being—
as the objects of its life-activity. There is no such limitation
imposed upon the being of man. The self-expression of his
being is neither limited to a particular segment, nor to a
particular quality of nature. He is neither instinctually
fitted to a specific environment, nor biologically tied to a
particular mode of life. His consciousness extends over to
the whole of nature, and the whole of nature is his object.
Indeed, his consciousness transcends all finitude and
reaches over to the infinite. Religion is man's consciousness
as consciousness of the infinite. In so far as consciousness
can reach out to the infinite, it is itself essentially infinite:
"The consciousness of the finite is nothing else than the
consciousness of the infinity of the consciousness . . . in
its consciousness of infinity, the conscious being is conscious of the infinity of its own being."

The anthropology of Feuerbach posits a correlation between a being and its object. This means that a being is
always given in such a way that it has objects. In terms of
its ontological constitution, a being is opened up to the objects it has. But its openness to the object means that the
object in its turn is capable of entering into the openness
of that being. The object is, so to speak, existentially disclosed to the being that has it: The disclosedness of the
object is the openness of the being to which it corresponds.
In this sense, the object is expressive of what a being essentially is; the object to which a subject essentially and
necessarily relates himself is nothing except the subject's
own, but objective, being.

Before becoming conscious of himself, that is, before
his consciousness acquires a reflexive relationship to itself,
man exists outside himself, or his consciousness is absorbed by the object. Feuerbach says that "man's self-
consciousness is his consciousness of the object. One knows
the man by the object which reflects his being; the object
lets his being appear to you; the object is his manifest
being, his true, objective ego. This is true not only of
intellectual but also of sensuous objects." Anything that
is an object of man's consciousness, whether actual or

possible, concrete or abstract, close by or farthest removed, expresses his being. The being of man is universal and infinite, because the universal and the infinite are the objects of his thought.

In view of Feuerbach's anthropological axiom, it is evident that the being of God reflects or manifests the being of man. The omniscience and omnipotence of God are the omniscience and omnipotence of man's own being. It is the perfection of his own being that appears to man as the perfection of God. The existentials constitutive of the being of man are feeling, willing, and thinking. According to Feuerbach, man "exists in order to think, love, and will." These activities are ends in themselves. As such, they are perfections, because everything that exists for its own sake is perfect. But in so far as these perfections belong to the being of man, he too is a perfect being, conscious of his own universality and infinity. His consciousness is his self-affirmation, self-love, joy in his own perfection, for "consciousness exists only in a plenitudinous, accomplished being." These characterizations of man's reality must naturally be taken in an ontological sense, that is, as characterizations of man in general; they are not applicable to a particular individual who is quite obviously far from being perfect, plenitudinous, and totally joyful. While talking about man, Feuerbach talks about man as the sum total of all actual and possible human qualities. The totality of these qualities is designated by the term *species*. "To be sure," says Feuerbach, "the human individual can, even must, feel and know himself to be limited—and this is what distinguishes him from the animal —but he can become conscious of his limits, his finiteness, only because he can make the perfection and infinity of his species the object either of his feeling, conscience, or thought."

Feuerbach's theory of religion, presented in the second section of the Introduction, is grounded in his anthropology and serves as an illustration of its fundamental principles. In the context of his anthropology, religion is a distinguished phenomenon, because the history of religion is the history of the objectifications or projections of man's being into a shifting pattern of superhuman and super-natural powers. Religion is the self-consciousness of man, because its object is the objective being of man. In religion, man "transposes his essential being outside himself before he finds it within himself. His own being becomes the object of his thought initially as another being." The history of religion has a progressive movement from lower to higher forms; in his religious consciousness, man's cultural and intellectual development is reflected: "Every progress in religion means therefore a deepening of man's knowledge of himself." That religion is not the realm of a separate and superior order of reality is "the hidden nature of religion which remains opaque to religion itself"; this hidden nature becomes "transparent to the thinker who makes it the object of his thought." With the dis-closure of the hidden nature of religion, religion loses all content in so far as this content is recognized and appropri-ated by man as his own, for nothing "is to be found in the essence and consciousness of religion which is not there in the being of man, which is not there in his con-sciousness of himself and the world."

The review article "On 'The Beginning of Philosophy'" takes up again one of the main themes of *Towards a Critique of Hegel's Philosophy*—the nature of philosophy —and offers in bold, vital strokes the definition of an em-pirically oriented philosophy which is "young" and "in-finite"—infinite because of the infinite richness of the ma-terial for its thought—as opposed to a philosophy beginning with itself which "finally becomes decrepit, weary of life, and disgusted with itself." Feuerbach rejects the view that philosophy occupied a special position in so far as it did not presuppose anything in order to make a beginning. In fact, the origin of philosophical knowledge is the same as that of any other kind of scientific knowledge: All sci-ence has to create its own object. It aims at transforming into an object that which does not yet exist as an object. The objects of everyday life are not the objects of science, because everyday life consists of an unquestioned acceptance, practical use, and a "natural" understanding of things; they become the objects of science only when the question as to their nature arises, that is, only when they become objects of scientific reflection.

Now in creating their objects, empirical sciences do not derive them from themselves, but from the given reality. Does philosophy create its object in the same way? As far as the "presuppositionless" philosophy is concerned, Feuerbach's answer is clearly no. This kind of philosophy does not begin, but only concludes with the empirical: "The spirit follows upon the senses, not the senses upon the spirit; the spirit is the end and not the beginning of things. The transition from empirical cognition to philosophy commands necessity, whereas the transition from philosophy to empirical cognition is only the luxury of arbitrariness." In an almost rhapsodic acclaim of the cognitive powers of natural science, Feuerbach exclaims that the goose quill is not only an "organ of revelation and the instrument of truth," but also "the telescope of astronomy, the soldering pipe of mineralogy, the hammer of geology, and the magnifying lense of the botanist." It is "more honorable and rational to begin with non-philosophy." By non-philosophy, Feuerbach means empirical reality existing in its own right as primary and autonomous, not as posited from the vantage point of an absolute philosophy.

In *The Necessity of A Reform of Philosophy*, Feuerbach emphatically rejects any philosophy that constitutes itself in response to an inner need of the history of philosophy, "which owes its existence to a philosophical need, as for example, the philosophy of Fichte in relation to that of Kant." Such a philosophy is an affair of the schools and does not correspond to "a need of mankind." Philosophy has previously built its speculative castles above and beyond the real world of man. It can acquire the character of a true and necessary philosophy only if it "harks to the need of the age as well as of mankind."

Feuerbach argues that the need of the age can no longer be satisfied by Christianity: "It is no longer able to respond to the needs either of the theoretical or the practical man

. . . for we have now discovered other interests for our heart than the eternal heavenly bliss, . . . because men have now appropriated to themselves all that is true, human, and anti-holy." The negation of Christianity, hitherto only an unconscious one, is now "being consciously willed and directly intended, the more so because Christianity has associated itself with forces inhibiting the basic drive of contemporary mankind—political freedom." This conscious negation of Christianity is synonymous with the beginning of a new age which necessitates "a new and openhearted philosophy which has ceased to be Christian, indeed, which is definitely un-Christian."

As Feuerbach sees it, the reality of the age lies in the fact that "religion and Church have been replaced by politics, the heaven by the earth, prayer by work, hell by material need, and the Christian by man." But if in practice, the Christian has been replaced by man, then this must also have the theoretical consequence of putting man in the place of the divine. If the basic drive of contemporary mankind is political freedom, then this new religion must have its highest point of reference in man.

The ultimate ground for transforming politics into religion is atheism, that is, the renunciation of a God who is other than man. Strange as it may sound, atheism alone is the real basis of state. If atheism is the self-assertion of the man who has appropriated God to himself, then the "true state is the unlimited, infinite, true, perfect, divine man. It is primarily the state in which man emerges as man; the state is man who relates himself to himself— the self-determining, the absolute man."

The works of Feuerbach that we have discussed so far convey a sense of urgency about his thought which is characteristic of those who, deeply dissatisfied with outrageous conditions in the area of their concern, have a "truth" to proclaim. In the case of Feuerbach the area of concern is German society as a whole, which still lagged behind the new reality created by the French Revolution. Feuerbach's own life was a prolonged victimization by a politically reinforced religious orthodoxy and a religiously reinforced political regime bent on crushing all criticism and free speech. Feuerbach believed that the degradation of man was a direct consequence of subordinating man, of deriving the purpose of his life, from a "higher" order of transcendent reality—the divine being of theology and the Absolute of the Hegelian philosophy. The positing of such an order meant the emptying of the very being and essence of man and their alienation to that order. All the sense of urgency in Feuerbach's philosophy comes from a realization of the necessity to restore to man his own alienated being and essence. Feuerbach's atheism, his denial of God, is the denial of the negation of man. This sense of urgency is keenest in Feuerbach's *Preliminary Theses on the Reform of Philosophy* and gives this work the character of a manifesto. The staccato effluxes of their aphoristic form certainly lend them concentrated power, surety of direction, and poignancy of intellectual penetration; but the aphoristic form also undermines their philosophical quality by obstructing a more elaborate and sustained argument: They lack a stringent epistemology and methodology to establish and substantiate Feuerbach's apercus and insights. The grand philosophical tradition, celebrating its triumphs of methodological rigor and conceptual precision in Kant and Hegel, sinks in Feuerbach to conceptual primitivity. Karl Löwith says: "With Feuerbach begins a new epoch of philosophical thinking which is outside the tradition; compared with what preceded it, it is certainly a relapse into conceptual and methodological primitivity, but looking ahead, it represents a creative attempt to reformulate the problems of philosophy in response to the altered existential consciousness of the new generation."[39]

Reverberating through history comes the opening statement of the *Theses:* "The secret of theology is anthropology. . . ." To Feuerbach, theology is essentially and structurally the same as speculative philosophy. Hence, anthropology is also the secret of speculative philosophy. The achievement of Feuerbach, a "real theoretical revolution,"[40] consists precisely in uncovering this secret. The term "secret" points to that which is really the case, that which is behind it all, but not known or recognized as such. Unquestionably modeled on the Feuerbachian secret hunting, Marx, too, discovers his great secret "that Hegel grasps the self-development of man as a process . . . that he thus grasps the nature of work and comprehends objective man . . . as the result of his own work."[41] Marx's secret is actually the secret of Feuerbach's secret. Let it be pointed out in passing that there is a link between the Feuerbachian "secret" and the Marxian concept of ideology which it is impossible to discuss in the present context. The secret of speculative philosophy is also the secret of Feuerbach's intellectual history: "God was my first thought, reason the second, and man the third and the last."[42] How does Feuerbach justify his claim that anthropology is the secret of theology and speculative philosophy?

According to Feuerbach, modern speculative philosophy was initiated by Spinoza. After the demolition of all rational metaphysics by Kant, it was restored by Schelling and consummated by Hegel. The reason why Spinoza is to be regarded as the initiator of speculative philosophy lies in his concept of Substance. Spinoza defines Substance as "that which is in itself and conceived through itself; in other words, that the conception of which does not need the conception of another thing from which it must be formed."[43] Thus understood, the Spinozian Substance is not different from the divine being or God of theology who is *causa sui*. All that exists, things as well as ideas, are just so many different modes in which the eternal and infinite Substance is manifested. Substance is the all-inclusive category of Spinoza in which even the distinction between creator and creature is eliminated. Beyond Substance there is no being and no God. Substance is not only all-inclusive, but also the ultimate, self-subsisting self-identity in the plurality of the attributes of reality. Substance, Divine Being, God is *Deus sive natura*. This is the famous pantheism of Spinoza according to which nature is itself God. The dichotomy of nature (the sum of all extended things) and spirit (the sum of all thinking things) is dissolved into the two attributes of substance—extension and thought. The conclusion that Feuerbach draws from this is that Spinoza is secretly affirming the divinity of matter and thought.

The restoration of speculative philosophy through Schelling is characterized by Feuerbach as the act of infusing into Spinoza's Substance—"this dead and phlegmatic thing" —the activity of spirit. The Absolute is now essentially activity and, thus, far removed from the inactive Substance of Spinoza. But the Absolute is also the identity of the real and the ideal in which all opposition between subject and object, spirit and nature is dissolved. The empirical phenomena are located in an hierarchical series of development as the manifestation of the Absolute and each is immediately the expression of the Absolute, that is, the one is not dialectically derived from the other. Although independent of each other, they are embedded in the common ground of the Absolute wherein their individual distinctions are submerged.

This conception of the Absolute is rejected by Hegel: "To pit this single assertion, that 'in the Absolute all is one,' against the organized whole of determinate and complete knowledge, or of knowledge which at least aims at and demands complete development—to give out its Absolute as the night in which, as we say, all cows are black —that is the very naïveté of vacuous knowledge."[44] The idea of the Absolute is an absolute certainty for Hegel. He differs from Schelling only in so far as he realizes the necessity to demonstrate the process through which the Absolute is mediated with appearance. The Hegelian Absolute is "self-activity, the power of self-differentiation." But it is still the Substance of Spinoza, albeit metamorphosed into spirit. Hegel is himself explicit about his dissatisfaction with this advance on the Spinozian Substance: "In my view . . . everything depends on grasping and expressing the ultimate truth not as Substance but as Subject as well. . . . If the generation which heard God spoken of as the One Substance was shocked and revolted

by such a characterization of his nature, the reason lay
partly in the instinctive feeling that in such a conception
self-consciousness was simply submerged, but not preserved."[45] And even if in Schelling Substance is, to use
a Feuerbachian phrase, "spirit-ualized" (*begeistert*), and
even if immediacy or intuition is conceived as thought, "it
is still a question whether this intellectual intuition does
not fall back into that inert, abstract simplicity [of the
Spinozian Substance] . . ." All this shows that Substance
and its metamorphoses, in the speculative philosophy of
German Idealism, represent nothing but transformation
of the Divine Being of theology into reason. The secret
of the Divine Being, and hence also of speculative reason,
is—and this is the Feuerbachian discovery—the being of
man himself. We have already ascertained the fundamental principle of Feuerbach's ontology according to
which the object corresponding to a being is that being
itself in its objectified form: The object is that through
which that being is revealed. The object of theology—the
Divine Being, and the object of speculative philosophy—
self-thinking reason, is therefore man himself, or once
again, the secret of theology is anthropology.

The method by which this truth is brought to light is
the inversion of the subject-object relationship in religion
and philosophy. Their real subject is man. Or, in the language of Feuerbach: "We need only turn the predicate
into the subject and thus, as subject, into object and principle—that is, only reverse speculative philosophy" in order
to have "the unconcealed, pure, and untarnished truth."

The inversion of idealism which Feuerbach had em-
ployed as an epistemological procedure in his *Critique
of Hegel's Philosophy* has now acquired the clarity and
decisiveness of a methodological principle. His formulations have now something of Nietzsche's "philosophizing
with the hammer." Feuerbach's demolition of idealism
proceeds employing dramatic phrases charged with an explosive power. "Atheism," he says "is inverted Pantheism."
Atheism is Feuerbach's term to denote the affirmation of
the being of man as the truth of the Divine Being, a truth

only concealed behind the Spinozian *Deus sive natura* as the objective form of man's being projected in its infinity and universality. Or again: "The essence of theology is the transcendent, i.e., the essence of man posited outside man; the essence of Hegel's *Logic* is transcendent thought; i.e., the thought of man posited outside man." On this account, metaphysics can now be exposed as "esoteric psychology." Metaphysics arrives at its categories through abstraction from reality only to interpret reality as the predicate of its abstract categories; metaphysics is the subjectivization of reality and its presentation now as a subject with its own inner development and activity. An exoteric, that is, real, metaphysics would be one which does not sever itself from "the so-called subjective spirit," i.e., man, because "one cannot separate the Absolute Spirit from the Subjective Spirit or the essence of man without being thrown back to the standpoint of theology, without being deluded into regarding the Absolute Spirit as being another spirit which is distinct from the being of man; i.e., without making us accept the illusion of a ghost of ourselves existing outside ourselves."

Feuerbach sums up his criticism of Hegel's philosophy by pointing to its abstractive and alienating function. Abstraction has the character of a *terminus technicus* in Feuerbach and means the positing of the essence of nature outside nature, the positing of the essence of man outside man, and the positing of the essence of thought outside the act of thinking. Guilty of abstraction in this sense, it has alienated man from himself, that is, it has surrendered up to a being abstracted from man that which is man's own real and concrete being. A new philosophy that will take into account the reality of man must be the "total negation of speculative philosophy"; it can only be derived "from the negation of Hegelian philosophy" as the culmination of the idealist-speculative philosophical tradition.

The new philosophy is akin to art which is "born out of the feeling that the life of this world is the true life." It is rooted, like art, in the decisive consciousness "that the human is the divine and the finite the infinite." A return to the human and the finite will be the source of a new poetry—and of a new philosophy—because "belief in the beyond is an absolutely unpoetical belief." It is also unphilosophical from the standpoint of a philosophy that corrects the inverted course of the speculative philosophy from the ideal to the real; that is, which constitutes itself in the transition from the ideal to the real. In so far as it is attuned to the real, the new philosophy has become practical philosophy. Feuerbach does not develop his concept of practice. It remains only an "embryo capable of development." Nevertheless, he conceives the role of philosophy as a critical-emancipatory thought which must generate a new practice directed towards overcoming the discrepancy between the infinite richness of man's being as the secret subject of religion and philosophy, and the misery of the concrete socio-political existence of man. As Feuerbach says elsewhere, the task of philosophy is to "open its eyes to human misery."[46] That such a concept of practice is profoundly inadequate was shown later by Marx. But in any case, Feuerbach's concept of philosophy is worlds removed from an academic philosophy devoted to knowledge as a problem internal to the tradition of philosophy. It is a philosophy of "existential" involvement and commitment.

Its immediate task is to begin with its antithesis, with that which it had hitherto left outside: "The philosopher must take into the text of philosophy that aspect of man which does not philosophize, but is rather opposed to philosophy and abstract thinking, or in other words, that which in Hegel has been reduced to a mere footnote." The antithesis of philosophy, or what Feuerbach calls non-philosophy is that "which is distinguished from thought, which is un-philosophical"; it is the "absolutely antischolastic . . . principle of sensualism." Feuerbach's new philosophy can be designated by a number of different names, but they are all identical in their import. It is realism in so far as its object is the real as the real core of the ideal; it is naturalism in so far as nature, the immanent, autonomous nature is the real substratum of all the predicates of the subject of theology and philosophy; it is materialism in so far as the terms nature and matter are interchangeable; and, finally, it is sensualism in so far as nature or matter is essentially sensuous.

The new philosophy is the unity of "head" and "heart," or of thought and sense perception. Feuerbach is most eloquent when talking about the senses: ". . . the sense is the need of the heart" which in its turn is "the source of suffering, finiteness, needs, and sensualism." Or: ". . . perception is the principle of life. . . . Perception gives being that is immediately identical with existence." Even if they lack the precision of philosophical epistemological terms, "head" and "heart" eminently express the whole humanist-emancipatory pathos of Feuerbach: "The heart makes revolutions, the head reforms; the head brings things into existence, the heart sets them in motion." The characterization of the heart reaches dithyrambic ecstasy as "the positively antitheological principle," as "the unbelieving, atheistic principle in man"; it "believes in nothing except itself; it believes only in the unshakeable, divine, and absolute reality of its own being." The new philosophy which has declared man to be divine, the new philosophy as "anthropotheism" is "the heart raised to intellect" and "speaks through the head in terms of the intellect only what the heart speaks in its own way."

In its return to nature, and to man as a natural being, the new philosophy is the "naturalization" of the knowledge about man and his world. This naturalization is the grounding of all science in nature. "A doctrine remains a hypothesis so long as it has not found its natural basis." An immanent nature as the ground of man's being and of his world, nature as "the inorganic body of man" is the most decisive concept of Feuerbach's philosophy. It is also the source of Marx's concept of nature as the key concept of his historical materialism.

The *Principles of the Philosophy of the Future* is a continuation of the *Preliminary Theses*, but contains—again within the limitations of an aphoristic form of phi-

losophizing—a much more substantiated and closely argued
account of Feuerbach's philosophy; its historical canvas
is also much wider so that both his critical and positive
propositions receive a greater clarity of definition and
surety of direction. We shall combine our discussion of
this work with an attempt to integrate all the elements of
Feuerbach's philosophy that we have considered so far
into a more systematic view.

The fundamental concern of Feuerbach is to inaugurate
a new philosophy which "joyfully and consciously recognizes the truth of sensuousness." The condition for the
possibility of such a philosophy is the refutation of the
speculative standpoint which, proceeding as it does from
the primacy of thought, ascribes to the sensuous only a
secondary and derivative ontological status. The refutation
of speculative philosophy is the refutation of speculative
consciousness which sees the truth of the real not in the
real itself but in the ideal. Feuerbach asks from the vantage point of his genetico-critical method the following
question: How is it possible to posit the ideal as an autonomous and self-subsisting order of reality? As we have
already seen, the ideal has its genesis in religious consciousness: It is the philosophical metamorphosis of what
religion regards as Divine Being. But again, wherein lies
the genesis of the Divine Being? In this context, it is essential to bear in mind that the philosophy of Feuerbach
does not seek to resolve the question as to the existence
or non-existence of God. It is only concerned with the
content which religious consciousness throughout its history has put into the category of God. In other words,
Feuerbach's criticism addresses itself to the historical forms
in which religious consciousness has articulated its conceptions of the Divine Being. The cornerstone of his philosophy is that the Divine Being thus conceived has its
genesis in the being of man: It is the hypostatization of
man understood as a species-being. In the words of Feuerbach: ". . . man's idea of God is the idea of the human
individual of his own species, . . . God as the totality
of all realities and perfections, is nothing other than the

totality of the qualities of the species compendiously put
together in him for the benefit of the limited individual,
but actually dispersed among men and realizing themselves
in the course of world history."

In the context of speculative philosophy, the Divine
Being of religion emerges as the *res cogitans* of Descartes,
the Substance of Spinoza, the Ego of Fichte, and the Absolute of Hegel. Speculative philosophy gives a rational-
conceptual form to the Divine Being of theology, just as
theology hypostatizes the species-being of man as the Divine Being. This, as we have already ascertained, is what
Feuerbach means when he asserts that anthropology is the
secret of theology and speculative philosophy. The God
of theology and the ideal principle of speculative philosophy are nothing but forms of human self-alienation existing independently and objectively. Feuerbach's insistence
on the anthropological substratum of theology and speculative philosophy contains a categorical imperative for man
to take back into himself all the richness of content—
infinity and universality—he has put into God or into his
speculative metamorphoses. The practical-emancipatory
value of this supersession of man's self-alienation would
be his elevation from a morally and socio-politically de-
graded, impoverished, unfree being into a free and dig-
nified being.

The principle in terms of which Feuerbach seeks to restore the independence of the real is none other than sensuousness. The real has the ontological determination of
being sensuous, and hence it is given through the senses:
"Taken in its reality or regarded as real, the real is the
object of the senses—the sensuous. Truth, reality, sensuousness are one and the same thing. Only a sensuous being
is a true and real being. Only through the senses is an
object given in the true sense, not through thought for
itself. The object given by and identical with ideation is
merely thought." Now, if the object is sensuous and given
through the senses, the perceiving subject cannot be exclusively active vis-à-vis a passively existing reality. In other

words, the active and world-positing subject of speculative philosophy is also passive in so far as it is acted upon by sensuous reality. Not only does the ego posit the world, but is also posited by the world. This is the very core of Feuerbach's theoretical revolution, that it destroys the basis of speculative epistemology which proceeds from a world-less subject-as-thought confronting a thought-less world. The subject of Feuerbach, in so far as sensuousness belongs to its essential ontological constitution, is from the very outset filled with the world, just as the world in its turn is the world of and for the subject. Thus, nature in Feuerbach's philosophy is the object of man; he is ontologically dependent on her; that is, he needs her in order to exist and realize himself. Only in this sense, that is, only as the absolute condition of man's self-objectification—the realization of himself as a species-being in the medium of an independently existing nature—does nature occupy a place in Feuerbach's philosophy. It has nothing to do with the metaphysical question as to what nature is in itself.

Feuerbach's principle of sensuousness plays a decisive role not only in establishing the primacy and independence of sensuous reality, but also in grounding the being of man in a human-social relationship. Once again, man in the sense of Feuerbach is to be distinguished from the purely rational subject of speculative philosophy. The whole man is the unity of reason and sensuousness: He is both mind and body. With respect to his body, man is a being of needs. The body is the rational limit of subjectivity, the concrete existence of man. That he is a sensuous being means that he stands in need of the means of life that exist outside himself, that he suffers pain, experiences the lack of things he needs but does not have, that he is subject to wishes and drives, that he experiences elation and depression, etc. Only as a sensuous being does man relate himself to real concrete being both actively and passively. Thus existing, man unites within himself thought and being, that is, overcomes the speculative dichotomy between thought and being. The categorical imperative of the new philosophy is: "Think as one who exists, as one who is

in the world and is part of the world, not as one in the
vacuum of abstraction, not as a solitary monad, not as an
absolute monarch, not as an unconcerned, extra-worldly
God; only then can you be sure that being and thought
are united in all your thinking." Man as the unity of
thought and being is both subject and object; as such,
he is necessarily referred to other subjects and objects
existing apart from himself. To be is to be in togetherness
with others. The being of man—the unity of thought and
being—is communal being. Thus, man can think, feel, and
act only because his subjectivity is grounded in a commonly shared objectivity. Feuerbach says: "You think only
because your thoughts themselves can be thought, and
they are true only if they pass the test of objectivity; that
is, when someone else, to whom they are given as objects,
acknowledges them as such. You see because you are
yourself a visible being, you feel because you are yourself
a feelable being. Only to an open mind does the world
stand open, and the openings of the mind are only the
senses." The principle of sensuousness thus constitutes the
being of man as both subject and object. But it also establishes the separate, independent existence of subject
and object, or in the language of Feuerbach, the distinction between I and You, a distinction that is dissolved in
the philosophy of identity: "The single man in isolation
possesses in himself the essence of man neither as a moral,
nor as a thinking being. The essence of man is contained
only in the community, in the unity of man with man—a
unity, however, which rests on the reality of the distinction
between I and You."

Feuerbach sums up his philosophy in the following
words: "The new philosophy makes man together with
nature the basis of man, the exclusive, universal, highest
object of philosophy; it makes anthropology together with
physiology the universal science." This philosophy was
acclaimed by Marx as containing a real theoretical revolution since Hegel's *Phenomenology* and *Logic*. But later
on, Marx rejected Feuerbach as another German ideologist
comparable to a clever fellow who "once got the idea

that people drown because they are possessed by the idea
of gravity. If they would get this notion out of their heads
by seeing it as religious superstition, they would be completely safe from all danger of water. For his entire life
he fought against the illusion of gravity while all statistics
gave him new and abundant evidence of its harmful effects. That kind of fellow is typical of the new revolutionary
philosophers in Germany."[47] Since Feuerbach's philosophy owes its historical significance almost completely to
the fact of its being a part of the intellectual history of
Marx, it is important to know the reasons that led Marx
from his initial enthusiasm for Feuerbach to his subsequent rejection of him. They will also tell us something
about the limitations of Feuerbach's philosophy.

III   FEUERBACH AND MARX

Marx's *Theses on Feuerbach*, "the first document in
which is deposited the brilliant germ of the new world
outlook,"[48] contain the first formulation of his profound
dissatisfaction and definitive break with the contemplative
standpoint of Feuerbach's materialism. It seems that the
criticism expressed in the *Theses* did not come suddenly
and abruptly, but had been maturing in Marx since the
initial stages of his encounter with Feuerbach. In a letter
to Arnold Ruge, written in 1843 at a time when Marx's
enthusiasm for Feuerbach was at its highest, he has the
following criticism to make: "Only in one respect are the
aphorisms of Feuerbach not to my liking: he is too much
concerned with nature and too little with politics. It is,
however, only through a link with politics that present
philosophy can emerge as truth."[49] From the very beginning, the fundamental concern of Marx was to transform philosophy from a contemplative into a practical
activity. His fascination with the method of Feuerbach's
criticism of religion and speculative philosophy can be
adequately grasped only if it is realized that Marx believed
to have discovered in it an effective instrument for a criti-

cism of the profane world as a prerequisite for the realization of philosophy. The criticism of Feuerbach, voiced in the letter to Ruge, was only overlaid for a time by the exciting prospect of applying the "theoretical revolution" of Feuerbach to the problems of politics and society. It was resumed in the *Theses* after Marx had convinced himself of the paltriness of the Feuerbachian revolution, and together with it of the inherent inability of philosophy qua philosophy to change the world.

Before Feuerbach's philosophy had any impact on Marx, the latter had already taken the decisive step of abandoning the contemplative standpoint in favor of a practical one. This, however, does not mean that Marx had altogether abandoned philosophy; the transition to practice was still a transition within philosophy, and was understood by Marx as a consequence emanating necessarily from the system of Hegel. Marx's intellectual beginnings—if we disregard his romantic outpourings before 1837—were anchored in the philosophy of Hegel. He describes, in a letter to his father dated 1837, the process of his unwilling "conversion" to Hegel. He had "read fragments of Hegel's philosophy and had found its grotesque craggy melody unpleasing."[50] But later, having read Hegel "from beginning to end" during a sickness precipitated by an "existential" crisis, he had found that he was "more and more chained to the current world philosophy from which I thought to escape." What was the reason for his fascination with Hegel? Marx writes: "Setting out from idealism . . . I hit upon seeking the Idea in the real itself. If formerly the gods had dwelt above the world, they had now become its center." Idealism in this context is taken by Marx to mean the standpoint that regards the gods; that is, the highest truth of being as existing in a transcendent realm separated from mundane reality. This idealist dichotomy of the real and the ideal is conceived by Hegel as their mediated identity; to him, all that is real is real only in so far as it has the Idea in itself. In seeking the Idea in the real, Marx is therefore identifying himself with the Hegelian standpoint. The "escape" from Hegel

is the theme of Marx's *Doctoral Dissertation* which poses
the question as to the very possibility of philosophy after
its culmination in Hegel. The *Dissertation* projects this
question into an analogous historical situation—that of the
post-Aristotelian philosophy. Epicureanism, Stoicism, and
Skepticism were the products of "self-consciousness" in
which philosophy, after its culmination in Aristotle, had
found a new element, like Themistocles who, "when
Athens was threatened with devastation, persuaded the
Athenians to leave it for good and found a new Athens
on the sea, on another element."[51] Himself condemned
to the fate of a successor to a total system, Marx in his
Dissertation turns for enlightenment to similarly situated
successors. The conclusion he draws is put in the form of
a "psychological law": "It is a psychological law that the
theoretical spirit, having become free in itself, turns into
practical energy. Emerging as *will* from Amenthes'
shadow world, it turns against worldly actuality which
exists outside it."[52] Having withdrawn itself from the
world into a total system—the shadow world of Amenthes
—philosophy returns to it; "like a practical person" spin-
ning "intrigues with the world," it "throws itself on the
bosom of the mundane siren."[53] Precisely because of its
inner transparency and perfection, the total system stands
opposed to an opaque and imperfect world. This is what
Marx means by the diremption of the world: "As philosophy has closed itself into a complete, total world . . .
the totality of the world is implicitly split . . ." As applied
to the philosophy of Hegel, "This split is driven to extremes because spiritual existence has become free, en-
riched to universality."[54] Philosophy qua system cannot
overcome this diremption; in returning to the world as
will, philosophy cannot force itself upon the world again
as a system whose "inner self-contentedness and rounded-
ness is broken down." In order to find itself, philosophy
must first lose itself as a system, for "the world's becoming
philosophical is at the same time philosophy's becoming
worldly, . . . its realization is at the same time its loss
[i.e., qua system], . . . what it combats outside is its own

inner defect [i.e., its abstract totality qua system from which the actual world with its contradictions is excluded] . . ." In his profound understanding of the nature of philosophy, Marx characterizes it as fundamentally critical. Its movement towards the world is its self-assertion as "criticism which measures individual existence against essence, particular activity against the Idea."[55] In this critical sense, philosophy cannot remain true to its own nature if it does not abandon contemplation and become practical; that is, address itself to the task of molding reality in the image of what it calls reason and freedom. Thus, as early as his *Doctoral Dissertation,* Marx determines philosophy as a practical activity called upon to oppose the irrationality and unfreedom of the world. He settles philosophy on the element of human self-consciousness and insists on its rebellious spirit: "Philosophy makes no secret of it. The confession of Prometheus —'to put it simply, I hate all the gods'—is its very own confession, its own motto against all heavenly and earthly gods who do not recognize human self-consciousness as the highest deity. There shall be none other beside this deity."[56]

It is against this background that Marx's enthusiastic reception of Feuerbach's method of inverting the subject-predicate relationship in theology and speculative philosophy is to be understood; because this method vindicated human self-consciousness—in Feuerbach the being of man as species-being—as the true and actual subject of all perfection, infinity, and universality attributed by religion and speculative philosophy to their highest being. Furthermore, the method of Feuerbach released empirical reality from its subordinate and derivative position, thus establishing nature as primary, self-subsisting, and intrinsically real. Thrilled by its emancipatory significance, Marx was quick to advise all speculative theologians and philosophers: "Free yourselves from the concepts and prepossessions of existing speculative philosophy if you want to get at things differently, as they are, that is to say, if you want to arrive at the *truth*. And there is no other road for you to *truth* and *freedom* except that leading through the Fire-brook [the *Feuer-bach*]. Feuerbach is the purgatory of the present times."[57] Marx himself applies the Feuerbachian method to Hegel's *Philosophy of the State,* and ascertains in a language strictly oriented on Feuerbach's terminology and diction: "Hegel makes the predicates, the objects, self-sufficient, but separated from their actual self-sufficiency, from their subject. Later the actual subject then appears as a result, while one should proceed from the actual subject and pay attention to its objectivization. . . . Hegel considers the universal not as the actual essence of what is the actual-finite, that is, what is existing and determinate, and he considers the actual *Ens* not as the *genuine subject* of the infinite."[58] It was due to Marx's primary concern with the actual socio-political world of man that he immediately left the Feuerbachian domain of the criticism of the religious world: "Man, who has found only the *reflection* of himself in the fantastic reality of heaven where he sought a supernatural being, will no longer be inclined to find the *semblance* of himself, only the non-human being, where he seeks and must seek his true reality."[59] What the true reality of man is, is the subject of the most profound, and theoretically the most fundamental work of the young Marx—the *Parisian Manuscripts* of 1844. In this work Marx formulates his first critique of political economy from the vantage point of a doctrine of man that is heavily indebted to Feuerbachian anthropology and naturalism. But it is also in the *Parisian Manuscripts* that Marx drifts away from the contemplative standpoint of Feuerbach and turns directly to Hegel, especially to the Hegel of the *Phenomenology.* A critical appropriation of the Hegelian dialectic of the Lord and the Slave leads Marx to the elaboration of a concept of man that, involving as it does the idea of the self-creation of man as a process anchored in labor as constitutive of man's essential being, transcends the scope of the contemplatively limited anthropology of Feuerbach.

At the heart of the *Parisian Manuscripts* is Marx's theory of communism which provides the focal point of their thematic perspective. The main themes of the work—critique of political economy, critique of Hegelian philosophy, and alienated labor—merge together and reveal their inner link in that theory: "*Communism* as *positive* overcoming of *private property* as *human self-alienation*, and thus as the actual *appropriation of the human* essence through and for man; therefore, as the complete and conscious restoration of man to himself within the total wealth of previous development, the restoration of man as a *social*, that is, human being. This communism as completed naturalism is humanism, as completed humanism it is naturalism. It is the *genuine* resolution of the antagonism between man and nature and between man and man; it is the true resolution of the conflict between existence and essence, objectification and self-affirmation, freedom and necessity, individual and species. It is the riddle of history solved and knows itself as this solution."[60] The dynamic core of this theory of communism is the concept of the essence of man. The condition of man in history and society is seen by Marx as determined by the conflict between his essence—what he truly and really is—and his existence—his actual mode of being in the context of alienated labor. The aim of Marx's critique of political economy is to show that although it regards self-objectifying labor as the source of wealth, it is unable to account for the crushing power of wealth—the product of labor—over labor, over man as a producing being: It is unable to account for "the complete domination of living men by dead matter."[61] In capitalist society, the "system of alienation" par excellence, the self-objectification of labor, has the character of the self-dehumanization of man. Alienated labor is the form that expresses the fact that the existence of man is at variance with his essence. Like political economy, Hegel, too, "views labor as the essence, the self-confirming essence of man"; that is why "Hegel's standpoint is that of modern political economy."[62] But labor in Hegel is the labor of Spirit, that is, abstracted from the concrete reality of man. However, albeit in a mystified form, the Hegelian self-alienation of the subject and its retraction by it have a critical thrust in so far as they point to the discrepancy between that which is and that which ought to be. Divested of its mystical garb, the subject of Hegel is the real, objective man: "The great thing in Hegel's *Phenomenology* and its final result—the dialectic of negativity as the moving and productive principle—is simply that Hegel grasps the self-development of man as a process, objectification as loss of the object, as alienation and transcendence of this alienation; that he thus grasps the nature of *labor* and comprehends objective man, authentic because actual, as the result of his *own labor*." [63] This great thing about Hegel's *Phenomenology* provides Marx with the basis for his specific concept of man which, although built into Feuerbachian anthropology, lies at the same time completely outside it.

Proceeding from Feuerbach, Marx characterizes man as a species-being. This means at the same time, as it does in Feuerbach, that man is a *"universal* and consequently free being." In distinction from the animal, man's life activity is not limited by a fixed mode of interchange with nature, but rather has the whole of nature as its object: "Nature is the *inorganic body* of man, that is, nature in so far as it is not the human body." [64] Not limited like the animal, man produces not in a single direction, but universally; because of the universal character of his interchange with nature, man reproduces the whole of nature. And in so far as he can transcend the context of immediate physical necessity, man, unlike the animal, creates "also in accordance with the laws of beauty." [65]

As a species-being, man is also a natural being. He does not approach nature from an outside position of "pure activity," but is from the very outset an integral part of nature: "That the physical and spiritual life of man is tied up with nature is another way of saying that nature is linked to itself, for man is a part of nature." [66] However, the link between man and nature has the character of a mediated relationship. Man as subjective nature is mediated through objective nature, just as objective nature is mediated through the subjective life activity—labor in the widest sense—of man. The epistemological significance of labor, a concept which finds its explication in Marx's later works, is already apparent in the *Parisian Manuscripts* when Marx attributes to it a world-constituting role. Man's interchange with nature, the medium of which is the life activity of man as productive activity, is the condition for the possibility of human objects. Nature is always nature as it has been worked upon, transformed, and integrated into certain perceptual patterns. But man as subjective nature is himself mediated through transformed or humanized nature. In Kantian terms, nature in the context of the anthropology of the *Parisian Manuscripts* is *phenomenon* and not *noumenon*. In the words of Marx: "*Human* objects are not natural objects as they immediately present themselves nor is *human* sense immediately and objectively *human* sensibility, human objectivity. Neither objective nor subjective nature is immediately presented in a form adequate to the *human* being."[67] The species-being of man—and here Marx has only the term in common with Feuerbach, but not its explication—consists in working upon nature so as to fashion it into the world of man: "In working upon the objective world, . . . man proves himself to be genuinely a *species-being*. This production is his active species-life. Through it nature appears as *his* work and his actuality. The object of labor is thus the *objectification of man's species-life:* he produces himself not only intellectually, as in consciousness, but also actively in a real sense and sees himself in a world he made."[68]

Marx's concept of man, as distinct from that of Feuerbach, is essentially social and historical. The object-creating activity is fundamentally social because from the very outset it is carried on within a social context. The reality of others is revealed to man in and through the object of labor. The subject-object of the interchange with nature is human collectivity. The interchange has the character of a historical process. Neither the reality of man nor the forms of his world and the mode of his interchange with nature are fixed. They result from previous socio-historical processes and are themselves such processes. History is the process of man's self-creation through his labor.

As mentioned earlier, these specific dimensions of Marx's concept of man are built into the Feuerbachian anthropology. Alienation, the basic theme of the *Parisian Manuscripts,* is understandable only with reference to the essence of man; alienation is the condition in which the essence of man and its self-manifestation as the world of man have the relationship of externality, foreignness, and domination to the actual empirical existence of man. The history of man is the history of his alienation from his own essence, culminating in capitalist society as the system of alienation par excellence. It is within this anthropological perspective that Marx interprets communism as the conscious restoration of man to himself, and sees in it the solution to the riddle of history.

Marx abandons this anthropological standpoint—and with this the whole of Feuerbachian humanism and naturalism—in his *Theses on Feuerbach* and the *German Ideology.* Marx says in the first *Thesis:* "The chief defect of all previous materialism (including Feuerbach's) is that the object, actuality, sensuousness is conceived only in the form of the *object or contemplation,* but not as *sensuous human activity, practice,* not subjectively. Hence, in opposition to materialism, the *active* side was developed by idealism—but only abstractly since idealism naturally does not know actual, sensuous activity as such. Feuerbach wants sensuous objects actually different from thought objects: but he does not comprehend human activity itself as objective."[69] This is quite obviously reminiscent of the characterization in the *Parisian Manuscripts* of labor as the process of man's self-creation, involving at the same time the "practical creation of an objective world." As in the *Parisian Manuscripts,* so also in the first *Thesis* "the *active* side" is associated with the idealist philosophy of Hegel. The Hegelian subject, even if in an abstract way, is actively involved in the production of its content, its objectifications. In other words, its relationship to its objectifications, the forms into which it alienates itself, is not contemplative, but practical, for only thus can it progressively supersede its self-alienation. The Hegelian subject is the activity of returning to itself from the object which it actively posits. The mediating activity is unknown to all materialism including that of Feuerbach. It does not realize that the object is essentially sensuous human activity in so far as it is posited as such by human labor, the activity of producing human objects. Hence, Feuerbach "does not comprehend human activity itself as *objective*." It would seem that Marx has not yet abandoned the framework of the *Parisian Manuscripts,* for what we have in the first *Thesis* is a more direct and definitive version of what he had already said. The sixth *Thesis,* however, makes it quite clear that Marx has completely abandoned the anthropological context of his concept of labor; the context is now socio-historical. Rejecting the idea of the essence of man, Marx relegates it to a social category: "But the essence of man is no abstraction inherent in each single individual. In its actuality it is the ensemble of social relationships." These social relationships do not have a fixed form; they are structured within a totality which is itself the result of its socio-historical process.

NOTES

1. D. Easton and K. Guddat, *Writings of the Young Marx on Philosophy and Society* (Garden City: Anchor Books, Doubleday, 1967), p. 416.
2. D. Rjazanov and V. Adoratskij, eds., *Marx-Engels-Gesamtausgabe* [hereafter MEGA], Abt. I, Bd. 3, pp. 209, 226.
3. Marx/Engels, *Selected Works,* Vol. II (Moscow: Foreign Languages Publishing House, 1962), p. 359.
4. Herbert Marcuse, *Ideen zu einer kritischen Theorie der Gesellschaft* (Frankfurt: Suhrkamp Verlag, 1969), pp. 26–27.
5. Louis Althusser, *For Marx* (London: Allen Lane; New York: Random House, 1969), pp. 32–34.

6. Heinrich Popitz, *Der entfremdete Mensch* (Frankfurt: Europäische Verlagsanstalt, 1967), p. 69.
7. Louis Althusser, op. cit., p. 46.
8. Ibid., p. 35.
9. Ibid., pp. 31–32.
10. Ibid., p. 45.
11. Martin Heidegger, *Being and Time*, Translated by John Macquarrie and Edward Robinson (Oxford, 1967), pp. 12–13.
12. Pp. 15–16 of this Introduction.
13. 14. 15. 16. 17. This volume, pp. 219 ff.
18. *The Logic of Hegel*, Translated by William Wallace (Oxford and New York: Oxford University Press, 1874), p. 328.
19. This volume, p. 118.
20. This volume, pp. 219 ff.
21. Ludwig Feuerbach, *Kleine Schriften* (Frankfurt: Suhrkamp, 1966), pp. 7 ff.
22. *Hegel: Texts and Commentary*, Translated by Walter Kaufmann (Garden City: Anchor Books, Doubleday, 1965), p. 10.
23. Hegel, *Sämtliche Werke*, Jubiläumsausgabe, 3rd. Edition, Bd. I (Stuttgart: Fr. Frommanns Verlag, 1949–59), p. 174.
24. Cf. *Hegel's Science of Logic*, Translated by A. V. Miller (New York: Humanities Press; London: Allen & Unwin, Ltd., 1969), p. 610.
25. Hegel, *Differenz des Fichte'schen und Schelling'schen Systems der Philosophie* (Hamburg: Felix Meiner Verlag, 1962), p. 12.
26. Ibid., p. 10.
27. Ibid., p. 12 ff.
28. Ibid., p. 11.
29. This volume, p. 53.
30. *Hegel's Science of Logic*, Translated by A. V. Miller (New York: Humanities Press, 1969), p. 68.
31. Ibid., p. 69.
32. Ibid., p. 69.
33. Ibid., p. 69.
34. F. Nicolin and O. Pöggeler, eds., *Enzyklopädie der Philosophischen Wissenschaften, 1830* (Hamburg: Felix Meiner Verlag, 1959), p. 243.
35. This volume, p. 1.

36. Marx/Engels, op. cit., p. 368.

37. Op. cit., p. 70: "All *explicata* to which the analytic of Dasein gives rise are obtained by considering Dasein's existence-structure. Because Dasein's characters of Being are defined in terms of existentiality, we call them *'existentialia.'* These are to be sharply distinguished from what we call *'categories'*—characteristics of Being for entities whose character is not that of Dasein."

38. Easton and Guddat, op. cit., p. 409.

39. Alfred Schmidt, *Der Begriff der Natur in der Lehre von Marx* (Frankfurt: Europaische Verlagsanstalt, 1962), pp. 143–44.

40. Easton and Guddat, op. cit., p. 285.

41. Ibid., p. 321.

42. This volume, pp. 247–48.

43. Hegel, *Ethics,* Edited by James Gutmann (New York: Hafner Publishing Co., 1949), p. 41.

44. Hegel, *Phenomenology of Mind,* Translated by J. B. Baillie (New York: Macmillan Company, 1955), p. 79.

45. Ibid., p. 80.

46. This volume, p. 125.

47. Easton and Guddat, op. cit., p. 405.

48. Marx/Engels, op. cit., p. 359.

49. MEGA, I, i. 2, p. 308.

50. Easton and Guddat, op. cit., p. 46.

51. Ibid., p. 53.

52. Ibid., p. 61.

53. Ibid., p. 52.

54. Ibid., p. 52.

55. Ibid., p. 61.

56. MEGA, I, i. 1, p. 10.

57. Easton and Guddat, op. cit., p. 95.

58. Ibid., p. 166.

59. Ibid., p. 249–50.

60. Ibid., p. 304.

61. Karl Marx, *Early Writings,* Translated by T. B. Bottomore (London: C. A. Watts & Co., New York: McGraw-Hill, 1963), p. 115.

62. Easton and Guddat, op. cit., p. 322.

63. Ibid., p. 321.

64. Ibid., p. 293.

65. Ibid., p. 295.

66. Ibid., p. 293.
67. Ibid., p. 326.
68. Ibid., p. 295.
69. Ibid., p. 400.

THE FIERY BROOK

Selected Writings of Ludwig Feuerbach

And there is no other road for you to *truth* and *freedom* except that leading *through* the brook of fire [the Feuerbach]. Feuerbach is the *purgatory* of the present times.

Karl Marx

Towards a Critique of
Hegel's Philosophy

German speculative philosophy stands in direct contrast
to the ancient Solomonic wisdom: Whereas the latter believes that there is nothing new under the sun, the former
sees nothing that is not new under the sun; whereas oriental man loses sight of differences in his preoccupation
with unity, occidental man forgets unity in his preoccupation with differences; whereas oriental man carries his indifference to the eternally identical to the point of an
imbecilic apathy, occidental man heightens his sensibility
for the manifold to the feverish heat of the *imaginatio
luxurians*. By German speculative philosophy, I mean that
philosophy which dominates the present—the philosophy
of Hegel. As far as Schelling's philosophy is concerned,
it was really an exotic growth—the ancient oriental idea
of identity on Germanic soil. If the characteristic inner
movement of Schelling's school is towards the Orient, then
the distinguishing feature of the Hegelian philosophy and
school is their move towards the Occident combined with
their belittlement of the Orient. The characteristic element
of Hegel's philosophy as compared to the orientalism of
the philosophy of identity is *difference*. In spite of everything, Hegel's philosophy of nature does not reach beyond
the involutions of zoophytes and mollusca to which, as is
known, acephales and gastropodes also belong. Hegel elevated us to a higher stage, i.e., to the class of *articulata*

whose highest order is constituted by *insects*. Hegel's spirit
is logical, determinate, and—I would like to say—entomo-
logical; in other words, Hegel's is a spirit that finds its
appropriate dwelling in a body with numerous protruding
members and with deep fissures and sections. This spirit
manifests itself particularly in its view and treatment of
history. Hegel determines and presents only the most striking differences of various religions, philosophies, times,
and peoples, and in a progressive series of stages, but he
ignores all that is common and identical in all of them.
The form of both Hegel's conception and method is that
of exclusive time alone, not that of tolerant space; his
system knows only *subordination* and *succession;* co-
ordination and coexistence are unknown to it. To be sure,
the last stage of development is always the *totality* that
includes in itself the other stages, but since it itself is a
definite temporal existence and hence bears the character
of particularity, it cannot incorporate into itself other
existences without sucking out the very marrow of their
independent lives and without robbing them of the meaning which they can have only in complete freedom. The
Hegelian method boasts of taking the same course as nature. It is true that it imitates nature, but the copy lacks
the life of the original. Granted, nature has made man the
master of animals, but it has given him not only hands to
tame animals but also eyes and ears to admire them. The
independence of the animal, which the cruel hand robs, is
given back to it by sympathetic ears and eyes. The love of
art breaks the chains that the self-interest of manual work
puts around the animal. The horse that is weighed down
under the groom's behind is elevated to an object of art
by the painter, and the sable that is slain by the furrier
for the purpose of turning its fur into a momentary orna-
ment of human vanity is preserved by natural science so
that it can be studied as a whole organism. Nature always
combines the monarchical tendency of time with the liberalism of space. Naturally, the flower cancels the leaf,
but would the plant be perfect if the flower only sat
brightly on a leafless stem? True, some plants do shed

their leaves in order to put all their energy into bringing
forth the blossom, but there are other plants in which the
leaf either appears later than the flower or simultaneously
with it, which proves that any presentation of the totality
of the plant requires the leaf as well as the flower. It is
true that man is the truth of the animal, but would the
life of nature, would the life of man itself be perfect
if animals did not exist independently? Is man's relationship with animals only a despotic one? Do not the forsaken
and the rejected find a substitute for the ingratitude, schem-
ing, and unfaithfulness of their fellow human beings in
the faithfulness of the animal? Does the animal not have
a power that consoles and heals his broken heart? Is not a
good, rational sense also part of animal cults? Could it
not be that we regard these cults as ludicrous because
we have succumbed to an idolatry of a different kind?
Does not the animal speak to the heart of the child in
fables? Did not a mere donkey once open the eyes of an
obdurate prophet?

The stages in the development of nature have, therefore,
by no means only a *historical* meaning. They are, indeed,
moments, but moments of a simultaneous totality of nature and not of a *particular* and *individual* totality which
itself would only be a moment of the universe, that is,
of the totality of nature. However, this is not the case with
the philosophy of Hegel in which only time, not space,
belongs to the form of intuition. Here, totality or the
absoluteness of a particular historical phenomenon or
existence is vindicated as predicate, thus reducing the
stages of development as independent entities only to a
historical meaning; although living, they continue to exist
as nothing more than shadows or moments, nothing more
than homoeopathic drops on the level of the *absolute.* In
this way, for example, Christianity—and, to be sure, taken
in its historical-*dogmatic* development—is determined as
absolute religion. In the interest of such a determination,
however, only the difference of Christianity from other
religions is accentuated, thus neglecting all that is common
to all of them; that is, the *nature* of religion which, as the

only absolute condition, lies at the base of all the different religions. The same is true of philosophy. The Hegelian philosophy, I mean the philosophy of *Hegel*, that is to say, a philosophy that is after all a particular and definite philosophy having an empirical existence—we are not concerned here with the character of its content—is defined and proclaimed as *absolute* philosophy; i.e., as nothing less than *philosophy itself*, if not by the master himself, then certainly by his disciples—at least by his orthodox disciples —and certainly quite consistently and in keeping with the teaching of the master. Thus, recently, a Hegelian—and a sagacious and thoughtful person at that—has sought to demonstrate—ceremoniously and, in his own way, thoroughly—that the Hegelian philosophy "is the *absolute reality of the idea* of philosophy."

But however sagacious the author is otherwise, he proceeds from the very outset uncritically in so far as he does not pose the question: Is it at all *possible* that a species realizes itself in *one* individual, art as such in *one* artist, and philosophy as such in one philosopher? And yet this is the main question; for what use to me are all the proofs that *this* particular person is the messiah when I do not believe at all that any messiah ever will, could, or must appear. Hence, if this question is not raised, it is quietly taken for granted that there must and does exist an aesthetic or speculative Dalai Lama, an aesthetic or speculative transubstantiation, and an aesthetic or speculative Day of Judgment. It is just this presupposition, however, that contradicts reason. "Only all men taken together," says Goethe, "cognize nature, and only all men taken together live human nature." How profound—and what is more—how true! Only love, admiration, veneration, in short, only passion makes the individual into the species. For example, in moments when, enraptured by the beautiful and lovable nature of a person, we exclaim: He is beauty, love, and goodness incarnate. Reason, however, knows nothing—keeping in mind the Solomonic wisdom that there is nothing new under the sun—of a real and absolute incarnation of the species in a particular individuality. It is true that the spirit or the consciousness is "species existing as species," but, no matter how universal, the individual and his head—the organ of the spirit—are always designated by a definite kind of nose, whether pointed or snub, fine or gross, long or short, straight or bent. Whatever enters into time and space must also subordinate itself to the laws of time and space. The god of limitation stands guard at the entrance to the world. Self-limitation is the condition of entry. Whatever becomes real, becomes so only as something determined. The incarnation of the species with all its plenitude into *one* individuality would be an absolute miracle, a violent suspension of all the laws and principles of reality; it would, indeed, be the *end of the world*.

Obviously, therefore, the belief of the Apostles and early Christians in the approaching end of the world was intimately linked with their belief in incarnation. Time and space are *actually already* abolished with the manifestation of the divinity in a particular time and form, and hence there is nothing more to expect but the *actual end* of the world. It is no longer possible to conceive the possibility of history; it no longer has a meaning and goal. *Incarnation* and *history* are absolutely incompatible; when deity itself enters into history, history ceases to exist. But if history nevertheless continues in the same way as before, then the theory of incarnation is in reality nullified by history itself. The manifestation of the deity, which is only a report, a narration for other later times—and hence only an object of imagination and recollection—has lost the mark of divinity, and relinquishing its miraculous and extraordinary status, it has placed itself on an equal footing with the other, ordinary phenomena of history in as much as it is itself *reproduced* in later times in a *natural* way. The moment it becomes the object of narration, it *ceases* to be a miracle. It is therefore not without reason that people say that time betrays all secrets. Consequently, if a historical phenomenon were actually the manifestation or incarnation of the deity, then it must extinguish—and this alone would be its proof—all the lights of history, par-

ticularly church lights, as the sun puts out the stars and
the day nocturnal lights; then it must illuminate the whole
earth with its rapturous divine effulgence and be for all
men in all times an absolute, omnipresent, and immediate
manifestation. For what is supernatural must also act *as
such beyond all limits of time;* and hence, what reproduces
itself in a natural way—maintains itself only through the
medium of either oral or written tradition—is only of mediated origin and integrated into a natural context.

The situation is the same with the theories of incarnation in the field of art and science. If Hegelian philosophy
were the absolute reality of the idea of philosophy, then
the immobility of reason in the Hegelian philosophy must
necessarily result in the immobility of time; for if time
still sadly moved along as if nothing had happened, then
the Hegelian philosophy would unavoidably forfeit its attribute of absoluteness. Let us put ourselves for a few
moments in future centuries! Will not the Hegelian philosophy then be chronologically a foreign and *transmitted*
philosophy to us? Will it be possible for us then to regard
a philosophy from other times, a philosophy of the past
as *our* contemporary philosophy? How else do philosophies
pass if it is not because men and epochs pass and posterity
wants to live not by the heritage of its ancestors but by
the riches acquired by itself? Will we therefore not regard
the Hegelian philosophy as an oppressive burden just as
medieval Aristotle once was to the Age of Reformation?
Will not an opposition of necessity arise between the old
and the new philosophy, between the unfree—because traditional—and free—because self-acquired—philosophy? Will
not Hegelian philosophy be relegated from its pinnacle
of the absolute reality of the Idea to the modest position
of a particular and definite reality? But is it not rational,
is it not the duty and task of the thinking man to anticipate
through reason the necessary and unavoidable consequences of time, to know in advance from the nature of
things what will one day automatically result from the
nature of time?

Anticipating the future with the help of reason, let us

therefore undertake to demonstrate that the Hegelian philosophy is really a definite and special kind of philosophy. The proof is not difficult to find, however much this philosophy is distinguished from all previous philosophies by its rigorous scientific character, universality, and incontestable richness of thought. Hegelian philosophy was born at a time when mankind stood, as at any other time, on a definite level of thought, when a definite kind of philosophy was in existence. It drew on this philosophy, linked itself with it, and hence it must itself have a definite; i.e., finite character. Every philosophy originates, therefore, as a manifestation of its time; its origin *presupposes its historical time*. Of course, it appears to *itself* as not resting on any presuppositions; and, in relation to earlier systems, that is certainly true. A later age, nevertheless, is bound to realize that this philosophy was after all based on certain presuppositions; i.e., certain accidental presuppositions which have to be distinguished from those that are *necessary* and *rational* and cannot be negated without involving absolute nonsense. But is it really true that the Hegelian philosophy does not begin with any presuppositions? "Yes! It proceeds from pure Being; it does not start from a *particular* point of departure, but from that which is purely indeterminate; it starts from that which is itself the beginning." Is that really so? And is it not after all a presupposition that philosophy has to begin at all? "Well, it is quite obvious that everything must have a beginning, philosophy not excepted." Quite true! But "beginning" here has the sense of accidental or indifferent; in philosophy, on the other hand, beginning has a *particular* meaning, the meaning of the first principle in itself as required by philosophical science. But what I would like to ask is: Why should beginning be taken in this sense? Is the notion of beginning not itself subject to criticism? Is it immediately true and universally valid? Why should it not be possible for me to abandon at the start the notion of beginning and, instead, turn directly to that which is real? Hegel starts from Being; i.e., the notion of Being or abstract Being. Why should I not be able to start from Being itself; i.e., real Being? Or,

again, why should I not be able to start from reason, since
Being, in so far as it is thought of and in so far as it is an
object of logic, immediately refers me back to reason? Do
I still start from a presupposition when I start from reason?
No! I cannot doubt reason and abstract from it without
declaring at the same time that both doubting and abstracting do not partake of reason. But even conceding
that I do base myself on a presupposition that my philosophizing starts directly from real Being or reason without
at all being concerned with the whole question of a beginning, what is so harmful about that? Can I not prove
later that the presupposition I had based myself on was
only formally and apparently so, that in reality it was
none at all? I certainly do not begin to think just at the
point when I put my thoughts on paper. I already know
how the subject matter of my thinking would develop. I
presuppose something because I know that what I presuppose would justify itself through itself.

Can it therefore be said that the starting point taken
by the Hegelian philosophy in the *Logic* is a general and
an absolutely necessary starting point? Is it not rather a
starting point that is itself determined, that is to say, determined by the standpoint of philosophy before Hegel?
Is it not itself tied up with (Fichte's) *Theory of Science?*
Is it not connected with the old question as to the first
principle of philosophy and with that philosophical view-
point which was essentially interested in a formal system
rather than in reality? Is it not linked with the first question
of all philosophy: What is the first principle? Is this connection not proved by the fact that the method of Hegel—
disregarding, of course, the difference of content which
also becomes the difference of form—is *essentially,* or at
least generally, the method of Fichte? Is this not also the
course described by the *Theory of Science* that that which
is at first *for us* is in the end also *for itself,* that therefore
the end returns to the beginning, and that the course
taken by philosophical science is a circle? Is it not so that
the circular movement, and indeed taken literally, becomes
an inner need or a necessary consequence where method;

i.e., the *presentation* of philosophy, is taken to be the essence of philosophy itself, where anything that is not a system (taken here in its narrow sense) is not philosophy at all? For only that which is a completed circle is a system, which does not just go on *ad infinitum,* but whose end rather returns to its beginning. The Hegelian philosophy is actually the most perfect *system* that has ever appeared. Hegel actually achieved what Fichte aspired to but did not achieve, because he concluded with an "ought" and not with an end that is also beginning. And yet, systematic thought is by no means the same as *thought as such,* or *essential* thought; it is only self-*presenting* thought. To the extent that I present my thoughts, I place them in time; an insight that contains all its successive moments within a simultaneity in my mind now becomes a sequence. I posit that which is to be presented as not existing and let it be born under my very eyes; I abstract from what it is prior to its presentation. Whatever I therefore posit as a beginning is, in the first instance, that which is purely indeterminate; indeed, I know nothing about it, for self-presenting knowledge has yet to become knowledge. Hence, strictly speaking, I can start only from the notion of a starting point; for whatever object I may posit, initially it will always have the nature of a starting point. In this regard, Hegel is much more consistent and exact than Fichte with his clamorous "I." But given that the starting point is indeterminate, then moving onward must mean determining. Only during the course of the movement of presentation does that from which I start come to determine and manifest itself. Hence, progression is at the same time retrogression—I return whence I started. In retrogression I retract progression; i.e., temporalization of thought: I restore the lost identity. But the first principle to which I return is no longer the initial, indeterminate, and unproved first principle; it is now mediated and therefore no longer the same or, even granting that it is the same, no longer in the same form. This process is of course well founded and necessary, although it rests only on the relationship of self-manifesting and self-presenting thought to thought in itself; i.e., to inner thought. Let us put it in the following way. I read the *Logic* of Hegel from beginning to end. At the end I return to the beginning. The idea of the Idea or the Absolute Idea contains in itself the idea of Essence, the idea of Being. I therefore know now that Being and Essence are moments of the Idea, or that the Absolute Idea is the *Logic in nuce.* Of course, at the end I return to the beginning, but, let us hope, *not in time,* that is, not in a way that would make me begin with the *Logic* all over again; for otherwise I would be necessitated to go the same way a second and a third time and so on with the result that my whole life will have become a circular movement within the Hegelian *Logic.* I would rather close the three volumes of the *Logic* once I have arrived at its end—the Absolute Idea, because I will then *know* what it contains. In the knowledge that I now have, I cancel the temporal process of mediation; I know that the Absolute Idea is the Whole, and I naturally need time to be able to realize for myself its processual form; however, this order of succession is completely indifferent here. The *Logic* in three volumes, i.e., the worked-out *Logic,* is not a goal *in itself,* for otherwise I would have no other goal in life than to go on reading it or to memorize it as a "paternoster." Indeed, the Absolute Idea itself retracts its process of mediation, *encompasses* this process *within itself,* and nullifies the reality of presentation in that it shows itself to be the first and the last, the one and all. And for this very reason, I, too, now shut the *Logic* and concentrate its spread into one idea. In the end, the *Logic* leads us, therefore, back to *ourselves,* i.e., to our inner act of cognition; mediating and self-constituting knowledge becomes *unmediated* knowledge, but not unmediated in the subjective sense of Jacobi because there is no unmediated knowledge in that sense. I mean a different kind of unmediatedness.

To the extent to which it is *self-activity,* thinking is an *unmediated* activity. No one else can think for me; only *through myself* do I convince myself of the truth of a thought. Plato is meaningless and non-existent for someone who lacks understanding; he is a blank sheet to one who cannot link ideas that correspond with his words. Plato in writing is only a *means* for me; that which is primary and *a priori,* that which is the *ground* to which all is ultimately referred, is understanding. To bestow understanding does not lie in the power of philosophy, for understanding is presupposed by it; philosophy only shapes my understanding. The *creation* of concepts on the basis of a particular kind of philosophy is not a real but only a formal creation; it is not creation out of nothing, but only the development, as it were, of a spiritual matter lying within me that is as yet indeterminate but, nevertheless, capable of assuming all determinations. The philosopher produces in me only the awareness of what I can know; he fastens on to my mental ability. In this sense, philosophy, issuing either from the mouth or the pen, goes back directly to its own *source;* it does not speak in order to speak—hence its antipathy against all pretty talk—but in order *not* to speak, that is, in order to *think;* it does not demonstrate—hence its contempt for all sophistic syllogistics—but only to show that what it demonstrates is *simply* in keeping with the very *principle* of all demonstration and reason, and that it is stringent thought; i.e., a thought that expresses to every thinking person a law of reason. To demonstrate is to show that what I am *saying* is *true,* is to lead expressed thought back to its source. The meaning of demonstration cannot, therefore, be grasped without reference to the meaning of *language.* Language is nothing other than the *realization of the species;* i.e., the "I" is mediated with the "You" in order, by eliminating their individual separateness, to manifest the unity of the species. Now, the element in which the word exists is air, the most spiritual and general medium of life. A demonstration has its ground only in the mediating activity of thought *for others.* Whenever I wish to prove something, I do so for others. When I prove, teach, or write, then I do so, I hope, not for myself; for I also know, at least in essentials, what I do not write, teach, and discuss. This is also the reason why one often finds it most difficult to

write about something which one knows best, which is
so perfectly certain and clear to oneself that one cannot
understand why others should not know it as well. A
writer who is so certain of the object he is to write about
that he would not even take the trouble to write about it
falls into a category of humor that is in a class by itself.
He defeats the purpose of writing through writing, and
jokes about proofs in his proofs. If I am to write and,
indeed, write well and in a fundamental way, then I must
doubt that the others know what I know, or at least that
they know it in the same way as I do. Only because of
that can I communicate my thoughts. But I also presuppose
that they should and *can* know them. To teach is not to
drum things into a person; rather, the teacher applies himself to an active capacity, to a capacity to learn. The artist
presupposes a sense of beauty—he cannot bestow it upon
a person—for in order that we take his works to be beautiful, in order that we accept and countenance them at all,
he must presuppose in us a sense of art. All he can do is
to cultivate it and give it a certain direction. Similarly,
the philosopher does not assume that he is a speculative
Dalai Lama, that he is the incarnation of reason itself.
In order that we recognize his thoughts as true, in order
that we understand them at all, he presupposes reason, as
a common principle and measure in us as well as in himself. That which he has learned, we should also be able to
know, and that which he has found we should also be able
to find *in ourselves* with the help of our own thinking.
Demonstration is therefore not a mediation through the
medium of language between thought, in so far *as it is
my thought,* and the thought of another person, in so far
as it is his thought—where two or three people assemble
in my name, I, reason, and truth am there among you—nor
is it a mediation of "I" and "You" to know the identity
of reason, nor, again, a mediation through which I verify
that my thought is not mine, but is rather thought *in and
for itself* so that it can just as well be mine as that of someone else. If we are indifferent in life as to whether our
thoughts are understood and acknowledged, then this in-

difference is shown only to this or that man or to this or that class of men because we regard them as people who are full of prejudices, corrupted by particular interests and feelings, incorrigible. Their number does not matter here at all. It is of course true that man can be self-sufficient because he knows himself to be a whole, because he distinguishes himself from himself, and because he can be the other to himself; man speaks to and converses with himself, and because he knows that his thought would not be his own if it were also not—at least as a possibility—the thought of others. But all this indifference, all this self-sufficiency and self-concern are only exceptional phenomena. In reality, we are not indifferent; the urge to communicate is a fundamental urge—the urge for truth. We become conscious and certain of truth only through the other, even if not through this or that accidental other. That which is true belongs neither to me nor exclusively to you, but is common to all. The thought in which "I" and "You" are united is a *true* thought. This unification is the confirmation, sign, and affirmation of truth only because it is itself already the truth. That which unites is true and good. The objection that, hence, theft too is true and good, because here, too, men are united, does not deserve to be refuted. In this case, each is only for himself.

All philosophers we know have *expressed*—i.e., *taught* —their ideas either orally, like Socrates, or in written form; otherwise they could not have become known to us. To express *thoughts* is to teach; but to teach is to demonstrate the truth of that which is taught. This means that demonstrating is not just a relationship of the thinker to himself or of a thought that is imprisoned within itself to itself, but the relationship of the thinker to others. Hence, the forms of demonstration and inference cannot be the *forms of reason*[1] as such; i.e., forms of an inner act of thought and cognition. They are only *forms of communication*, modes of expression, representations, conceptions; in short, forms in which thought manifests itself. That is why a quick-witted person can be ahead of his demonstrating teacher; even with the first thought, he anticipates in no

time the ensuing sequence of deductions which another
person must go through step by step. A genius for thinking
is just as much innate to man, and exists just as much to
a certain degree in all men—in the form of receptivity—
as a genius for art. The reason why we regard the forms
of communication and expression as the basic forms of
reason and thought lies in the fact that, in order to raise
them to the clarity of consciousness, we present our fundamental thoughts to ourselves in the same way as we present
them to another person, that we first teach ourselves these
fundamental thoughts which directly spring from our
genius for thinking—they come to us we know not how—
and which are perhaps innate to our being. In short, the
reason lies in the fact that we express and articulate our
thoughts in thought itself. Demonstrating is therefore only
the means through which I strip my thought of the form
of "mine-ness" so that the other person may recognize it as
his own. Demonstrating would be senseless if it were not
also *communicating.* However, the communicating of
thoughts is not material or *real* communication. For example, a push, a sound that shocks my ears, or light is real
communication. I am only passively receptive to that which
is material; but I become aware of that which is mental
only through myself, only through self-activity. For this
very reason, what the person demonstrating communicates
is not the *subject matter itself,* but only the medium; for
he does not instil his thoughts into me like drops of medi-
cine, nor does he preach to deaf fishes like Saint Francis;
rather, he addresses himself to *thinking* beings. The main
thing—the understanding of the thing involved—he does
not give me; he *gives* nothing at all—otherwise the philosopher could really produce philosophers, something
which so far no one has succeeded in achieving. Rather,
he presupposes the faculty of understanding; he shows
me—i.e., to the other person as such—my understanding
only in a mirror. He is only an actor; i.e., he only embodies
and represents what I should reproduce in myself in imi-
tation of him. Self-constituting and systematic philosophy
is dramatic and theatrical philosophy as opposed to the

poetry of introspective material thought. The person demonstrating says and points out to me: "This is rational,
this is true, and this is what is meant by law; this is how
you must think when you think truly." To be sure, he
wants me to grasp and acknowledge his ideas, but not as
his ideas; he wants me to grasp them as generally rational;
i.e., also as mine. He only expresses what is my own understanding. Herein lies the justification for the demand that
philosophy should awaken, stimulate thought, and not
make us the captives of its oral or written word—a communicated thought is precisely thought externalized into
word—which always has a mentally deadening effect. Every
presentation of philosophy, whether oral or written, is to
be taken and can only be taken in the sense of a means.
Every system is only an expression or image of reason,
and hence only an object of reason, an object which reason—a living power that procreates itself in new thinking
beings—distinguishes from itself and posits as an object
of criticism. Every system that is not recognized and appropriated as just a *means, limits* and warps the mind for
it sets up the indirect and formal thought in the place of
the direct, original, and material thought. It kills the spirit
of invention; it makes it impossible to distinguish the *spirit*
from the *letter* for together with the thought—herein lies
the limitation of every system as something external—it also
necessarily insists on retaining the word, thus failing to
capture, indeed denying completely the original meaning
and determination of every system and expression of
thought. All presentation, all demonstration—and the presentation of thought is demonstration—has, according to its
original determination—and that is all that matters to us—
the cognitive activity of the other person as its ultimate aim.

Moreover, it is quite obvious that presentation or demonstration is also an end *for itself,* since every means must,
in the first instance, be an end. The form must itself be
instructive, that is, objectively expressed. The presentation
of philosophy must itself be philosophical—the demand
for the identity of form and content finds herein its justification. The presentation is, of course, *systematic* to the

extent to which it is itself philosophical. By virtue of being so, the presentation comes to have a value *in and for itself*. For that reason the systematizer is an artist—the history of philosophical system is the picture gallery of reason. Hegel is the most accomplished philosophical artist, and his presentations, at least in part, are *unsurpassed models of scientific art sense* and, due to their rigor, *veritable means for the education and discipline of the spirit*. But precisely because of this, Hegel—in keeping with a general law which we cannot discuss here—made form into essence, the being of thought for others into being in itself, the *relative goal* into the *final goal*. Hegel, in his presentation, aimed at anticipating and imprisoning the intellect itself and compressing it into the system. The system was supposed to be, as it were, reason itself; all immediate activity was to dissolve itself completely in mediated activity, and the presentation of philosophy was *not to presuppose anything*, that is, nothing was to be left over in us and nothing within us—a complete emptying of ourselves. The Hegelian system is the *absolute self-externalization* of reason, a state of affairs that expresses itself, among other things, in the fact that the empirical character of his natural law is pure speculation. The true and ultimate reason for all complaints about formalism, neglect of subjectivity, etc., lies solely in the fact that Hegel compresses everything into his presentation, that he proceeds abstractly from the pre-existence of the intellect, and that he does not appeal to the intellect within us. It is true that Hegel retracts the process of mediation in what he calls the result, but in so far as form is posited as objective essence, one is again left in doubt as to the objectivity or subjectivity of the process of mediation. Hence, those who claim that the process of the mediation of the Absolute is only a formal one may well be materially right, but those who claim the opposite, that is, those who claim objective reality for this process, may not, at least formally, be in the wrong.

The Hegelian philosophy is thus the culminating point of all speculative-systematic philosophy. With this, we have discovered and mooted the reason underlying the beginning of the *Logic*. Everything is required either to present (prove) itself or to flow into, and be dissolved in, the presentation. The presentation ignores that which was known before the presentation: It must make an absolute beginning. But it is precisely here that the limits of the presentation manifest themselves immediately. Thought is prior to the presentation of thought. That which constitutes the starting point within the presentation is primary only for the presentation but not for thought. The presentation needs thought which, although always present within thinking, emerges only later.[2] The presentation is that which is mediated in and for itself; what is primary is therefore never immediate even within the presentation, but only posited, dependent, and mediated, in that it is determined by the determinations of thought whose certainty is self-dependent and which are prior to and independent of a philosophy presenting and unfolding itself in time. Thus, presentation always appeals to a higher authority—and one which is *a priori* in relation to it. Who would think that this is not also the case with the "being" of the Hegelian *Logic?* "Being is that which is immediate, indeterminate, self-same, self-identical, and undifferentiated." But are not the notions of immediacy and identity presupposed here? "Being merges into Nothingness; it disappears immediately into its opposite: its truth is the very movement of its disappearing." Does Hegel not take perceptions for granted here? Is disappearing a notion or is it rather a sensuous perception? "Becoming is restlessness, the restless unity of being and nothingness; existence is this unity having come to rest." Is not a highly doubtful perception simply taken for granted here? Can a skeptic not object that rest is a sensory illusion, that everything is rather in constant motion? What, therefore, is the use of putting such ideas at the starting point, even if only as *images?* But it may be objected that such assumptions as the notions of sameness and identity are quite evident and natural. How else could we conceive of being? These notions are the necessary means through which we cognize being as primary. Quite right! But is being, at least for us, immediate? Is it not rather that wherefrom we cannot abstract the Primary? Of course, the Hegelian philosophy is aware of this as well. Being, whence the *Logic* proceeds, presupposes on the one hand the *Phenomenology,* and on the other, the Absolute Idea. Being (that which is primary and indeterminate) is revoked in the end as it turns out that it is *not* the *true* starting point. But does this not again make a *Phenomenology* out of the *Logic?* And being only a *phenomenological* starting point? Do we not encounter a conflict between appearance and truth within the *Logic* as well? Why does Hegel not proceed from the true starting point? "Indeed, the true can only be a result; the true has to prove itself to be so, that is, it has to present itself." But how can it do so if being itself has to presuppose the Idea, that is, when the Idea has already in itself been presupposed as the Primary? Is this the way for philosophy to constitute and demonstrate itself as the truth so that it can no longer be doubted, so that skepticism is reduced once and for all to absurdity? Of course, if you say A, you will also have to say B. Anyone who can countenance being at the beginning of the *Logic* will also countenance the Idea; if this being has been accepted as proved by someone, then he must also accept the Idea as proved. But what happens if someone is not willing to say A? What if he says instead, "Your indeterminate and pure being is just an abstraction to which nothing real corresponds, for real is only real being? Or else prove if you can the reality of *general* notions!" Do we not thus come to those general questions that touch upon the truth and reality not only of Hegel's *Logic* but also of philosophy altogether? Is the *Logic* above the dispute between the Nominalists and Realists (to use old names for what are natural contraries)? Does it not contradict in its first notions sense perception and its advocate, the intellect? Have they no right to oppose the *Logic?* The *Logic* may well dismiss the voice of sense perception, but, then, the *Logic* itself is dismissed by the intellect on the ground that it is like a judge who is trying his own case. Have we therefore not

the same contradiction right at the outset of the philosophical science as in the philosophy of Fichte? In the latter case, the contradiction is between the *pure* and the
empirical, real ego; in the former, it is between the pure
and the empirical, real being. "The pure ego is no longer
an ego"; but, then, the pure and empty being, too, is no
longer being. The *Logic* says: "I abstract from determinate
being; I do not predicate of determinate being the unity
of being and nothingness." When this unity appears to
the intellect as paradoxical and ridiculous it quickly sub-
stitutes determinate being by pure being, for now it would,
of course, be a contradiction for being not to be nothingness as well. But the intellect retorts: "Only determinate
being is being; in the notion of being lies the notion of
absolute determinateness. I take the notion of being from
being itself; however, all being is determinate being—that
is why, in passing, I can also posit nothingness which
means 'not something' or 'opposed to being' because I
always and inseparably connect 'something' with being. If
you therefore leave out determinateness from being, you
leave being with no being at all. It will not be surprising
if you then demonstrate that indeterminate being is nothingness. Under these circumstances this is self-evident. If
you exclude from man that which makes him man, you
can demonstrate without any difficulty whatsoever that he
is not man. But just as the notion of man from which you
have excluded the specific difference of man is not a
notion of man, but rather of a fabricated entity as, for
example, the Platonic man of Diogenes, so the notion of
being from which you have excluded the content of being
is no longer the notion of being. Being is diverse in the
same measure as things. Being is one with the thing that
is. Take away being from a thing, and you take away
everything from it. It is impossible to think of being in
separation from specific determinations. Being is not a particular notion; to the intellect at least, it is all there is."

Therefore, how can the *Logic,* or any particular philosophy at all, reveal truth and reality if it begins by contradicting sensuous reality and its understanding *without*

resolving this contradiction? That it can prove *itself* to be true is not a matter of doubt; this, however, is not the question. A twosome is needed to prove something. While proving, the thinker splits himself into two; he contradicts himself, and only after a thought has been and has overcome its own opposition, can it be regarded as proved. To prove is at the same time to refute. Every intellectual determination has its antithesis, its contradiction. Truth exists not in unity with, but in refutation of its opposite. Dialectics is not a monologue that speculation carries on with itself, but a dialogue between speculation and empirical reality. A thinker is a dialectician only in so far as he is his own *opponent.* The zenith of art and of one's own power is to doubt oneself. Hence, if philosophy or, in our context, the *Logic* wishes to prove itself true, it must refute rational empiricism or the intellect which denies it and which alone contradicts it. Otherwise all its proofs will be nothing more than *subjective* assurances, so far as the intellect is concerned. The antithesis of being—in general and as regarded by the *Logic*—is *not nothingness,* but *sensuous* and *concrete* being.

Sensuous being denies logical being; the former contradicts the latter and vice versa. The resolution of *this* contradiction would be the proof of the reality of logical being, the proof that it is not an abstraction, which is what the intellect now takes it to be.

The only philosophy that proceeds from no presuppositions at all is one that possesses the courage and freedom to doubt *itself,* that produces itself out of its *antithesis.* All modern philosophies, however, begin only with themselves and not with what is in opposition to them. They presuppose philosophy; that is, what they understand by philosophy to be the immediate truth. They understand by mediation only *elucidation,* as in the case of Fichte, or *development,* as in the case of Hegel. Kant was critical towards the old metaphysics, but not towards himself. Fichte proceeded from the assumption that the Kantian philosophy was the truth. All he wanted was to raise it to "science," to link together that which in Kant had a dichotomized existence, by deriving it from a common principle. Similarly, Schelling proceeded from the assumption that the Fichtean philosophy was the established truth, and restored Spinoza in opposition to Fichte. As far as Hegel is concerned, he is a Fichte as mediated through a Schelling. Hegel polemicized against the Absolute of Schelling; he thought it lacked the moment of reflection, apprehension, and negativity. In other words, he imbued the Absolute Identity with Spirit, introduced determinations into it, and fructified its womb with the semen of the Notion (the ego of Fichte). But he, nevertheless, took the truth of the Absolute for granted. He had no quarrel with the existence or the objective reality of Absolute Identity; he actually took for granted that Schelling's philosophy was, in its essence, a true philosophy. All he accused it of was that it lacked *form*. Hence, Hegel's relationship to Schelling is the same as that of Fichte to Kant. To both the true philosophy was already in existence, both in content and substance; both were motivated by a purely "scientific," that is, in this case, *systematic* and *formal* interest. Both were critics of certain specific qualities of the existing philosophy, but not at all of its essence. That the Absolute existed was beyond all doubt. All it needed was to prove itself and be known *as such*. In this way it becomes a result and an object of the mediating Notion; that is, a "scientific" truth and not merely an assurance given by intellectual intuition.

But precisely for that reason the proof of the Absolute in Hegel has, in principle and essence, only a formal significance, notwithstanding the scientific rigor with which it is carried out. Right at its starting point, the philosophy of Hegel presents us with a contradiction, the contradiction between truth and science, between essence and form, between thinking and writing. The Absolute Idea is assumed, not formally, to be sure, but essentially. What Hegel premises as stages and constituent parts of mediation, he thinks are determined by the Absolute Idea. Hegel does not step outside the Idea, nor does he forget it. Rather, he already thinks the antithesis out of which the Idea should produce

itself *on the basis of its having been taken for granted.* It
is already proved substantially before it is proved formally.
Hence, it must always remain unprovable, always subjective for someone who recognizes in the antithesis of the
Idea a premise which the Idea has itself established in advance. The externalization of the Idea is, so to speak, only
a dissembling; it is only a pretense and nothing serious—
the Idea is just playing a game. The conclusive proof is
the beginning of the *Logic,* whose beginning is to be taken
as the beginning of philosophy as such. That the starting
point is being is only a formalism, for being is here not
the true starting point, nor the truly Primary. The starting
point could just as well be the Absolute Idea because it
was already a certainty, an immediate truth for Hegel
before he wrote the *Logic;* i.e., before he gave a scientific form of expression to his logical ideas. The Absolute
Idea—the Idea of the Absolute—is its own indubitable certainty as the Absolute Truth. It posits itself in advance as
true; that which the Idea posits as the other, again presupposes the Idea according to its essence. In this way, the
proof remains only a formal one. To Hegel, the thinker,
the Absolute Idea was absolute certainty, but to Hegel,
the author, it was a formal uncertainty. This contradiction between the thinker who is without needs, who can
anticipate that which is yet to be presented because everything is already settled for him, and the needy writer who
has to go through a chain of succession and who posits
and objectifies as formally uncertain what is certain to the
thinker—this contradiction is the process of the Absolute
Idea which presupposes being and essence, but in such a
way that these on their part already presuppose the Idea.
This is the only adequate reason required to explain the
contradiction between the actual starting point of the
Logic and its real starting point which lies at the end. As
was already pointed out, Hegel in his heart of hearts was
convinced of the certainty of the Absolute Idea. In this regard, there was nothing of the critic or the skeptic in him.
However, the Absolute Idea had to demonstrate its truth,
had to be released from the confines of a subjective intel-

lectual conception—it had to be shown that it also existed for *others*. Thus understood, the question of its proof had an essential, and at the same time an inessential, meaning: It was a necessity in so far as the Absolute Idea had to prove itself, because only so could it demonstrate its necessity; but it was at the same time superfluous as far as the inner certainty of the truth of the Absolute Idea was concerned. The expression of this superfluous necessity, of this dispensable indispensability or indispensable dispensability is the Hegelian method. That is why its end is its beginning and its beginning its end. That is why being in it is already the certainty of the Idea, and nothing other than the *Idea in its immediacy*. That is why the Idea's lack of self-knowledge in the beginning is, in the sense of the Idea, only an ironical lack of knowledge. What the Idea says is different from what it thinks. It says "being" or "essence," but actually it thinks only for itself. Only at the end does it also say what it thinks, but it also retracts at the end what it had expressed at the beginning, saying: "What you had, at the beginning and successively, taken to be a different entity, that I am myself." The Idea itself is being and essence, but it does not yet confess to be so; it keeps this secret to itself.

That is exactly why, to repeat myself, the proof or the mediation of the Absolute Idea is only a formal affair. The Idea neither creates nor proves itself through a *real other*—that could only be the empirical and concrete perception of the intellect. Rather, it creates itself out of a formal and apparent antithesis. Being is in itself the Idea. However, to prove cannot mean anything other than to bring the other person to my own conviction. The truth lies only in the unification of "I" and "You." The Other of pure thought, however, is the sensuous intellect in general. In the field of philosophy, proof therefore consists only in the fact that the contradiction between sensuous intellect and pure thought is disposed, so that thought is true not only for itself but also for its opposite. For even if every true thought is true only through itself, the fact remains that in the case of a thought that expresses an antithesis, its credibility will remain subjective, one-sided, and doubtful so long as it relies only on itself. Now, logical being is in direct, unmediated, and abhorrent contradiction with the being of the intellect's empirical and concrete perception. In addition, logical being is only an indulgence, a condescension on the part of the Idea, and, consequently, already that which it must prove itself to be. This means that I enter the *Logic* as well as intellectual perception only through a violent act, through a transcendent act, or through an immediate break with real perception. The Hegelian philosophy is therefore open to the same accusation as the whole of modern philosophy from Descartes and Spinoza onward—the accusation of an unmediated break with sensuous perception[3] and of philosophy's *immediate* taking itself for granted.

The *Phenomenology* cannot be seen as invalidating this accusation, because the *Logic* comes *after* it. Since it constitutes the antithesis of logical being it is always present to us, it is even necessarily brought forth by the antithesis and provoked by it to contradict the *Logic,* all the more so because the *Logic* is a new starting point, or a beginning from the very beginning, a circumstance which is *ab initio* offensive to the intellect. But let us grant the *Phenomenology* a positive and actual meaning in relation to the *Logic*. Does Hegel produce the Idea or thought out of the other-being of the Idea or thought? Let us look at it more closely. The first chapter deals with "Sensuous Certainty, the This and Meaning." It designates that stage of consciousness where sensuous and particular being is regarded as true and real being, but where it also suddenly reveals itself as a general being. "The 'here' is a tree"; but I walk further and say: "The 'here' is a house." The first truth has now disappeared. "The 'now' is night," but it is not long before "the 'now' is day." The first alleged truth has now become "stale." The "now" therefore comes out to be a general "now," a simple (negative) manifold. The same is the case with "here." "The 'here' itself does not disappear, but remains in the disappearance of the house, tree, and so on, and is indifferent to being the house, tree, etc. Therefore, this shows itself again as *mediated simplicity* or *generality*." The particular which we mean in the context of sensuous certainty is something we cannot even express. "Language is more truthful; here, we ourselves directly cancel our opinions, and, since it is the general which is true in sensuous certainty and which alone is expressed by language, we cannot possibly express a sensuous entity as intended." But is this a dialectical refutation of the reality of sensuous consciousness? Is it thereby proved that the general is the real? It may well be for someone who is certain in advance that the general is the real, but not for sensuous consciousness or for those who occupy its standpoint and will have to be convinced first of the unreality of sensuous being and the reality of thought. My brother is called John, or, if you like, Adolph, but there are innumerable people besides him who are called by the same name. Does it follow from this that my brother John is not real? Or that Johnness is the truth? To sensuous consciousness, all words are names—*nomina propria*. They are quite indifferent as far as sensuous consciousness is concerned; they are all signs by which it can achieve its aims in the shortest possible way. Here, language is irrelevant. The reality of sensuous and particular being is a truth that carries the seal of our blood. The commandment that prevails in the sphere of the senses is: An eye for an eye and a tooth for a tooth. Enough of words, come down to real things! *Show* me what you are talking about! To sensuous consciousness it is precisely language that is unreal, nothing. How can it regard itself, therefore, as refuted if it is pointed out that a particular entity cannot be expressed in language? Sensuous consciousness sees precisely in this a refutation of language but not a refutation of sensuous certainty. And it is perfectly justified, too, because otherwise we would have to feed ourselves on mere words instead of on things in life. The content of the whole first chapter of the *Phenomenology* is, therefore, for sensuous consciousness nothing but the reheated cabbage of Stilpo, the Megarican —only in the opposite sense. It is nothing but a verbal

game in which thought that is already certain of itself as
truth plays with natural consciousness. Consciousness,
however, does not let itself be confounded; it holds firmly
to the reality of individual things. Why just the "here"
and not "that which is here?" Why just the "now" and
not "that which is now?" In this way, the "here" and the
"now" will never become a mediated and general "here,"
a mediated and general "now" for sensuous consciousness or for us who are its advocates and wish to be convinced of something better and different. Today is now,
but tomorrow is again now, and it is still completely the
same unchanged and incorrigible now as it was yesterday. Here is a tree, there a house, but when there, I again
say "here"; the "here" always remains the old "everywhere" and "nowhere." A sensuous being, a "this," passes
away, but there comes another being in its place which is
equally a "this." To be sure, nature refutes this individual,
but it soon corrects itself. It refutes the refutation in that
it puts another individual in place of the previous one.
Hence, to sensuous consciousness it is sensuous being that
lasts and does not change.

The same unmediated contradiction, the same conflict
that we encounter at the beginning of the *Logic* now confronts us at the beginning of the *Phenomenology*—the conflict between being as the object of the *Phenomenology*
and being as the object of sensuous consciousness. The
"here" of the *Phenomenology* is in no way different from
another "here" because it is actually general. But the real
"here" is distinguished from another "here" in a real way;
it is an exclusive "here." "This 'here' is, for example, a
tree. I turn around and this truth has disappeared." This
can, of course, happen in the *Phenomenology* where turning around costs nothing but a little word. But, in reality,
where I must turn my ponderous body around, the "here"
proves to be a very real thing even behind my back. The
tree delimits my back and excludes me from the place it
already occupies. Hegel does not refute the "here" that
forms the object of sensuous consciousness; that is, an
object for us distinct from pure thought. He refutes only

the logical "here," the logical "now." He refutes the *idea* of "this-being," *haecceitas*. He shows the untruth of an individual being in so far as it is determined as a (theoretical) reality in imagination. The *Phenomenology* is nothing but a phenomenological Logic. Only from this point of view can the chapter on sensuous certainty be excused. However, precisely because Hegel did not really immerse himself in sensuous consciousness, did not think his way into it because in his view sensuous consciousness is an object in the sense of an object of self-consciousness or thought; because self-consciousness is merely the externalization of thought *within* the self-certainty of thought; so the *Phenomenology* or the *Logic*—both have the same thing in common—begins with itself as its own immediate presupposition, and hence with an unmediated contradiction, namely, with an absolute break with sensuous consciousness. For it begins, as mentioned already, not with the "other-being" of thought, but with the *idea of the "other-being" of thought*. Given this, thought is naturally certain of its victory over its adversary in advance. Hence, the humor with which thought pulls the leg of sensuous consciousness. But this also goes to show that thought has not been able to refute its adversary.

Quite apart from the significance of the *Phenomenology*, Hegel started, as was already mentioned, from the assumption of Absolute Identity right from the earliest beginnings of his philosophical activity. The idea of Absolute Identity, or of the Absolute, was simply an objective truth for him. It was not just a truth for him, but absolute truth, the Absolute Idea itself—absolute, that is, beyond all doubt and above all criticism and skepticism. But the idea of the Absolute was, according to its positive meaning, at the same time only the idea of objectivity in opposition to the idea of subjectivity, as in the Kantian and Fichtean philosophy. For that reason, we must understand the philosophy of Schelling not as "absolute" philosophy—as it was to its adherents[4]—but as the antithesis of critical philosophy. As we know, Schelling wanted in the beginning to go in an opposite direction to idealism. His natural philosophy was actually reversed idealism at first, which means that a transition from the latter to the former was not difficult. The idealist philosopher sees life and reason in nature also, but he means by them his own life and his own reason. What he sees in nature is what he puts into it; what he gives to nature is therefore what he takes back into himself—nature is objectified ego, or spirit looking at itself as its own externalization. Idealism, therefore, already meant the unity of subject and object, spirit and nature, but together with the implication that in this unity nature had only the status of an object; that is, of something posited by spirit. The problem was, therefore, only to release nature from the bondage to which the idealist philosopher had subjected it by chaining it to his own ego, to restore it to an independent existence in order to bestow upon it the meaning it received in the philosophy of nature. The idealist said to nature, "You are my *alter* ego," while he emphasized only the ego so that what he actually meant was: "You are an outflow, a reflected image of myself, but nothing particular just by yourself." The philosopher of nature said the same thing, but he emphasized the "alter": "To be sure, nature is your ego, but your *other* ego, and hence real in itself and distinguished from you." That is why the meaning of the identity of spirit and nature was also a purely idealistic one in the beginning. "Nature is only the visible organism of our intellect." (Schelling, in the Introduction to the *Project for a System of the Philosophy of Nature*.) "The organism is itself only a mode of perception of the intellect." (Schelling, in *The System of Transcendental Idealism*.) "It is obvious that the ego constructs itself while constructing matter. . . . This product—matter—is therefore completely a construction by the ego, although not for an ego that is still identical with matter." (Ibid.) "Nature shall be the visible spirit, and spirit, invisible nature." (Schelling, in the Introduction to *Ideas for a Philosophy of Nature*.) The philosophy of nature was supposed to begin only from what is objective, but at the same time to arrive at the same result at which idealism arrived through and out of itself. "The necessary tendency of all natural science is to arrive at the intellect from nature." (Schelling, in *The System of Transcendental Idealism.*) "The task of the philosophy of nature is to show the primacy of the objective and to derive the subjective from it! All philosophy must strive either to produce the intellect out of nature or nature out of the intellect." (Ibid.) That is why the philosophy of nature, with all its integrity, left idealism undisturbed, for all it wanted was to demonstrate *a posteriori* what idealism had said of itself *a priori*. The only difference between the two lay in the course taken, in method. Nevertheless, basic to the opposite course, there was an opposite intuition, or at least it had to emerge unavoidably from this opposite course. It was bound to happen that nature thus received a meaning *for itself*. The object had already been released from the confines of subjective idealism in so far as it had also been posited as the object of a *particular* science. If not in itself, nature was nevertheless not something derivative or posited for natural science, but rather something primary and independent. In this way, nature received a meaning that was opposed to the idealism of Fichte. But even so the meaning which nature had in and for idealism—that is, one which was diametrically opposed to the meaning of nature in the philosophy of nature—was to retain its validity as if nothing had happened, and idealism was to continue to exist undiminished and with all its rights and pretensions. Consequently, we now have two independent and mutually opposed truths instead of the only absolutely decisive and autonomous truth of the Fichtean ego—the truth of idealism, which denies the truth of the philosophy of nature, and the truth of the philosophy of nature, which in its turn denies the truth of idealism. For the philosophy of nature it is nature alone that exists, just as for idealism it is only spirit. For idealism, nature is only object and accident, but for the philosophy of nature it is substance, i.e., both subject and object, something which only intelligence within the context of idealism claims to be. However, two truths, two "Absolutes," is a contradiction. How do we

find a way out of this conflict between a philosophy of
nature that negates idealism and an idealism that negates
the philosophy of nature? Only by turning the *predicate*
wherein both concur into the *subject*—this would then be
the Absolute or that which is purely and simply independent—and the subject into the predicate. In other words, the
Absolute is nature *and* spirit. Spirit and nature are only
predicates, determinations, forms of one and the same
thing; namely, of the Absolute. But what then is the Absolute? Nothing other than this "and," that is, the unity of
spirit and nature. But are we really making any progress
in taking this step? Did we not have this unity already in
the notion of nature? For the philosophy of nature is a
science not of an object that is opposed to the "I," but of
an object that is itself both subject and object—the philosophy of nature is at the same time idealism. Further,
the connection between the notions of subject and object
within the notion of nature was precisely the supersession
of the separation—effected by idealism—between mind and
non-mind, hence the supersession of the separateness of
nature and spirit. What is it, therefore, through which the
Absolute distinguishes itself from nature? The Absolute is
the Absolute Identity, the absolute subject-object, whereas
mind is the subjective subject-object. Oh, what brilliance!
And how surprising! Suddenly, we find ourselves on the
standpoint of idealistic dualism: We deprive nature at
the same time of that which we give it. Nature is the
subject-object with the *plus* of objectivity. That means that
the positive notion of nature—provided that the *plus* gives
us a notion whereby nature is not suspended into the
vacuum of the Absolute, but still remains nature—is that
of *objectivity;* and similarly the notion of the spirit—in so
far as it is spirit—is not a vague, nameless entity, but the
notion of *subjectivity* in as much as the *plus* of subjectivity constitutes its distinguishing feature. But are we the
cleverer for this approach than we were initially? Do we
not have to bear again the same old cross of subjectivity
and objectivity? If the Absolute is now cognized, that is,
if it is brought out of the darkness of absolute indetermi-

nateness where it is only an object of imagination and phantasy into the light of the notion, then it is cognized either as spirit or as nature. Hence, there is no science of the Absolute as such, but either the science of the Absolute as nature or that of the Absolute as spirit; that is, either the philosophy of nature or of idealism, or if both together, then only in such a way that the philosophy of nature is only the philosophy of the Absolute as nature, while idealism is only the philosophy of the Absolute as spirit. But if the object of the philosophy of nature is the Absolute as nature, then the positive notion is just the notion of nature, which means that the predicate again becomes the subject and the subject—the Absolute—becomes a vague and meaningless predicate. Hence, I could just as well delete the Absolute from the philosophy of nature, for the Absolute applies equally to spirit as to nature; as much to one particular object as to another opposite object; as much to light as to gravity. In the notion of nature, the Absolute as pure indeterminateness, as *nihil negativum*, disappears for me, or if I am unable to banish it from my head, the consequence is that nature vanishes before the Absolute. That is also the reason why the philosophy of nature did not succeed in achieving anything more than evanescent determinations and differences which are in truth only imaginary, only ideas of distinctions but not real determinations of knowledge.

But precisely for that reason the positive significance of the philosophy of Schelling lies solely in his philosophy of nature compared to the limited idealism of Fichte, which knows only a negative relationship to nature. Therefore, one need not be surprised that the originator of the philosophy of nature presents the Absolute only from its real side, for the presentation of the Absolute from its ideal side had already occurred in Fichteanism before the philosophy of nature. Of course, the philosophy of identity restored a lost unity, but not by objectifying this unity as the Absolute, or as an entity common to and yet distinguished from nature and spirit—for thus understood, the Absolute was only a mongrel between idealism and the philosophy of nature, born out of the conflict between idealism and the philosophy of nature as experienced by the author of the latter—but only in so far as the notion of this unity meant the notion of nature as both subject and object implying the restoration of nature to its proper place.

However, by not being satisfied with its rejection of subjective idealism—this was its positive achievement—and by wanting itself to acquire the character of absolute philosophy, which involved a misconception of its limits, the philosophy of nature came to oppose even that which was positive in idealism. Kant involved himself in a contradiction—something necessary for him but which cannot be discussed here—in so far as he misconceived the affirmative, rational limits of reason by taking them to be *boundaries*. Boundaries are arbitrary limits that are removable and ought not to be there. The philosophy of identity even rejected the positive limits of reason and philosophy together with these boundaries. The unity of thought and being it claimed to have achieved was only the unity of *thought* and *imagination*. Philosophy now became beautiful, poetic, soulful, romantic, but for that matter also transcendent, superstitious, and *absolutely uncritical*. The very condition of all criticism—the distinction between "subjective" and "objective"—thus melted into thin air. Discerning and determining thought came to be regarded as a finite and *negative* activity. No wonder then that the philosophy of identity finally succumbed, irresistibly and uncritically, to the mysticism of the Cobbler of Görlitz.

It was in the context of this philosophy that Hegel's own philosophizing began, although Hegel was by no means a disciple bound to the originator of that philosophy. Rather, they were friends. Hegel restored philosophy by rescuing it from the realm of imagination. A Hegelian applies with perfect justification to Hegel what Aristotle remarked of Anaxagoras; namely, that he (Anaxagoras), as one among drunks, was the only sober thinker among the philosophers of nature. With Hegel the unity of thought and being acquired a rational meaning, which is not, however, above criticism. Hegel's principle is the thinking spirit. He incorporated into philosophy the element in which rationalism has its being; namely, the intellect. In spite of the assurance to the contrary, the intellect, both as a matter of fact and with respect to its own reality, was excluded from the idea of the Absolute; in Hegel, it became a moment of the Absolute itself. The metaphysical expression of this state of affairs is the statement that the negative, the other or that which is an object of reflection, is to be conceived not only as negative and finite, but also as positive and essential. There is therefore a negative and critical element in Hegel even if what really determines his thinking is the idea of the Absolute. Although he recognized that the Absolute lacked intellect or the principle of form—both are to him one and the same—and although he actually defined the Absolute differently from Schelling by attributing to it the principle of form, thus raising form to the level of essence, the fact remains that for Hegel form—and this is indeed necessarily included in its notion —simultaneously means something formal, and the intellect again means something negative. It was assumed that the content of the philosophy of the Absolute was true, speculative, and profound; all it lacked was the form of the notion. The notion—form or intellect—was posited as essential to the extent that its absence meant a defect. However, this defect must be only a formal affair if the content has been assumed as true—herein can be seen the proof of what we said earlier about the method of Hegel. This means that philosophy is not concerned with anything except notion or form. The content—even if it is to be produced internally by philosophy's self-activity inasmuch as it is contained in the form of the notion—is always given: The business of philosophy is solely to apprehend it by critically distinguishing the essential from the non-essential or from that which is contributed by the peculiar form of intuition or sensuousness. Philosophy in Hegel has therefore no genetico-critical sense, although it certainly has a critical one. A genetico-critical philosophy is one that does not dogmatically demonstrate

or apprehend an object given through perception—for what
Hegel says applies unconditionally to objects given immediately, i.e., those that are absolutely real and given
through nature—but examines its *origin;* which questions whether an object is a real object, only an idea, or
just a psychological phenomenon; which, finally, distinguishes with utmost rigor between what is subjective
and what is objective. The genetico-critical philosophy is
mainly concerned with those things that are otherwise
called secondary causes. Indeed, its relationship to absolute
philosophy—which turns subjective psychological processes
and speculative needs, for example, Jakob Böhme's process through which God is mediated, into the processes of
the Absolute—is, to illustrate by analogy, the same as the
relationship of that theological view of nature which takes
comets or other strange phenomena to be the immediate
workings of God to the purely physicist or natural philosophical view which sees, for example, the cause of the
gallnut in the innocent sting of an insect rather than looking upon it, as theology does, as a sign of the existence
of the Devil as a personal being. The Hegelian philosophy
is, uniquely, a rational mysticism. Hence it fascinates in
the same measure as it repels. The mystical-speculative
souls, for whom it is an unbearable contradiction to see
the mystical united with the rational, find it repulsive because they find the notion disappointing, and destructive
of the very mystical fascination they cherish. It is equally
repulsive to rational heads who find the union of the rational and the mystical abhorrent. The unity of the subjective and the objective as enunciated and placed at the
summit of philosophy by Schelling, a unity that is still
basic to Hegel although placed by him—but only according to form—in the right place; namely, at the end of philosophy as the Result. This unity is both a fruitless and
a harmful principle because it eliminates the distinction
between "subjective" and "objective" even in the case of
particulars, and renders futile the genetico-critical thought,
indeed, negates the very question about truth. The reason
why Hegel conceived those ideas which express only sub-

jective needs to be objective truth is because he did not go back to the source of and the need for these ideas. What he took for real reveals itself on closer examination to be of a highly dubious nature. He made what is secondary primary, thus either ignoring that which is really primary or dismissing it as something subordinate. And he demonstrated what is only particular, what is only relatively rational, to be the rational in and for itself. Thus, as a consequence of the lack of a genetico-critical mode of enquiry, we see nothingness—a conception that is extremely proximate to the idea of the Absolute—play its role right at the beginning of the *Logic*. But what is this nothingness? "By the shadow of Aristotle!" Nothingness is that which is absolutely devoid of thought and reason.[5] Nothingness cannot be thought at all, because to think is to determine, as Hegel himself says. If nothingness were conceived, it would come to be determined, and hence it would no longer be nothingness. As has been rightly said, of the non-essent there is no knowledge.[6] We call nothingness that to which no concept corresponds (Wolf). Thought can think only that which is because thought is itself an essent, a real activity. The pagan philosophers have been criticized for not being able to overcome the eternity of matter and the world. However, to them, matter meant being; it was the sensuous expression of being. What they have been criticized for is that they *made use of thought*. But have the Christians really done away with the eternity; that is, the reality of being? All they have done is to place it into a particular being, into the being of God which they thought of as its own ground and as being without beginning. Thought can never go beyond being, because it cannot go beyond itself; because reason consists only in positing being; because only this or that being, but not the genesis of being itself, can be thought. The activity of thinking authenticates itself as a well-grounded and real activity precisely through the fact that its first and last notion is that of being without beginning. The Augustinian nothingness, which appears to be so impressive and profound to speculative thinkers precisely because there is nothing behind it, is simply an expression of *absolute arbitrariness* and *thoughtlessness*. This amounts to saying that I cannot conceive of any other ground of the world except absolute arbitrariness; that is, I cannot conceive of any other ground except no ground at all, except as just an empty act of will. But in a mere act of will reason disappears and I do not advance something which could be an object for thought, which could be called a ground; what I say is as much as nothing. Hence all I express is my own ignorance, my own arbitrariness. Nothingness is an absolute self-deception, *proton pseudos,* the absolute lie in itself. The thought of nothingness is thought contradicting itself. He who thinks nothingness thinks precisely nothing. Nothingness is the negation of thought; it can therefore only be thought at all in so far as it is made into *something.* In the moment nothingness is thought of, it is also not thought of, for I also think the opposite of nothingness. "Nothingness is simple sameness with itself." Oh really? But are simplicity and sameness then not *real* determinations? Do I really think nothingness when I think simple sameness? Do I therefore not deny nothingness the moment I posit it? "Nothingness is complete vacuity, complete absence of determination and content, complete undifferentiatedness in itself." What? Is nothingness undifferentiated in itself? Do I then not posit something in nothingness in exactly the same way in which nothingness in *creatio ex nihilo* is posited as quasi-matter in so far as the world is supposed to be created out of nothingess? Can I then speak of nothingness without contradicting myself? Nothingness is complete vacuity. But what is vacuity? Vacuity is where there is nothing, but at the same time where there should be or can be something. In other words, vacuity is the expression for capacity. Now this would make nothingness into an entity, and an entity whose capacity to contain is the greatest. But you say that it is absolutely without determination and content. However, I cannot think of something that lacks all determination and content, for it is impossible to have a notion of something that lacks all determination. By using the word "lack," I give expression to the fact that something is missing, that a default is involved. This means that I think of content and determination as primary because they are positive, or, in other words, I think nothingness through something which is not nothingness. I set nothingness in relation to that which is full of content. But this also means that where I set things in relation to one another I at the same time posit determinations. Thought is a determinate, i.e., an affirmative activity to such a degree that that which is absolutely indeterminate becomes something determinate the moment it is thought; that through the very act of thought the idea of nothingness reveals itself directly as thoughtlessness, as an untrue thought, as something that just simply cannot be thought. If it were really possible to think nothingness, the distinction between reason and unreason, thought and thoughtlessness would disappear. In that case it would be possible to think and justify any and everything, even the greatest impossibility and nonsense. This also explains why the most senseless fantasies and the most preposterous miracle-mongering could flourish as long as the idea of a *creatio ex nihilo* was held to be true, for they naturally followed from the idea of nothingness which, as a sanctified authority, stood at the head of creation. Nothingness is the *limit* of reason. A follower of Kant would of course interpret this limit—as all other limits—in the sense of the limitation of reason. Nothingness, however, is a rational limit, a limit which reason itself imposes upon itself and which is an expression of its essence and reality because nothingness is simply the absence of all reason. If it were possible for reason to think nothingness, it would in that case have taken leave of itself.

And yet "there does exist a difference in whether something or nothing is intuited or thought. Therefore, to intuit or think nothingness does have a meaning; it is there in our intuition or thought, or rather it is vacuous thought or intuition itself." However, vacuous thought is no thought at all. Vacuous thought is nonsense, thought only imagined, but which does not really exist. If to think

nothingness should have a meaning—and a meaning it
surely has; namely, that of being no thought at all—and,
indeed, one such that it confers objectivity on nothingness,
then knowledge of nothingness must also mean knowledge.
And hence, if I were to say of an unknowing person that
he knew *nothing,* I would be open to the retort that I am
nevertheless attributing knowledge to him: that the person concerned *knows* nothing means that he is not unknowing. Nothingness is here a short and telling expression for want of thoroughness, competence, rationality,
vagueness, etc. It has the same semantic level as in the
following proposition: That which contradicts itself is nothing. Nothing has only a tautological sense here. What I am
saying is that the subject of the proposition is self-
contradictory, self-refuting, irrational. Here nothing has
only a linguistic meaning. However, one could further object that "in spite of everything, nothingness has its existence in the medium of thought and imagination. Hence
the assertion that nothingness, although existing in thought
and imagination, has no real existence; what it is, is found
only in thought and imagination." Admittedly, it occurs
in our thought and imagination, but must it for that reason have a place in Logic? A ghost, too, can be imagined
by us, but does it for that reason figure as a real being
in psychology? Of course, it has a place in philosophical
discussion, but only because philosophy has to enquire
into the origin of the belief in ghosts. And what after all
is nothingness if not a ghost haunting the speculative imagination? It is an idea that is no idea, a thought that is no
thought, just as a ghost is a being that is no being, a body
that is no body. And, after all, does nothingness not owe
its existence to darkness, like a ghost? Is not the idea of
darkness the same thing for sensuous consciousness as the
idea of nothingness for abstract consciousness? Hegel himself says: "Nothingness is here the pure absence of Being
—*nihil privativum*—as darkness is the absence of light."
That is, an affinity between darkness and nothingness is
conceded here, an affinity which manifests itself in the
fact that the eye is just as little able to perceive darkness

as the intellect is able to think nothingness. But it is precisely this unmistakable affinity between the two that leads us to the recognition of their common origin. Nothingness, as the opposite of being, is a product of the oriental imagination which conceives of that which has no being as having being; which opposes death to life as an autonomous rational principle; which opposes darkness to light as if it were not just the pure absence of light but something positive in itself. Thus, darkness as an entity opposed to light has as much or as little reality as nothingness has opposed to being—indeed, there is a much less rational basis for its reality. But darkness is substantialized only where man is not yet able to make the distinction between what is subjective and what is objective; where he makes his subjective impressions and feelings into objective qualities, where the horizon of his ideational power is highly limited, where his own local standpoint appears to him as the standpoint of the world or the universe itself, and where, therefore, the disappearance of light appears to him as a real movement and darkness as the going down of the source of the light itself—i.e., the sun—and, finally, where he can, therefore, explain to himself the phenomenon of "darkening" by assuming the existence of a particular being that is hostile to light and which he also believes to be involved, in the form of a dragon or a snake, in a struggle with the being of light as at the occurrence of a solar eclipse. However, the idea of darkness as a definite being that is hostile to light has its source only in the darkness of the intellect: This darkness exists only in imagination. In nature, there is no real antithesis of light. Matter in itself is not darkness, but rather that which is illuminable, or that which is unilluminated only for itself. The light, to use scholastic terms, is only the reality (*actus*) of a possibility (*potentia*) that lies in matter itself. Hence, all darkness is only relative. Even density is not antithetical to light. Quite apart from the density of transparent diamonds and crystals, there are bodies that, even when made dense—oil-besmeared paper, for example—become transparent. Even the densest and

the darkest bodies become transparent if cut into thin
laminae. Of course, there does not exist an absolutely
transparent body, but this rests—not considering the ac-
companying empirical circumstances—on the "itselfness"
of a body and is just as natural as the fact that one and
the same thought becomes changed in the minds of the
different people who take it up. This change rests on their
independence and self-activity. However, this self-activity
does not, for that matter, express an opposition to the
activity of the being who is communicating and revealing
his thoughts. It is the same thing with the idea of nothingness as with the Zoroastrian conception of night. Nothingness is only the limit imposed upon human thought; it
does not emanate from thought, but rather from non-
thought. Nothingness is just nothing; that is all that can
be said of it. Hence nothingness constitutes its own refutation. Fantasy alone is responsible for making a substance
out of nothingness, but only by way of metamorphosing
nothingness into a ghost-like, being-less being. It can,
therefore, be said that Hegel did not enquire into the
genesis of nothingness, thus accepting it at its face value.
In view of the analysis of the meaning of nothingness just
given, the opposition between being and nothingness as
such is by no means—let it be said in passing—a universal
and metaphysical opposition.[7] Rather it falls into a definite
area—the relationship of individual to general being—of
the imagining and reflecting individual to the species. The
species is *indifferent* to the individual. The reflecting individual carries the consciousness of the species within
himself, which means that he can transcend his "now-
being," regard it as of no consequence, and anticipate by
imagination a "not-being" in opposition to his "now-being"
—"not-being" has meaning only as an imagined opposite
of "now-being." A man can say to himself: "What am
I worth? What meaning is there in life? What in death?
Who is going to bother whether I exist or not? And, once
I am dead, I am without pain and consciousness anyway."
Not-being is here taken, and given independent existence,
as a state of pure apathy and non-sentience. The unity of

being and nothingness has its positive meaning only as the *indifference* of the species or of the consciousness of the species towards the particular individual. However, the opposition itself between being and nothingness exists only in the imagination, for being, of course, exists in reality— or rather it is the real itself—but nothingness, not-being, exists only in imagination and reflection.

However, just as it is with nothingness in the *Logic*, so it also is with other matters in the philosophy of Hegel. Hegel disregarded—and not accidentally, but rather as a consequence of the spirit of German speculative philosophy since Kant and Fichte—the secondary causes (which are, however, very often the primary causes and are truly grasped only when they are grasped not only empirically, but also metaphysically; i.e., philosophically) together with the *natural* grounds and causes of things which form the fundamental principles of the genetico-critical philosophy. From the extremes of a hypercritical subjectivism, we are, in Hegel's philosophy, hurled into the extremes of an uncritical objectivism. Of course, the natural and psychological ways of explaining things in the early days of philosophy were superficial, but only because one did not see logic in psychology, metaphysics in physics, and reason in nature. If, on the other hand, nature is understood as it should be understood—as objective reason—then it is the only canon equally as true of philosophy as of art. The *summum bonum* of art is human form (taken not only in the narrowest sense, but also in the sense of poetry); the *summum bonum* of philosophy is human *being*. Human form cannot be regarded as limited and finite, because even if it were so the artistic-creative spirit could easily remove the limits and conjure up a higher form from it. The human form is rather the genus of the manifold animal species; it no longer exists as species in man, but as genus. The being of man is no longer a particular and subjective, but a universal being, for man has the whole universe as the object of his drive for knowledge. And only a cosmopolitan being can have the cosmos as its object. It is true that the stars are not the objects of an immediate sensuous perception, but they obey the same laws as we do. All speculation that would rather go beyond nature and man is therefore futile—as futile as the kind of art that would like to give us something higher than human form, but gives us only distortions. Futile, too, is the speculative philosophy that has risen against Hegel and is in vogue now—the speculative philosophy of the positivists. For instead of going beyond Hegel, it has actually retrogressed far behind Hegel in so far as it has failed to grasp precisely the most significant directions suggested by Hegel and his predecessors, Kant and Fichte, in their own characteristic ways. Philosophy is the science of reality in its truth and totality. However, the all-inclusive and all-encompassing reality is nature (taken in the most universal sense of the word). The deepest secrets are to be found in the simplest natural things, but, pining away for the Beyond, the speculative fantast treads them under his feet. The only source of salvation lies in a return to nature. It is wrong to look upon nature as contradicting ethical freedom. Nature has built not only the mean workshop of the stomach, but also the temple of the brain. It has not only given us a tongue whose *papillae* correspond to intestinal *villi*, but also ears that are enchanted by the harmony of sounds and eyes that only the heavenly and generous being of light ravishes. Nature opposes only fantastic, not rational, freedom. Each glass of wine that we drink one too many of is a very pathetic and even peripatetic proof that the servilism of passions enrages the blood; a proof that the Greek *sophrosyne* is completely in conformity with nature. As we know, the maxim of the Stoics—and I mean the rigorous Stoics, those scarecrows of the Christian moralists—was: Live in conformity with nature.

NOTES

1. Hence the so-called forms of logical judgments and conclusions are not active forms of thought, not causal rela-

tions of reason. They presuppose the metaphysical concepts of generality, particularity, individuality, of the whole and the part, of necessity, of cause and effect. They are thought of only through these concepts; hence, as forms of thought, they are posited, derived, and not original. Only metaphysical relationships are logical; only metaphysics, as the science of categories, is the true, *esoteric* logic. This is the profound insight of Hegel. The so-called logical forms are only abstract and elementary forms of language; but speech is not thought, for otherwise the greatest chatterer would be the greatest thinker. What we normally call thought is only the translation into an idiom comprehensible to us of a highly gifted but more or less unknown author who is difficult to understand. The so-called logical forms have their validity only in this translation, not in the original. Hence, they belong not to the "optics," but only to the "dioptric" [belonging to the use of optical instruments. Tr.] of the spirit, a domain which is, of course, still unknown.

2. What the term "presentation" connotes here is the same as "positing" in Hegel's philosophy. For example, the concept is already a judgment, but not yet posited as such; similarly, the judgment is in itself a conclusion, but not posited, not realized, as such. That which precedes presupposes that which succeeds, but the former must nevertheless emerge as itself and for itself, so that the latter, which in reality is prior, may again be posited for itself. As a consequence of this method, Hegel also gives independent status to determinations that have no reality in themselves. This is what happens in the case of being at the beginning of the *Logic*. What other meaning can being have except that of real, actual being? What therefore is the concept of being supposed to be as distinct from the concept of existence and reality? The same holds true for the forms of judgments and syllogisms, which, as special logical relationships, are given an independent character by Hegel. Thus the affirmative and negative judgments are meant to express a particular relationship; namely, that of immediacy, whereas singular, particular, and universal judgments are meant to express the relationship of reflexion. But all these different forms of judgments are only empirical modes of speech that have to be reduced to a judgment wherein the predicate contains the essential difference, the

nature, the species of the subject before they can express a logical relationship. The same holds true for the assertive and problematic judgment. In order that the judgment inherent in the concept may be posited, these forms must also be posited as particular stages, and the assertive judgment must again be an immediate judgment. But what kind of logical relationship must lie at the base of these forms of judgments? Does this not lie at the base of the subject that makes judgments?

3. There is, of course, an unavoidable break which lies in the nature of science as such; however, there is no necessity for it to be an unmediated break. It is mediated by philosophy by the fact that it produces itself out of non-philosophy.

4. The Hegelian philosophy, too, can be correctly known, appreciated, and judged only if one realizes that, notwithstanding the fact that it has formally incorporated Fichteanism into itself, it constitutes the antithesis of Kantianism and Fichteanism in its content.

5. Hegel designates nothingness as privative of thought. "Already at the level of existence thought-less nothingness becomes a limiting factor." *Logic*, Vol. III, p. 94.

6. See also Aristotle's *Analytica Posteriora*, Bk. II, c. 7, § 2, and Bk. I, § 10.

7. In Greek philosophy, the opposition between being and not-Being is obviously an abstract expression of the opposition between affirmation and negation, between reality and unreality in the sense of truth and untruth. At least in Plato's *Sophist* this opposition has obviously no other meaning than the opposition between truth and untruth. Hence, the central concept, around which the whole dialogue revolves, is the concept of difference; for where there is no difference, there is also no truth; where everything can be true without distinction, as with the Sophists, nothing is true.

Introduction to the
Essence of Christianity (1841)

I THE BEING OF MAN IN GENERAL

Religion has its genesis in the *essential difference* between man and the animal—the animals have *no* religion. Although it is true that the old uncritical zoographers attributed to the elephant, among other laudable qualities, the virtue of religiousness, the fact is that such a thing as the religion of elephants belongs to the realm of fable. Cuvier, one of the greatest authorities on the animal world, concludes from the evidence provided by his own investigations that the elephant possesses no higher degree of intelligence than the dog.

But what constitutes the essential difference between man and the animal? The most simple, general, and also the most widely held answer to this question is *consciousness*. Consciousness, however, is to be taken here in the strict sense, for consciousness in the sense of the feeling of self, in the sense of the ability to distinguish one sensuous object from another, to perceive—even judge—external things according to definite sensuous characteristics emanating from them, consciousness in this sense cannot be denied of the animal. Strictly speaking, consciousness is given only in the case of a being to whom his *species,* his *mode of being* is an object of thought. Although the animal experiences itself as an individual—this is what is meant by saying that it has a feeling of itself—it does not do so as a species. It is in this sense that the animal lacks consciousness, for consciousness deserves to be called by that name only because of its link with *knowledge*. Where there is consciousness in this sense, there is also the capacity to produce systematic knowledge or science. Science is the *consciousness of species*. In life we are concerned with individuals, but in science, with species. Only a being to whom his own species, his characteristic mode of being, is an object of thought can make the essential nature of other things and beings an object of thought.

Thus understood, the animal has a simple, but man a twofold, life. In the case of the animal the inner life is one with the outer, whereas in the case of man there is an inner *and* an outer life. The inner life of man is constituted by the fact that man relates himself to his species, to his mode of being. Man thinks, that is to say, he converses, enters into a dialogue *with himself*. The animal, on the other hand, cannot perform the function characteristic to its species without the existence of another individual external to itself. But man can perform the *functions characteristic to his species*—thought and speech—in isolation from another individual. Man is in himself both "I" and "You"; he can put himself in the place of another precisely because his species, his essential mode of being—not only his individuality—is an object of thought to him.

The characteristic human mode of being, as distinct from that of the animal, is not only the basis, but also the object of religion. But religion is the consciousness of the infinite; hence it is, and cannot be anything other than, man's consciousness of *his* own essential nature, understood not as a finite or limited, but as an infinite nature. A really finite being has not even the slightest inkling, let alone consciousness, of what an infinite being is, for the mode of consciousness is limited by the mode of being. The consciousness of the caterpillar, whose life is confined to a particular species of plant, does not extend beyond this limited sphere; it is, of course, able to distinguish this plant from other plants, but that is the entire extent of its knowledge. In a case where consciousness is so limited but where, precisely because of this limitation, it is also infallible and unerring, we speak of instinct rather than consciousness. Consciousness in the strict sense, or consciousness properly speaking, and consciousness of the infinite cannot be separated from each other; a limited consciousness is no consciousness; consciousness is essentially infinite and all-encompassing. The consciousness of the infinite is nothing else than the consciousness of the infinity of consciousness. To put it in other words, in its consciousness of infinity, the conscious being is conscious of the infinity of its own being.

But what is the being of man of which he is conscious, or what is that which constitutes in him his species, his humanity proper?[1] Reason, Will, and Heart. To a complete man belongs the power of thought, the power of will, and the power of heart. The power of thought is the light of knowledge, the power of will is the energy of character, the power of heart is love. Reason, love, and power of will are perfections of man; they are his highest powers, his absolute essence in so far as he is man, the purpose of his existence. Man exists in order to think, love, and will. What is the end of reason? Reason. Of love? Love. Of will? The freedom to will. We pursue knowledge in order to know; love in order to love; will in order to will, that is, in order to be free. Truly to be is to be able to think, love, and will. Only that which exists for its own sake is true, perfect, and divine. But such is love, such is reason, and such is will. The divine trinity in man, but transcending the individual man, is the unity of reason, love, and will. Reason (imagination, fantasy, conception, opinion), will, and love or heart are powers that man does not possess, although he is nothing without them but is what he is through them. As elements constituting his essence which he neither possesses nor makes, they are the very powers that animate, determine, and govern him —divine, absolute powers that he is powerless to resist.[2]

Is it at all possible for the feeling man to resist feeling, for the loving man to resist love, for the rational man to resist reason? Who has not experienced the irresistible power of musical sounds? And what else is this power if not the power of feeling? Music is the language of feeling —a musical note is sonorous feeling or feeling communicating itself. Who has not experienced the power of love, or at least not heard of it? Which is the stronger—love or the individual man? Does man possess love, or is it rather love that possesses man? When, impelled by love, a man gladly sacrifices his life for his beloved, is this his own strength that makes him overcome death, or is it rather the power of love? And who has not experienced the silent power of thought, given that he has truly experienced the activity of thinking? When, submerged in deep reflection, you forget both yourself and your surroundings, is it you who controls reason, or is it rather reason that controls and absorbs you? Does not reason celebrate its greatest triumph over you in your enthusiasm for science? Is not the drive for knowledge simply an irresistible and all-conquering power? And when you suppress a passion, give up a habit, in short, when you win a victory over yourself, is this victorious power your own personal power existing, so to speak, in isolation, or is it rather the energy of will, the power of morality which imposes its rule over you and fills you with indignation of yourself and your individual weaknesses?[3]

Man is nothing without the objects that express his being. The truth of this proposition is borne out by great men whose lives we emulate in so far as they reveal the essence of man. They had only one basic and dominant passion— the realization of the goal which constituted the essential object of their activity. But the object to which a subject essentially and necessarily relates himself is nothing except the subject's own objective being. If an object is common to several individuals belonging to the same species, but differing in terms of their characteristics, it is still, at least in so far as it is an object to each of them according to their respective differences, their own objective being.

In this sense the sun is the common object of the planets,

but it is not an object for the Earth in the same way as it is for Mercury, Venus, Saturn, or Uranus. Each planet has its own sun. The sun which lights and warms Uranus —and the way it does so—has no physical (only an astronomic or scientific) existence for the Earth. Not only does the sun appear different, but it really is another sun on Uranus than on the Earth. Hence, Earth's relationship to the sun is at the same time the Earth's relationship to itself, to its own being, for the measure of the magnitude and intensity of light which is decisive as to the way the sun is an object for the earth is also the measure of the Earth's distance from the sun, that is, the measure that determines the nature of the Earth. The sun is therefore the mirror in which the being of each planet is reflected.

Thus, man becomes conscious of himself through the object that reflects his being; man's self-consciousness is his consciousness of the object. One knows the man by the object that reflects his being; the object lets his being appear to you; the object is his manifest being, his true, objective ego. This is true not only of intellectual but also of sensuous objects. Even those objects which are farthest removed from man are manifestations of his own specific mode of being because, and in so far as, they are objects for him. Even the moon, the sun, the stars say to man: Γνῶθι σεαυτόν—know thyself. That he sees them, that he sees them the way he does, bears witness to his own nature. The animal is moved only by the rays of light, which are essential for its life, but man is also moved by the rays from the remotest star, which are indifferent to his life. Only man knows pure, intellectual, disinterested joys and emotions; only man celebrates the theoretical feasts of vision. The eye that looks into the starry heavens, that contemplates the light that bears neither use nor harm, that has nothing in common with the earth and its needs, this eye contemplates its own nature, its own origin in that light. The eye is heavenly in its nature. Hence, it is only through the eye that man rises above the earth; hence theory begins only when man directs his gaze towards the heavens. The first philosophers were astronomers. The

heavens remind man of his destination, remind him that
he is destined not merely to act, but also to contemplate.

What man calls Absolute Being, his God, is his own
being. The power of the object over him is therefore the
power of his own being. Thus, the power of the object
of feeling is the power of feeling itself; the power of the
object of reason is the power of reason itself; and the
power of the object of will is the power of the will itself.
The man whose being is determined by sound is governed
by feeling, at least by a feeling that finds its corresponding
element in sound. But only the sound that is charged with
content, meaning, and feeling possesses power over feeling
—not sound as such. Feeling is determined only by that
which is charged with feeling, that is, only by itself, by
its own being. The same is true of the will, and the same
of reason. Therefore, whatever the object of which we
become conscious, we always become conscious of our
own being; we cannot set anything in motion without setting ourselves in motion. And since willing, feeling, and
thinking are perfections, essences, and realities, it is impossible that while indulging in them we experience reason,
feeling, and will as limited or finite; namely, as worthless.
Finiteness and nothingness are identical; finiteness is only
a euphemism for nothingness. Finiteness is a metaphysical,
a theoretical expression, while nothingness is a pathological, a practical one. That which is finite to the intellect
is nothing to the heart. But it is impossible to be conscious
of will, feeling, and reason, only as finite powers, because
every perfection, every power, every being is the immediate verification and confirmation of itself. One cannot love,
will, or think without experiencing these activities as perfections; one cannot perceive oneself to be a loving, willing,
and thinking being without experiencing an infinite joy in
being so. Consciousness is given when a being is its own
object; consequently, it is nothing by itself and as distinct
from the being that is conscious. How else could it be
conscious of itself? Therefore it is impossible to be conscious of a perfection as an imperfection; impossible to

experience feeling as limited; impossible to experience thought as limited.

Consciousness is self-sustained activity, self-affirmation, and self-love—it is joy in one's own perfection. Consciousness is the characteristic mark of a perfect being; consciousness exists only in a plenitudinous, accomplished being. Even human vanity confirms this truth. A man sees himself in the mirror; he is pleased with his form. This feeling of pleasure is a necessary, involuntary consequence of the perfect beauty of his form. A beautiful form is perfect in itself; it is, in view of its perfection, necessarily pleased with itself—hence the necessary urge to behold itself in its own mirror. A man is self-complacent when he is enamored of his own looks, but not when he admires the human form in himself. Indeed, he must even admire this form, for he simply cannot imagine any other form that is more beautiful, more noble than the human form.[4] Naturally, every being loves itself, loves the way it is— and this is how it should be. Being is a good. "Anything," says Bacon, "that deserves to be, also deserves to be known." Everything that exists is of value, is a being possessing a distinction; that is why it affirms and asserts itself. But the highest form of self-affirmation, the form that is itself a matter of distinction, a bliss, a good—that form is consciousness.

Every limitation of reason, or of human nature in general, rests on a delusion, an error. To be sure, the human individual can, even must, feel and know himself to be limited—and this is what distinguishes him from the animal—but he can become conscious of his limits, his finiteness, only because he can make the perfection and infinity of his species the object either of his feeling, conscience, or thought. But if his limitations appear to him as emanating from the species, this can only be due to his delusion that he is identical with the species, a delusion intimately linked with the individual's love of ease, lethargy, vanity, and selfishness; for a limit which I know to be mine alone, humiliates, shames, and disquiets me. Hence, in order to free myself of this feeling of shame, this uneasiness, I

make the limits of my individuality the limits of man's being itself. What is incomprehensible to me is incomprehensible to others; why should this worry me at all? It is
not due to any fault of mine or of my understanding; the
cause lies in the understanding of the species itself. But it
is a folly, a ludicrous and frivolous folly to designate that
which constitutes the nature of man and the absolute nature of the individual, the essence of the species, as finite
and limited. Every being is sufficient to itself. No being
can deny itself, its own nature; no being is intrinsically
limited. Rather, every being is in itself infinite; it carries
its God—that which is the highest being to it—within itself.
Every limit of a being is a limit only for another being that
is outside and above it. The life of the ephemera is extraordinarily short as compared with animals whose life
span is longer; and yet this short span of life is just as long
for them as a life of many years for others. The leaf on
which the caterpillar lives is for it a world, an infinite
space.

That which makes a being what it is, is its talent, its
power, its wealth, and its adornment. How can it possibly
regard its being as nothing, its abundance as lack, or its
talent as incapacity? If plants could see, taste, and judge,
each would claim its own blossom to be the most beautiful; for its understanding and taste would be limited by the
productive power of its being. What the productive power
of a plant has brought forth as its highest achievement,
that must be confirmed and recognized as the highest also
by its taste, its power of judgment. What the nature of a
being affirms, that cannot be denied by its understanding,
taste, and judgment; otherwise this intellect, this power of
judgment would not be that belonging to this particular
being, but rather to some other being. The measure of
being is also the measure of the understanding. If the being concerned is limited, its feeling and understanding
would be limited, too. But, to a limited being, its limited
understanding is not a limitation. On the contrary, it is
perfectly happy and satisfied with it; it experiences, praises,
and values it as a glorious, divine power; and the limited

understanding praises, in its turn, the limited being to whom it belongs. Both harmonize so completely that the question of any discord between them does not arise. The understanding of a being is its horizon. The horizon of your being is limited by what you can see, just as what you can see is limited by the horizon of your being. The eye of the animal does not see beyond what it needs. And so far as the power of your being, so far as your unlimited feeling of self reaches—so far are you God. The conflict in human consciousness between understanding and being, between the power of thought and the power to produce, is only an individual conflict having no general significance; but it is a conflict only in appearance. He who has written a bad poem and knows it to be bad, is in his knowledge—and hence in his being—not so limited as he who, having written a bad poem, thinks it is good.

In keeping with this, if you therefore think the infinite, you think and confirm the infinity of the power of thought; if you feel the infinite, you feel and confirm the infinity of the power of feeling. The object of reason is reason as its own object; the object of feeling is feeling as its own object. If you have no sensibility, no feeling for music, you perceive in the most beautiful music nothing more than what you perceive in the wind that whistles past your ears or in the brook that rushes past your feet. What is it in the sound that grips you? What do you perceive in it? What else if not the voice of your own heart? Hence, feeling addresses itself to feeling; hence, feeling is comprehensible only to feeling, that is, to itself—because the object of feeling is feeling itself. Music is a monologue of feeling. But even the dialogue of philosophy is in reality a monologue of reason—thought speaking to thought. The colorful splendor of crystals ravishes the senses, but only the laws of crystallonomy interest reason. The rational alone is the object of reason.[5]

Hence, all that has, in the sense of superhuman speculation and theology, the significance only of the derivative, the subjective, the means, or the organ, has in truth the significance of the original, of the divine, of the essential being, and of the object itself. If, for example, feeling is the essential organ of religion, the essence of God expresses nothing else than the essence of feeling. The true, albeit hidden, sense of the saying "Feeling is the organ of the divine" is that feeling is the noblest, the most excellent, i.e., the divine, in man. How could you perceive the divine through feeling if feeling itself were not divine? The divine can be known only through that which is itself divine—"God can be known only through himself." The Divine Being perceived by feeling is in reality nothing but the being of feeling itself which is enraptured and fascinated by itself—feeling that is blissful in itself, intoxicated wth joy.

This goes to explain that where feeling is made the organ of the infinite, the subjective essence of religion, the object of religion loses its objective value. Hence, it is understandable that ever since feeling became the mainstay of religion, the otherwise sacred content of Christian belief fell to indifference. If, from the standpoint of feeling, some value is still conceded to the content of Christianity, the fact remains that this value owes itself to feeling which is perhaps only accidentally connected with the object of religion; if some other object would excite the same feelings, it would be just as welcome. But the object of feeling is reduced to indifference precisely because feeling is proclaimed to be the subjective essence of religion only where it is also in actual fact its objective essence, even if it is not —at least not directly—expressed as such. I say directly, for indirectly this is certainly admitted when feeling, as such, is declared to be religious, that is, when the difference between what are characteristically religious and what are irreligious—or at least non-religious—feelings is eliminated —a consequence necessitated by the standpoint which holds feeling alone to be the organ of the divine. For what other reason do you have to regard feeling as the organ of the infinite, of the divine, if not because of the essential nature of feeling? But is not the nature of feeling in general also the nature of every special feeling, whatever its object? The question therefore is: What makes feeling religious? Perhaps its specific object? Not at all, for this object is a religious one only if it is not an object of cold intellect or memory, but of feeling. What then? The answer is: The nature of feeling of which every feeling, whatever be its object, partakes. Feeling has thus been declared sacred simply on the ground that it is feeling; the ground of the religiousness of feeling is its nature and lies in itself. But is not feeling itself thereby pronounced to be the absolute, the divine? If it is only through itself that feeling is good or religious, i.e., sacred or divine, does it then not have its god within itself?

But if you want, on the one hand, to give feeling an unequivocal object, and, on the other, to interpret what your feeling truly is without letting any foreign element interfere with your reflection, what else can you do except make a distinction between your individual feelings and the universal essence and nature of feeling; what else can you do except separate the essence of feeling from the disturbing and contaminating influences with which feeling is bound up in you as a particular individual? Hence, what you can alone have as an object of thought, express as the infinite, determine as the essential nature of the infinite is merely the nature of feeling. You have no other determination of God here than the following one: God is pure, unlimited, free feeling. Every other God, whom you posited here, would be a God imposed upon your feeling from outside. From the point of view of the orthodox form of belief, which is decisive as to the manner in which religion relates itself to an external object, feeling is atheistic; it denies an objective God—it is its own God. From the standpoint of feeling, the denial of feeling is only the denial of God. You are either only too cowardly or too limited to admit in words what your feeling tacitly affirms. Bound to external considerations and unable to grasp the inner sublimeness of feeling, you recoil from acknowledging the religious atheism of your heart, thus destroying the unity of your feeling with itself by perpetrating on yourself the delusion of an objective being separate from feeling. This act of self-delusion throws you

back to the old questions and doubts: Is there a God or
not? The questions and doubts vanish—they are, indeed,
impossible—when feeling is defined as the essence of religion. Feeling is your innermost power, and yet it is a
power that is separate from and independent of you; existing inside you, it is above you; it is your very own being,
yet it seizes hold of you as another being. In short, it is
your God. How can it therefore be possible for you to
distinguish from this being in you another objective being?
How can you get beyond your feeling?

But feeling has been taken here only as an example.
The same holds true of every other power, faculty, po-
tentiality, reality, or activity—the name is of no consequence—which one determines as the essential organ of an
object. Whatever has the significance of being subjective
or from the side of man has for that very reason the significance of being also objective or from the side of the
object. It is simply impossible for man to get beyond the
true horizon of his being. It is true that he can imagine
individuals of a different, and allegedly higher, kind, but
he cannot conceive of himself in abstraction from his
species, from his mode of being. The essential determinations he attributes to those other individuals must always
be determinations emanating from his own being—determinations in which he in truth only projects himself, which
only represent his self-objectifications. It may certainly be
true that thinking beings exist also on other planets; but
by assuming their existence, we do not change our standpoint, we only enrich it quantitatively not qualitatively;
for just as the same laws of motion apply on other planets
as they do here, so also the same laws of feeling and
thought apply there as here. In fact, the reason why we
project life on other planets is not that there are beings
different from ourselves there, but that there may be more
beings there identical with or similar to our being.[6]

II THE ESSENCE OF RELIGION IN GENERAL

What we have so far maintained concerning the general relationship between man and his object, and between man and sensuous objects, is particularly true of man's relationship to the religious object.

In view of its relation to the objects of the senses, the consciousness of the object can be distinguished from self-consciousness; but, in the case of the religious object, consciousness and self-consciousness directly coincide. A sensuous object exists apart from man, but the religious object exists within him—it is itself an inner, intimate object, indeed, the closest object, and hence an object which forsakes him as little as his self-consciousness or conscience. "God," says Augustine, for example, "is nearer, more closely related to us and therefore more easily known by us than sensuous and physical things."[7] Strictly speaking, the object of the senses is in itself indifferent, having no relevance to our disposition and judgment. But the object of religion is a distinguished object—the most excellent, the first, the highest being. It essentially presupposes a critical judgment—the discrimination between the divine and the non-divine, between that which is worthy of adoration and that which is not.[8] It is in this context, therefore, that the following statement is unconditionally true: The object of man is nothing else than his objective being itself. As man thinks, as is his understanding of things, so is his God; so much worth as a man has, so much and no more has his God. The consciousness of God is the self-consciousness of man; the knowledge of God is the self-knowledge of man. Man's notion of himself is his notion of God, just as his notion of God is his notion of himself—the two are identical. What is God to man, that is man's own spirit, man's own soul; what is man's spirit, soul, and heart—that is his God. God is the manifestation of man's inner nature, his expressed self; religion is the solemn unveiling of man's hidden treasures, the avowal of his innermost thoughts, the open confession of the secrets of his love.

But if religion, i.e., the consciousness of God, is characterized as the self-consciousness of man, this does not mean that the religious man is directly aware that his consciousness of God is his self-consciousness, for it is precisely the absence of such an awareness that is responsible for the peculiar nature of religion. Hence, in order to eliminate this misunderstanding, it would be better to say that religion is the first, but indirect, self-consciousness of man. That is why religion precedes philosophy everywhere, in the history of mankind as well as in the history of the individual. Man transposes his essential being outside himself before he finds it within himself. His own being becomes the object of his thought first as another being. Religion is the essential being of man in his infancy; but the child sees his essential being, namely, man outside himself, as a child; a man is object to himself as another man. Hence, the historical development occurring within religions takes the following course: What an earlier religion regarded as objective, is now recognized as subjective; i.e., what was regarded and worshiped as God, is now recognized as something human. From the standpoint of a later religion, the earlier religion turns out to be idolatry: Man is seen to have worshiped his own essence. Man has objectified himself, but he has not yet recognized the object as his own essential being—a step taken by later religion. Every progress in religion means, therefore, a deepening of man's knowledge of himself. But every religion, while designating older religions as idolatrous, looks upon itself as exempted from their fate. It does so necessarily, for otherwise it would no longer be religion; it sees only in other religions what is the fault— if a fault it can be called—of religion as such. Because its object, its content, is a different one, because it has superseded the content of earlier religions, it presumes to be exalted above the necessary and eternal laws that constitute the essence of religion; it gives itself to the illusion that its object, its content, is superhuman. However, the hidden nature of religion, which remains opaque to religion itself, is transparent to the thinker who makes it the object of his thought. And our task consists precisely in showing that the antithesis of the divine and human is illusory; that is, that it is nothing other than the antithesis between the essential being of man and his individual being, and that consequently the object and the content of the Christian religion are altogether human.

Religion, at least the Christian religion, is the expression of how man relates to himself, or more correctly, to his essential being; but he relates to his essential being as to another being. The Divine Being is nothing other than the being of man himself, or rather, the being of man abstracted from the limits of the individual man or the real, corporeal man, and objectified, i.e., contemplated and worshiped as another being, as a being distinguished from his own. All determinations of the Divine Being are, therefore, determinations of the being of man.[9]

In relation to the predicates—attributes or determinations—of God, this is admitted without hesitation, but by no means admitted in relation to the subject of these predicates, in relation to the being in which they are grounded. The negation of the subject is taken to mean the negation of religion, atheism, but not the negation of the predicates. That which has no determinations, also has no effect upon me; that which has no effect upon me, also does not exist for me. To eliminate all determinations of a being is the same as to eliminate that being itself. A being without determinations is a being that cannot be an object of thought; it is a nonentity. Where man removes all determinations from God, God is reduced to a negative being, to a being that is not a being. To a truly religious man, however, God is not a being without determinations, because he is a definite, real being to him. Hence, the view that God is without determinations, that he cannot be known, is a product of the modern era, of modern unbelief.

Just as reason can be, and is, determined as finite only where man regards sensual enjoyment, religious feeling,

aesthetic contemplation, or moral sentiment as the absolute, the true, so the view as to the unknowability or indeterminateness of God can be fixed as a dogma only
where this object commands no interest for cognition,
where reality alone claims the interest of man or where
the real alone has for him the significance of being an
essential, absolute, divine object, but where at the same
time this purely worldly tendency is contradicted by a still-
existing remnant of old religiosity. By positing God as
unknowable, man excuses himself to what is still left of
his religious conscience for his oblivion of God, his sur-
render to the world. He negates God in practice—his mind
and his senses have been absorbed by the world—but he
does not negate him in theory. He does not attack his
existence; he leaves it intact. But this existence neither
affects nor incommodes him, for it is only a negative
existence, an existence without existence; it is an existence
that contradicts itself—a being that, in view of its effects,
is indistinguishable from non-being. The negation of determinate, positive predicates of the Divine Being is nothing else than the negation of religion, but one which still
has an appearance of religion, so that it is not recognized
as a negation—it is nothing but a subtle, sly atheism. The
alleged religious horror of limiting God by determinate
predicates is only the irreligious wish to forget all about
God, to banish him from the mind. He who is afraid to be
finite is afraid to exist. All real existence, that is, all existence that really is existence, is qualitative, determinate
existence. He who seriously, truly believes in the existence
of God is not disturbed even by grossly sensuous qualities
attributed to God. He who regards the fact of his existence
as an insult, he who recoils from that which is gross, may
just as well give up existing. A God to whom his determinateness is an insult lacks the courage and strength to exist.
Determinateness is the fire, the oxygen, the salt of existence. An existence in general, an existence without qualities, is an insipid and preposterous existence. But there is
nothing more, and nothing less, in God than what religion
puts in him. Only when man loses his taste for religion,

that is, when religion itself becomes insipid, does God become an insipid existence.

Moreover, there is yet a milder way of denying the divine predicates than the direct one just described. One admits that the predicates of the Divine Being are finite and, more particularly, human determinations, but one rejects the idea of rejecting them. One even defends them on the ground that they are necessary for man; that being man, he cannot conceive God in any way other than human. One argues that although these determinations have no meaning in relation to God, the fact is that God, if he is to exist for man, can appear to man in no other way than he does, namely, as a being with human attributes. However, this distinction between what God is in himself and what he is for man destroys the peace of religion as well as being an unfeasible and unfounded distinction. It is not at all possible for me to know whether God as he is in and for himself is something different from what he is for me. The manner in which he exists for me is also the totality of his existence for me. The determinations in terms of which he exists for me contain also the "in-itself-ness" of his being, his essential nature itself; he exists for me in a way in which he can exist for me alone. The religious man is completely satisfied with how he sees God in relation to himself—and he knows nothing of any other relation—for God is to him what he can be to man at all. In the distinction made above, man transgresses the boundaries of himself, his being and its absolute measure, but this transcending is only an illusion. For I can make the distinction between the object as it is in itself and the object as it is for me only where an object can really appear different from what it actually appears to me. I cannot make such a distinction where the object appears to me as it does according to my absolute measure; that is, as it must appear to me. It is true that my conception can be subjective; that is, one which is not bound by the essential constitution of my species. However, if my conception corresponds to the measure of my species, the distinction between what something is in itself and what it is for me ceases; for in that case this conception is itself an absolute one. The measure of the species is the absolute measure, law, and criterion of man. Yet religion has the conviction that its conceptions and determinations of God are such as every man ought to have if he is to have true conceptions, that these are conceptions necessitated by human nature, that they are indeed objective, conforming to the nature of God. To every religion, the gods of other religions are only conceptions of God; but its own conception of God is itself its God—God as it conceives him to be, God genuinely and truly so, God as he is in himself. Religion is satisfied only with a complete and total God—it will not have merely an appearance of God, it can be satisfied with nothing less than God himself, God in person. Religion abandons itself if it abandons God in his essential being; it is no longer true if it renounces its possession of the true God. Skepticism is the archenemy of religion. But the distinction between object and concept, between God as he is in himself and as he is for me, is a skeptical, that is, irreligious distinction.

That which is subsumed by man under the concept of "being-in-itself," that which he regards as the most supreme being or as the being of which he can conceive none higher, that is the Divine Being. How can he therefore still ask, what this being is in itself? If God were an object to the bird, he would be an object to it only as a winged being—the bird knows nothing higher, nothing more blissful than the state of being winged. How ludicrous would it be if this bird commented: "God appears to me as a bird, but I do not know what he is in himself." The highest being to the bird is the "bird-being." Take from it its conception of "bird-being," and you take from it its conception of the highest being. How, therefore, could the bird ask whether God in himself were winged? To ask whether God is in himself what he is for me, is to ask whether God is God; it is to raise oneself above God and to rebel against him.

Given, therefore, the situation in which man is seized by the awareness that religious predicates are mere anthropomorphisms, his faith has also come under the sway of doubt and unbelief. And if this awareness does not lead him to the formal negation of the predicates and thence to the negation of the being in which they are grounded, it is only due to an inconsistency for which his faint-heartedness and irresolute intellect are responsible. If you doubt the objective truth of the predicates, you must also doubt the objective truth of the subject to which they belong. If your predicates are anthropomorphisms, their subject, too, is an anthropomorphism. If love, goodness, and personality are human determinations, the being which constitutes their source and, according to you, their pre-supposition is also an anthropomorphism; so is the existence of God; so is the belief that there is a God—in short, all presuppositions that are purely human. What tells you that the belief in a God at all is not an indication of the limitedness of man's mode of conception? Higher beings—and you assume that such beings exist—are perhaps so blissful in themselves, so at unity with themselves that they are not exposed to a tension between themselves and a higher being. To know God and not to be God, to know blissfulness and not to enjoy it, is to be in conflict with oneself, is to be delivered up to unhappiness.[10]

You believe in love as a divine attribute because you yourself love, and believe that God is a wise and benevolent being because you know nothing better in yourself than wisdom and benevolence. You believe that God exists, that therefore he is a subject or an essence—whatever exists is also an essence, whether it is defined as a substance, a person, or in any other way—because you yourself exist, are yourself an essence. You know no higher human good than to love, to be wise and good. Equally, you know no other happiness than to exist, to be a being, for your consciousness of good and happiness derives itself from your consciousness of being and existing yourself. God to you exists, is a being for the same reason that he is to you a wise, blissful, and benevolent being. The distinction between the divine attributes and the divine essence is only this. To you the essence, the existence does not appear as

an anthropomorphism, because the fact of your own being
brings with it the necessity of conceiving the existence of
God, whereas the attributes appear to you as anthropomorphisms, because their necessity—the necessity that God is
wise, good, just, etc.—is not an immediate necessity identical with the being of man, but is mediated by his self-
consciousness, by the activity of his thought. I may be
wise or unwise, good or bad, but I am a being—I exist.
Man's existence is to him the first datum, the sustaining
ground of his conceptions, the presupposition of all his
predicates. Hence, man is prepared to concede that the
predicates of God are anthropomorphic, but not the existence of God; to him it is a settled, inviolable, absolutely
certain, and objective truth. And yet, this distinction is
only an apparent one. The necessity of the subject lies only
in the necessity of the predicate. Your being is the being
of man; the certainty and reality of your existence lie in
the certainty and reality of your human attributes. What
the subject is—its being—lies only in the predicate; the
predicate is the truth of the subject; the subject is only the
personified, existing predicate. The distinction between subject and object corresponds to the distinction between existence and essence. The negation of the predicate is therefore the negation of the subject. What remains of the being
of man if you take away its attributes? Even in the language of ordinary life one speaks of the divine not in terms
of its essence, but in terms of its attributes—providence,
wisdom, omnipotence.

The certainty of the existence of God, which has been
held by man to be more certain than even his own existence, depends therefore on the certainty of the attributes
of God—it does not have the character of immediate certainty. To the Christian, only the existence of a Christian
God is a certainty, just as to the pagan only that of a pagan
god is certain. The pagan did not doubt the existence of
Jupiter, because Jupiter as a divine being was not repulsive
to him. He could not conceive of a god with any other
attributes, because these attributes were to him a certainty,

a divine truth. The truth of the predicate alone ensures the existence of the subject.

That which man conceives to be true is also that which he immediately conceives to be real because, originally, only the real is true to him—true in opposition to that which is merely conceived, dreamed, or imagined. The concept of being, of existence, is the original concept of truth. In other words, man originally makes truth dependent on existence, but only later existence dependent on truth. Now God is the essence of man, regarded by him as the highest truth. But God, or religion—both are the same—varies according to the determination in terms of which man comprehends his essence, in terms of which he regards it as the highest being. This determination, which is decisive for man's idea of God, is to him the truth and, precisely for that reason, also the highest existence, or existence itself. For, strictly speaking, only the highest existence is existence, and deserves this name. Therefore, God is a really existing being for the same reason that he is this particular being. The attribute or determination of God is nothing else than the essential attribute of man himself, and the thus-determined man is what he is, has his existence, his reality, in his determinateness. You cannot take away from a Greek the quality of being a Greek without taking away his existence. Hence, it is of course true that for a particular religion—that is, relatively—the certainty of the existence of God is immediate; for just as arbitrarily or necessarily the Greek was Greek, so necessarily were his gods Greek beings, so necessarily were they really existing beings. In view of its understanding of the world and man, religion is identical with the essence of man. However, it is not man who stands above the conceptions essential to his being; rather, it is these conceptions that stand above him. They animate, determine, and govern him. This goes to show that the necessity to prove, and the possibility to doubt, how and whether existence is related to being or quality is abolished. That which I sever from my being can only be doubtful. How could I therefore doubt God who is my essence? To doubt God would be to doubt my-

self. Only when God is conceived abstractly, when his predicates are arrived at through philosophical abstraction, does
the distinction or separation arise between subject and
predicate, existence and essence—only then does the illusion arise that the existence or the subject is something
different from the predicate, something immediate, indubitable, or distinct from the predicate which is subject to
doubt. But this is only an illusion. A God whose predicates
are abstract also has an abstract existence. Existence, being,
is as varied as the qualities predicated of it.

The identity of subject and predicate is borne out clearly
by the course taken by religion in its development, a course
which is identical with that taken by human culture. As
long as man is a mere natural being, his God is a mere
natural deity. Where man lives in houses, he encloses his
gods in temples. A temple expresses the value which man
attaches to beautiful buildings. Temples in honor of religion are in truth temples in honor of architecture. With
man's progress to culture from a state of primitive sav-
agery, with the distinction between what is proper and
what is improper for man, there also arises the distinction
between what is proper and what is improper for
God. God expresses man's notion of majesty, highest
dignity, religious sentiment, and highest feeling of propriety. Only at a later stage did the culturally more advanced
artists of Greece embody in their statues of gods the concepts of dignity, spiritual grandeur, rest without
movement, and serenity. But why did they regard these
qualities as divine attributes? Because they held these attributes in themselves to be divine. Why did they exclude
all repulsive and low emotions? Because they regarded
these emotions as something improper, undignified, unhuman, and, consequently, ungodlike. The Homeric gods
eat and drink—this means that eating and drinking are
divine pleasures. Physical strength is a quality of the
Homeric gods—Zeus is the strongest of all gods. Why? Because physical strength in itself was something glorious
and divine to the Greeks. The highest virtue to ancient
Germans was the virtue of the warrior; that is why their

highest god was the god of war—Odin; that is why war to them was "the primeval or the oldest law." The first, true divine being is not the quality of divinity, but the divinity or the deity of quality. In other words, that which theology and philosophy have so far regarded as God, as the absolute and essential, is not God; but that which they did not regard as God, is precisely God—quality, determination, and reality par excellence. A true atheist, that is, an atheist in the ordinary sense, is therefore he alone to whom the predicates of the Divine Being—for example, love, wisdom, and justice—are nothing, not he to whom only the subject of these predicates is nothing. And the negation of the subject is by no means also necessarily the negation of the predicates as they are in themselves. The predicates have a reality of their own, have an independent significance; the force of what they contain compels man to recognize them. They prove their truth to man directly through themselves. They are their own proof and evidence. Goodness, justice, and wisdom do not become chimeras if the existence of God is a chimera, nor do they become truths simply because the existence of God is a truth. The concept of God depends on the concept of justice, kindness, and wisdom—a God who is not kind, not just, and not wise is no God. But these concepts do not depend on the concept of God. That a quality is possessed by God does not make it divine; God possesses it, because it is in itself divine, because without it God would be a defective being. Justice, wisdom, and, in fact, every determination which constitutes the divinity of God, is determined and known through itself; but God is known and determined by the predicates. Only in the case where I think that God and justice are identical, that God is immediately the reality of the idea of justice or of any other quality, do I think of God as self-determined. But if God, the subject, is that which is determined, and the quality or the predicate is that which determines him, then the predicate, and not the subject, in truth deserves the primacy of being, the status of divinity.

Only when it happens that a number of contradictory

qualities are combined into one being, which is then conceived in the form of a person, that is, when personality
is particularly emphasized, does one forget the origin of
religion, does one forget that that which reflective thought
looks upon as the predicate distinguishable or separable
from the subject was originally the true subject. Thus, the
Greeks and the Romans deified the accidents as
substances; virtues, mental states, and emotions, were as
independent beings. Man, particularly the religious man,
is the measure of all things, of all reality. Whatever im-
presses man, whatever makes a particular impression on
his mind—and it may be merely some strange, inexplicable
sound or note—he hypostatizes into a particular deity.
Religion encompasses all the objects of the world; think
of anything existing, and you will find that it has been the
object of religious veneration. Nothing is to be found in
the essence and consciousness of religion that is not there
in the being of man, that is not there in his consciousness
of himself and the world. Religion has no particular content of its own. Even the emotions of fear and dread had
their temples in Rome. The Christians, too, hypostatized
their mental states into beings and qualities of things, their
dominant emotions into powers dominating the world. In
short, they hypostatized the qualities of their being—
whether known or unknown to them—into self-subsisting
beings. Devils, goblins, witches, ghosts, angels, etc., con-
tinued to be sacred truths as long as the religious disposition held its uninterrupted sway over mankind.

In order not to acknowledge the identity of the divine
and human predicates, and hence of the divine and human
essence, one takes recourse to the idea that God, as an
infinite being, has an infinite plenitude of various predicates, of which we know only some in this world, and
indeed, those that are similar or analogous to our own;
but the others, by virtue of which God is a totally different
being from the being of man or from anything similar to
it, we shall only know in the future—in the world hereafter. However, an infinite plenitude or multitude of predicates which are truly different—and so different that the

knowledge of the one does not immediately posit and lead
to the knowledge of the other—realizes its truth only in
an infinite plenitude or multitude of different beings or
individuals. Thus, the being of man is infinitely rich in
different kinds of predicates, but precisely for that reason
it is infinitely rich in different kinds of individuals. Each
new man is, so to say, a new predicate, a new talent added
to mankind. Mankind possesses as many qualities, as many
powers, as the number of its members. Although the individual partakes of the same power that is inherent in
all men, it is so constituted in him that it appears to be a
new and unique power. The secret of the inexhaustible
plenitude of the divine determinations is, therefore, nothing else than the secret of the being of man which is infinitely diverse, infinitely determinable, and—precisely for
these reasons—sensuous. Only in sensuousness, only in
space and time, does an infinite being—a being that is really
infinite and plentiful in predicates—exist. Where there are
truly different predicates, there are truly different times.
One man is an excellent musician, an excellent writer, and
an excellent physician; but he cannot make music, write,
and cure at one and the same time. Time, and not the
Hegelian dialectic, is the power by means of which an-
titheses and contradictions are united in one and the same
being. However, the infinite plurality of different predicates
must remain an unreal conception if it is seen in con-
junction with the concept of God, but in disjunction with
the being of man. Thus, it must remain a fantasy—a conception of sensuousness, lacking the essence and truth of
sensuousness. Thus, it must remain a conception that
stands in direct contradiction with the Divine Being as an
intellectual—that is, abstract, simple, and unique being—for
the predicates of God are of such a nature that possessing
one implies possessing all the others, because there is no
real difference between them. If, therefore, the present
predicates do not involve the future ones, the present God
does not involve the future God, then the future God
does not involve the present—they are two different beings.[11] But this distinction contradicts the unity, unique-

ness, and simplicity of God. Why is a certain predicate a predicate of God? Because it is of divine nature, that is, because it expresses no limitation, no defect. Why are other predicates so? Because, however different they may be among themselves, they concur in this: They equally express perfection and unlimitedness. Hence, I can imagine innumerable predicates of God, because they must all concur in the abstract concept of the Godhead, because they must have in common that which makes every single predicate into a divine attribute or predicate. This is the case with Spinoza. He speaks of an infinite plurality of the attributes of the divine substance, but he does not name any besides thought and extension. Why? Because it is a matter of complete indifference to know them; because they are, indeed, in themselves indifferent and superfluous; because despite these innumerable predicates, I would still be saying the same as with the two predicates of thought and extension. Why is thought an attribute of substance? Because according to Spinoza, it is comprehended through itself, because it is something that cannot be divided, that is, perfect and infinite. Why extension or matter? Because they express the same thing in relation to themselves. That means that substance can have an indefinite number of predicates, because it is not their determinateness, their difference, but their non-difference, their sameness, which makes them attributes of substance. Or rather, substance has such an infinite number of predicates, only because—and this is, indeed, strange—it has really no predicate, no definite, real predicate. The indeterminate One existing in thought is supplemented by the indeterminate manifoldness existing in the imagination. Because the predicate is not *multum,* it is *multa.* In truth, the positive predicates are thought and extension. With these two, infinitely more is said than with nameless innumerable predicates; for they say something definite; they enable me to know something. But substance is too indifferent, too passionless to be enthusiastic about, or be on the side of, something; in order to be something, it prefers to be nothing.

Now, if it is accepted that whatever the subject or being involves lies solely in its determinations—in other words, the predicate is the true subject—it is also clear that if the divine predicates are determinations of the being of man, their subject, too, is the being of man. The divine predicates are general, on the one hand, but personal, on the other. The general ones are metaphysical, but they provide religion with ultimate points of reference, with a foundation; they are not the characteristic determinations of religion. It is the personal predicates alone on which the essence of religion is grounded, in which the divine nature of religion is objectified. Such personal predicates are, for example, that God is a Person, that he is the moral Lawgiver, the Father of men, the Holy One, the Just, the Merciful. It is obvious from these and other determinations—or at least it will be clear later—that as personal determinations these predicates are purely human determinations, and that, consequently, man's relationship to God in religion is his relationship to his own being. For these predicates are to religion not man's conceptions or images of God distinct from God as he is in himself, but truths and realities. Religion knows nothing of anthropomorphisms—anthropomorphisms are not anthropomorphisms to it. The essence of religion is precisely that it regards the attributes of God as the being of God. That these attributes are images is shown only by the intellect, which reflects on religion and, while defending them, denies them before its own tribunal. But in the view of religion, God is a real Father, real Love, real Mercy; for it takes him to be a real, living, personal attribute. Indeed, these and corresponding determinations are precisely those that are most offensive to the intellect, and which it denies in its reflection on religion. Subjectively, religion is emotion; hence, objectively also, emotion is to it an attribute of the Divine Being. It regards even anger as not unworthy of God, provided that nothing evil is associated with it.

But it is important to note here—and the phenomenon in question is an extremely remarkable one, characterizing the innermost essence of religion—that the more human the being of God is, the greater is the apparent difference between God and man; that is, the more is the identity of the human and the Divine Being denied by theology or the self-reflection of religion, and the more is the human—taken in the sense in which it is as such the object of man's consciousness—depreciated.[12] The reason for this is to be found in the following: Because the positive and essential basis of the conception or determination of God can only be human, the conception of man as an object of consciousness can only be negative, that is, hostile to man. In order to enrich God, man must become poor; that God may be all, man must be nothing. But he also does not need to be anything for himself, because everything for himself, everything he takes from himself, is not lost, but preserved in God. Since man has his being in God, why then should he have it in and for himself? Why should it be necessary to posit and have the same thing twice? What man withdraws from himself, what he lacks in himself, he only enjoys in an incomparably higher and richer measure in God.

As a consequence of their vow of chastity, the monks repressed sexual love in themselves; but, for that matter, they had in the Virgin Mary the image of woman; in God, in heaven, the image of love. The more an ideal, imagined woman was the object of their real love, the more easily could they dispense with woman in flesh and blood. The greater the significance they attached to the annihilation of sensuality, the greater was for them the significance of the heavenly Virgin: She occupied in their mind a place even more prominent than that of Christ or God. The more the sensuous is denied, the more sensuous is the God to whom it is sacrificed. Whatever is sacrificed to God is something particularly cherished, but also something that is particularly pleasing to God. That which is the highest to man is also the highest to his God; that which pleases man pleases God also. The Hebrews did not sacrifice to Jehovah unclean, loathsome animals, but those they valued most; those they ate themselves were also the food of God.[13] Where, therefore, the denial of sensuousness leads to its hypostatization as a certain being, or to its transformation into an offering pleasing to God, there the highest value is attached to sensuousness; there the renounced sensuousness is restored precisely through the fact that God takes the place of the sensuous being that has been renounced. The nun weds herself to God; she has a heavenly bridegroom, and the monk, a heavenly bride. But the heavenly virgin is obviously the form in which a general truth concerning the essence of religion appears. Man affirms in God what he denies in himself.[14] Religion abstracts from man, from the world. But it can abstract only from defects and limits, whether real or imaginary; it can abstract only from the illusory but not from the real, positive being of the world and man. Hence, it must reincorporate into its negation and abstraction that wherefrom it abstracts, or believes to abstract. And thus, in fact, religion unconsciously places in God all that it consciously denies, provided, of course, that the negated is something essential, true, and, consequently, something that cannot be negated. Thus, in religion man negates his reason—he knows nothing of God through his own reason; his thoughts are only earthly; he can only believe in what God reveals. But, for that matter, the thoughts of God are human and earthly; like man, he has plans in his head —he makes allowance for the circumstances and intellectual powers of man, like a teacher for his pupils' capacity to understand; he calculates exactly the effect of his gifts and revelations; he keeps an eye on man in all his doings; he knows everything—even the most earthly, the meanest, or the worst. In short, man denies his knowledge, his thought, that he may place them in God. Man renounces himself as a person only to discover God, the omnipotent and the infinite, as a personal being; he denies human honor, the human ego, only to have a God that is selfish, egoistic, who seeks in everything only himself, his honor, his advantage, only to have a God whose sole concern is the gratification of his own selfishness, the enjoyment of his own ego.[15] Religion further denies goodness as a quality of man's being; man is wicked, corrupt, and incapable of good; but, in contrast, God is only good—the good being. It is demanded of man to conceive the good as God, but does this not make goodness an essential determination of man? If I am absolutely, i.e., by nature, wicked and unholy, how can holiness and goodness be the objects of my thought—no matter whether these objects are given to me internally or externally? If my heart is wicked, my understanding corrupt, how can I perceive and feel the holy to be holy, the good to be good? How can I perceive a beautiful painting as beautiful if my soul is by nature ugly, and hence incapable of perceiving aesthetic beauty? Even if I am not a painter and do not have the power to produce something beautiful out of myself, my feeling and understanding are aesthetic since I perceive beauty in the world outside. Either the good does not exist for man, or if it does, it reveals the holiness and goodness of the being of man. That which is absolutely against my nature, with which I have nothing in common, I also cannot think or feel. Holiness stands in contrast to me as an individual, but in unity with my human essence. The holy is a reproach to my sinfulness; in it I recognize myself as a sinner, but in my idea of holiness I also know that I am not, and I reproach myself for not being what I ought to be, what I can be according to my nature. An ought without the possibility of conforming to it is a ludicrous chimera which cannot take hold of the mind. But in so far as I acknowledge goodness as my essential determination, as my law, I acknowledge it, consciously or unconsciously, as my own nature. A being other than mine, and differing from me according to its nature, does not concern me. I can perceive sin as sin only if I perceive it as involving me in a contradiction with myself; that is, as a contradiction between my personality and essence. As a contradiction of the divine; that is, of a being other than mine, the feeling of sin is inexplicable, meaningless.

The distinction between Augustinianism and Pelagianism consists only of this: What the former expresses in the form characteristic to religion, the latter expresses in the form characteristic to rationalism. Both say the same thing, both see the good as belonging to man; but Pelagianism does it directly, in a rationalistic, moral form, whereas Augustinianism does it indirectly, in a mystical, that is, religious form.[16] That which is ascribed to the God of man is in truth ascribed to man himself; that which man predicates of God, he in truth predicates of himself. Augustinianism would only then be true—and true, indeed, in a sense opposed to Pelagianism—if the devil were the God of man, if man, aware that he was himself a devil, worshiped and celebrated the devil as the highest expression of his own being. But as long as man worships a good being as God, that long does he behold his own goodness in God.

The doctrine of the fundamental corruption of man's nature and the doctrine that man is incapable of good are identical, and concur in the view that, in truth, man is unable to do anything by himself and through his own power.

The denial of human power and activity would be true only if man also denied the existence of moral activity in God; that is, if he were to say with the Oriental nihilist or pantheist: The Divine Being is absolutely without will, inactive, indifferent, and ignorant of the distinction between good and evil. But he who defines God as an active being—and, indeed, as morally active, as a moral and critical being, as a being that loves, works, and rewards good, and punishes, rejects, and condemns evil—he who so defines God only apparently denies human activity. In actual fact, he regards it as the highest, the most real activity. He who attributes action to man declares human activity to be divine. He says: A God who does not act, that is, does not act morally or humanly, is no God. He therefore makes the notion of God dependent on the notion of activity, or rather human activity, for he knows of none higher.

Man—and this is the secret of religion—objectifies[17] his being, and then again makes himself the object of this objectified being, transformed into a subject, a person. He thinks of himself as an object, but as an object of an ob-

ject, as an object to another being. Thus, here man is an
object to God. That man is good or evil is not indifferent
to God. No! God is keenly and deeply concerned whether
man is good; he wants him to be good and blissful—and
both necessarily belong together. The reduction of human
activity to nothingness is thus retracted by the religious
man through the fact that he turns his sentiments and
actions into an object of God, man into a purpose of God
—that which is an object in mind is a purpose in action—
and the divine activity into a means of man's salvation.
God acts, that man may be good and felicitous. Thus,
while in appearance the greatest humiliation is inflicted
upon man, in truth he is exalted to the highest. Thus, in
and through God, the aim of man is man himself. It is
true that the aim of man is God, but the aim of God is
nothing except the moral and eternal salvation of man;
that means that the aim of man is man himself. The divine
activity does not distinguish itself from the human.

How could the divine activity work on me as its object,
indeed, work in me, if it were essentially foreign to me?
How could it have a human aim, the aim to make man
better and happy, if it were not itself human? Does not
the aim determine the act? When man makes it his goal
to morally improve himself, his resolutions and projects
are divine; but, equally, when God has in view the salvation of man, both his aims and his corresponding activity
are human. Thus, in God man confronts his own activity
as an object. But because he regards his own activity as
existing objectively and as distinct from himself, he necessarily receives the impulse, the urge, to act not from himself, but from this object. He looks upon his being as existing outside himself, and he looks upon it as the good;
hence it is self-evident, a tautology, that he receives the
impulse to good from where he deposits it.

God is the most subjective, the very own being of man,
but set apart from himself. That means that he cannot
derive his actions purely out of himself, or that all good
comes from God. The more subjective, the more human
God is, the more man exteriorizes his subjectivity, his hu-

manity, because God is in reality the exteriorized self of man which he, however, reappropriates. As the activity of the arteries drives the blood into the extremities, and the action of the veins leads it back again, as life basically consists in a constant systole and diastole, so is it also in religion. In the religious systole man's being departs from itself into an outward projection; man disowns, rejects himself; in the religious diastole his heart again embraces his rejected being. God alone is the being whose actions originate within himself, whose activity flows out of himself—thus operates the repelling force in religion; God is the being who acts in me, with me, through me, upon me, and for me; he is the principle of my salvation, of my good sentiments and actions, and hence my own good principle and essence—thus operates the attracting force in religion.

The course of religious development, as delineated in general above, consists more specifically in this, that man progressively appropriates to himself what he had attributed to God. In the beginning, man posits his essence completely and without distinction outside himself. This is illustrated particularly by his belief in revelation. That which to a later epoch or to a culturally advanced people is revealed by reason or nature is revealed to an earlier epoch, or to a culturally backward people, by God. All human urges, however natural—even the urge for cleanliness—were conceived by the Israelites as positive divine commandments. This example again shows us that man's image of God is the more debased and the more commonly human the more man denies himself. Can the degradation, the self-abnegation of man sink to lower depths than when he denies himself even the power and ability to fulfill by himself, out of his own resources, the requirements of ordinary decency?[18] In comparison, the Christian religion distinguished the urges and emotions of man according to their character and content. It made only the good emotions, only the good sentiments, and only the good thoughts the revelations and workings of God, that is, his sentiments, emotions, and thoughts; for what God

reveals is a determination of God himself; that which fills
the heart overflows the lips; the nature of the effect reveals
the nature of the cause; the character of the revelation
points to the character of the being that reveals itself. A
God who reveals himself only in good sentiments is himself a God whose essential quality is only moral goodness.
The Christian religion separated inward moral purity from
external physical purity; the Israelite religion identified the
two.[19] In contrast to the Israelite, the Christian religion
is the religion of criticism and freedom. The Israelite re-
coiled from doing anything that was not commanded by
God; even in external things he was without will; even his
food fell within the jurisdiction of religious authority. On
the other hand, the Christian religion left all these external things to the autonomy of man, that is, it posited
in man what the Israelite posited outside himself—in God.
Israel is the most perfect embodiment of religions positiv-
ism; that is, of the type of religion that posits the essential
being of man outside man. As compared with the Israelite,
the Christian is an *esprit fort,* a free spirit. That is how
things change. What yesterday still passed for religion, has
ceased to be so today; and what is regarded as atheism
today will be religion tomorrow.

NOTES

1. The uninspired materialist says: "Man is distinguished from
   the animal only by consciousness; he is an animal, but
   one possessing consciousness in addition." He does not
   take into account that a being who awakes to consciousness
   is thereby qualitatively changed. Moreover, what we have
   just said is by no means intended to belittle the animal.
   This is not the place to go deeper into this question.
2. "A strong opinion expresses itself even at the cost of life."
   —Montaigne
3. Whether this distinction between the individual—naturally,
   a word that, like all other abstract words, is highly indeterminate, equivocal, and misleading—and love, reason, or

will is borne out by nature or not, is quite irrelevant to the theme of the present work. Religion abstracts from man his powers, qualities, and essential determinations and deifies them as independent beings, no matter whether each one of them is singly turned into a being—as in polytheism—or all of them are turned into one being—as in monotheism. That means that this distinction must also be made while explaining these divine beings and tracing their origin. Moreover, it is not only indicated by the object, it is also linguistically and, which is the same, logically evidenced; for man distinguishes himself from his mind, his heart, as if he were a being without them.

4. "Nothing is more beautiful to man than man himself." (Cicero, *de natura deorum*, lib., 1.) And this is no sign of limitation, for man also regards other beings as beautiful besides himself, delights in the beautiful forms of animals, in the beautiful forms of plants, in the beauty of nature in general. But only a form that is absolutely perfect can delight without envy in the form of other beings.

5. "The intellect is percipient only to the intellect and to that which flows from it."—Reimarus. (*Wahrheit der natürlichen Religion*, IV. Abt., § 8.)

6. "It is probable that the ability to enjoy music and mathematics is not unique to man, but extends to many other beings as well."—Christ. Hugenius (*Cosmotheoros*, Lib. I.) This means that a quality does not change; the capability for music, for mathematics is the same; only the number of those capable of enjoying them should be unlimited.

7. *De Genesi ad litteram*, Lib., V, c. 16.

8. "You do not realize that it is easier to know than to worship God."—Minucius Felix, *Octavianus*, c. 24.

9. "The perfections of God are the perfections of our own soul, but God possesses them boundlessly. . . . We possess only some powers, some knowledge, some good; but God possess them in their entirety and perfection." (Leibniz, *Théodicée*, Préface.) "Everything by which the human soul is distinguished is inherent also in the Divine Being. Everything which is excluded from God also does not belong to the essential determinations of the soul." (St. Gregorius Nyss, *de anima*, Lips. 1837, p. 42.) "The most excellent and important among all forms of knowledge is therefore self-knowledge; for if one knows himself he can also

know God." (Clemens Alexandrinus, *Paedag.*, Lib., iii, c. 1.)

10. Hence in the world hereafter the conflict between God and man ceases. There, man is no longer man—at the most, only in fantasy. He no longer has a will of his own, no longer has a will that is distinguished from that of God; consequently, he also no longer has a being that is specifically his own—and what kind of a being is a being without will? In the world hereafter man is one with God; there, the antithesis between God and man vanishes. But where there is only God, there is no longer God. Where there is nothing contrasting majesty, there is also no majesty.

11. For religious belief there is no other difference between the present and the future God than that the former is an object of belief, conception, and fantasy, whereas the latter is an object of the immediate; i.e., of personal and sensuous conception. He is the same God both here and in the world hereafter, but here he is opaque, whereas in the other world he is transparent.

12. However great may the similarity between the creator and the creature be conceived, the dissimilarity between both must be conceived even greater. (Later. Conc. Can. 2. Summa Omn. Conc. Carranza. Antw. 1559, p. 326.) The last distinction between man and God, between the finite and the infinite being in general, to which the religio-speculative imagination soars is the distinction between something and nothing, between *ens* and *nonens;* for only in nothingness is all community with other beings annulled.

13. *Cibus Dei,* Leviticus iii, 2.

14. "He who despises himself," says Anselm, "is honored by God. He who dislikes himself is liked by God. Therefore, be small in your own eyes so that you may be big in the eyes of God; for you shall be the more valued by God, the more contemptuous you are of men." (Anselmi Opp., Parisiis 1721, p. 191.)

15. "God can only love himself, can think only of himself, can only work for himself. In making man, God pursues his own advantage, his own glory." (Vide P. Bayle, *Ein Beitrag zur Geschichte der Philo. u. Mensch.*)

16. Pelagianism negates God and religion—"by ascribing too much power to the will, they weaken the power of pious prayer." (Augustinus, *de natura et gratia contra Pelagium,*

c. 58.) It has only the Creator, i.e., Nature, as its basis, not the Saviour, the God proper of religion—in short, it negates God, but, in return, elevates man into God, in so far as it makes man a being who does not need God, who is self-sufficient and independent. (On this point, see *Luther Against Erasmus and Augustine,* 1. c., c. 33.) Augustinianism negates man, but, in return, it lowers God to the level of man, even to the disgrace of a death on the cross for the sake of man. The former puts man in the place of God; the latter puts God in the place of man. Both lead to the same result; the distinction between them is only apparent, a pious illusion. Augustinianism is only reversed Pelagianism—that which the latter posits as subject, the former posits as object.

17. Man's religious, namely, original, self-objectification is, moreover, to be distinguished from that occurring in reflection and speculation; the latter is arbitrary, the former necessary—as necessary as art and language. In the course of time, theology naturally coincides with religion.

18. Deuteronomy xxiii: 12, 13.

19. See, for example, Genesis xxxv: 2; Leviticus xi: 44 and xx: 26. Also, the *Commentary* of Le Clerc on these passages.

On "The Beginning of Philosophy"

"Philosophy distinguishes itself from all empirical science through the fact that its subject matter is not given to it and that it does not have at its disposal any fundamental principles or method with which to approach its subject matter. Philosophy does not presuppose anything. It is precisely in this fact of non-presupposition that its beginning lies—a beginning by virtue of which it is set apart from all other sciences. This act of dispensing with all presuppositions constitutes the very concept of philosophy as it emerges simultaneously with the beginning of philosophy. . . . To presuppose means to base a consideration on something already given." This is how the beginning of philosophy and its first concept are defined in J. F. Reiff's essay entitled "On the Beginning of Philosophy." However, this definition is by no means absolutely valid or as free of all presuppositions as it is meant to be. It is true that the empirical sciences have actually evolved an existence of their own, and that therefore their subject matter and method are given. But this was not the case as long as these sciences were in their formative stages. All science aims not at abolishing its object—God forbid!—but only at making into an object that which does not as yet exist as an object. But that which does not exist as an object is, understandably, not given at all, and hence all science has to begin without having a datum of its own;

i.e., without having a secure ground under its feet. And what is that which does not exist as an object? For science, everything—even the most tangible, ordinary, and everyday thing, as long as it is only an object of ordinary, everyday life, or an object of the ordinary view of things, but not that of science. A very instructive and interesting example is furnished by the air. It is one of the most essential, proximate, indispensable, and obtrusive external things, and yet it made fools of physicists and philosophers for such a long time before even its elementary properties—weight and expansiveness—became objects for us! Nothing would therefore be more absurd than to characterize the "Beyond, or the realm of the spirits" and similar things or nonsense as not being objects, as unapproachable and mysterious. The realm of the spirits had opened itself to men long before the realm of the air was still closed to them; sooner did they live in the light of another than in that of this world, and sooner did they know the treasures of the heaven than those of the earth. What is nearest to man is precisely that which is most remote to him—because it has no air of mystery about it, it is no mystery to him; because it is always given to him as an object, it is never an object for him.

To turn that which is not given as such into an object, to make comprehensible that which is not comprehensible; that is, to elevate something from being an object of ordinary, everyday life to an object of thought—i.e., an object of knowledge—is an absolute, a philosophical act— an act to which philosophy or knowledge in general owes its existence. What follows directly from this is that the beginning of philosophy is not just its own beginning as a particular kind of knowledge distinguished from that of the empirical sciences, but the beginning of any knowledge whatsoever. This is confirmed by history itself. Philosophy is the mother of all sciences. The first philosophers were explorers of nature—as are philosophers in the modern era. This is something which the author of the present work also happily points out, although according to him this occurs not at the beginning, as he should have shown, but only at the end of philosophy. If the beginning of both philosophical and empirical knowledge is originally one and the same act, then the task of philosophy should obviously be to bear in mind from the very outset this common origin and, hence, to take as its starting point not its distinction from the empirical science but its identity with it. It may later part company with the empirical science, but if it proceeds from it separately right from the beginning, then it will never be able to make friends with it in a genuine way, which is after all what we desire. For the inevitable consequence of beginning separately must be that philosophy will remain unable to transcend its position as a separate science and will be similar in its attitude, as it were, to that of an oddly hyperdelicate person who believes that even so much as touching the empirical tools would be enough to compromise his dignity, as if the goose quill alone were the organ of revelation and the instrument of truth and not, equally, the telescope of astronomy, the soldering pipe of mineralogy, the hammer of geology, and the magnifying lens of the botanist. To be sure, an empiricism that is unable or unwilling to raise itself to the level of philosophical thought is limited and poor. But equally limited is a philosophy that is unable to descend to the level of empiricism. But how does philosophy come down to the level of empiricism? Simply by appropriating the results of empirical research? No. The answer is, only by acknowledging that empirical activity, too, is a philosophical activity, that seeing is also thinking, that the senses, too, are the organs of philosophy. Modern philosophy differed from scholastic philosophy precisely through the fact that it combined sensuous experience and the activity of thought; in opposition to all thought that was divorced from real things, it postulated that philosophizing was possible only under the guidance of the senses. If, therefore, we recalled to our mind the way modern philosophy began, we would at the same time grasp the true beginning of philosophy. Philosophy does not arrive at reality in the end; rather, it begins with it. This alone is the natural or the appropriate course taken

by philosophy and not the one that our author describes
in keeping with the spirit of the speculative philosophy
since Fichte. The spirit follows upon the senses, not the
senses upon the spirit; the spirit is the end and not the
beginning of things. The transition from empirical cognition to philosophy commands necessity, whereas the transition from philosophy to empirical cognition is only the
luxury of arbitrariness. A philosophy that begins with the
empirical remains eternally young, whereas a philosophy
that concludes with the empirical finally becomes decrepit,
weary of life, and disgusted with itself. For if we begin
with reality and remain within it, we would never cease
to need philosophy, because empirical cognition leaves us
in the lurch at every step, thus forcing us back to philosophical thought. A philosophy that concludes with the
empirical is therefore finite, whereas a philosophy that
begins with the empirical is infinite. The latter always has
material for thought, whereas the former ends up in a
blind alley. A philosophy that begins with thought without
reality ends up, in consequence, with thought-less reality.
The writer of these lines would not mind at all if, because
of what he has just said, he is accused of subscribing to
empiricism. As far as he is concerned, it is at least more
honorable and rational to begin with non-philosophy and
end with philosophy than vice versa, like many a "great"
philosopher of Germany—*exempla sunt odiosa*—to open his
life with philosophy and close it with non-philosophy.
Moreover, the way from empirical reality to philosophy
can be demonstrated quite clearly from the speculative
point of view also. If, as cannot be doubted, nature is the
basis of spirit, but not in the sense of that mystical teaching
which derives the luminous spirit from the dark nature,
holding that light can arise only out of darkness. If nature
is the basis of spirit in the sense that nature itself is light,
then the objectively founded beginning or the true basis
of philosophy must also be nature. Philosophy must begin
with its antithesis, with its alter ego, otherwise it will always
remain subjective and, hence, always a prisoner of the
ego. A philosophy that presupposes nothing is a philosophy

that presupposes itself; it is a philosophy that begins directly with itself.

Reiff determines the "ego, i.e., pure ego" as the absolute
starting point of philosophy as follows: "A given as such,
and in so far as it is given at all to the ego, is something
other than the ego. But it is not given as other; rather,
the ego distinguishes the given from itself as its other; it
grasps itself in distinction from it; it enunciates that the
given is not ego but its other. By distinguishing itself from
that which is given, the ego establishes the given as other
than itself. In this way the given has already vanished; it
has become merely the other in relation to the ego. As this
other, it has its existence only in the distinguishing act of
the ego." But this ego which is separate from things,
which posits and thereby at the same time cancels its own
other, is this ego not hypothetical? Is it not rather an ego
that is seen from a particular standpoint? Is this standpoint
simply necessary and absolute? Is it a standpoint whereupon philosophy has to base itself in order to be what it
is? Is an object nothing else besides being an object? Certainly, it is the other of the ego. But can I not turn this
around and say that it is the ego that is the other, i.e.,
the object of the object, and that, consequently, the object
is also an ego? What enables the ego to posit the other?
Only the fact that the ego is the same in relation to the
object what the object is in relation to the ego. But the
ego concedes this only in an indirect way, that is, by turning its own passivity into activity. However, he who makes
the ego itself the object of criticism knows that the ego's
activity of positing the object expresses, in actual truth,
nothing but its own positedness by the object. However,
if the object is not only something posited, but also (to
continue in this abstract language) something which itself
posits, then it is clear that the presuppositionless ego, which
excludes the object from itself and negates it, is only a
presupposition of the subjective ego against which the object must protest; consequently, the ego cannot be a universal and sufficient principle of deduction as our author
takes it to be. Hence, contrary to this type of philosophy

which starts from the position of taking itself for granted,
which is already in complete possession of itself while still
at the point of its beginning, which is primarily and essentially interested in answering the question: How is the
ego able to suppose the existence of the world, or of an
object? Contrary to this type of philosophy there is another
which creates itself objectively; which starts from its antithesis and asks itself the opposite, but much more interesting and fruitful question: How are we able to suppose the existence of an ego that thus inquires and can
thus inquire?

It is correct that nothing can impinge upon or enter into
the ego for which there is no ground, or at least no pre-
disposition, within the ego itself; it is correct that, in so far
as every determination from outside is at the same time
a self-determination, the object itself is nothing else but
the objective ego. But just as the ego posits itself in and
verifies itself through the object, so, equally, does the object posit itself in and verify itself through the ego. The
reality of the ego in the object is at the same time the
reality of the object in the ego. If, as held by obtuse materialism and empiricism, the impressions from the object
alone were decisive, then the animals could already, even
have to, be physicists. If, on the other hand, the ego alone
mattered, then beings different from the ego could not
receive the same or analogous impressions from the same
objects. To be sure, the impression on the ego is "different
from that made by the finger on wax"; however, the impression on wax is also different from that on talc, chalk,
or on any other body. Talc is mild and soft, and yet it is
far from being as yielding and characterless as wax; any
attempt to penetrate with a finger into the being of
calcareus densus must founder on its impertinent com-
pactness. The reason I can make an impression on wax
without receiving from it any in return, or, at best, only
the smeary one of the *semper aliquid haeret*, lies in the
quality of its own characterlessness; just as, on the other
hand, the reason I cannot pierce into chalk without feeling
the resistance offered by it lies in its own rock-firm

strength. Already Theophrastus has noted in his treatise on the varieties of stone that "the different kinds of stone must be treated differently," that is, exactly like human beings who, endowed as they are with egos, would be least willing to, and just cannot, be treated all in the same way.

Hence, there is no point in attributing to the virtuosity and universality of the ego alone that which also belongs to the vitality and individuality of things, and, consequently, affects the non-ego as well as the ego in the same or in an analogous way. The warmth of the spring sun which lures the human ego from the schackles of frosty bureaucracy into free air also draws lizards and blind worms out of their hiding places into light. The *stapelia hirsuta* has not only for us but also for the carrion fly the smell of carrion, otherwise it would not be tempted to entrust it with its eggs. The rock crystal, which offers no resistance to its penetration by the rays of the light, allows us, to the greatest pleasure of our eyes, to see through it also. A piece of wax, which does not arouse any feelings in us, makes a superficial impression even on water, whereas the more solemn limestone, which slumps down to the very bottom of the water, also weighs our ego down to the ground. How happy we would be if nature revealed its charms only to our ego! Oh how happy! Because no honey insect or wax moth would then destroy our beehives, no weevil our corn fields, and no cabbage caterpillar our vegetable gardens. However, that which tastes sweet and pleasant to us is also palatable to beings other than us.

Or must taste and smell be below the dignity of the human ego because possessing them involves it in competition and rivalry with weevils and cabbage caterpillars? Should it be better for taste and smell, or the senses in general, to no longer belong to our ego? Should they rather belong to beings apart from and below us? But would you not feel utterly miserable, both physically and mentally, if your eyes went blind, your ears deaf, and your taste and smell blunt? Would you not then cry out in great pain a thousand times a day: "Oh, if I could only get back my senses!" Would this not be confessing and declaring that the senses do belong to your ego, and that you—I say you, you yourself, not just your body—would be a wretched cripple without the senses or with only imperfect senses? Or must not the ego which has become defective and crippled through the loss of the senses, as, for example, yours, or at least mine which is so honest as to confess that it has lost a part of itself if it has lost a part of its body, must not this ego be the speculative ego? What kind of an ego would this speculative ego then be? How should it then be possible at all to speak of "common sensation, instinct, sense, etc." if this ego is different from the real ego? How could it still retain the name ego if it were to deny its affinity with the empirical ego? The speculative ego would rather claim no other distinction over our empirical ego than that it is the ego under which everyone who says "I" can be subsumed indiscriminately—the ego that has been purged of all the particularities, inessentials, and accidentalities of the empirical. But, obviously, the body is not to be counted among these particularities and accidentalities. This means that the body—at least, the speculative body—belongs also to the speculative ego; for it is hard to see why we should grant the difference between the necessary and the contingent only to the ego and not to the body as well; it is hard to see why we shall not be permitted to purge the body just as well as the ego of all unseemliness and contingency.

The ego is corporeal; this has no other meaning than that the ego is not only active but also passive. And it is wrong to derive the passivity of the ego from its activity, or to present it as activity. On the contrary: the passivity of the ego is the activity of the object. Because the object, too, is active, the ego is passive—a passivity of which the ego need not be ashamed, for the object belongs to the innermost being of the ego.

But precisely because of this, it is one-sided and partial in the highest degree to want to consider and present all the determinations of the ego in isolation from the objects, i.e., as the self-determinations of the ego; moreover, this would be completely impossible to carry out, because the ego's own power is by no means sufficient to satisfy all its needs. It must therefore borrow the means it lacks from the objective world, that is to say, from its own body. Thus, for example, "the sensation of animal warmth" of which the ego partakes according to psychology is obviously of purely physical origin. But how does this rhyme together with an ego that creates everything out of itself? How does the disturbing fire of animal warmth enter into the "gnostic calm of an ego that is concentrated in itself?" Perhaps because animal warmth can assert its own autonomy and independence in the face of changing external temperature? But even this independence has its limit, which immediately reminds us of the inseparability of the subject and object. People have suddenly died on the equator when the temperature approached 40°C. Or is the animal body so identical with the ego that the ego derives out of itself whatever it derives out of the body? However, the ego is "open to the world" by no means "through itself" as such, but through itself as a corporeal being, that is, through the body. In relation to the abstract ego, the body is the objective world. It is through the body that the ego is not just an ego but also an object. To be embodied is to be in the world; it means to have so many senses, i.e., so many pores and so many naked surfaces. The body is nothing but the porous ego. Or should only the sensation of animal warmth qua sensation belong to the ego? But what is sensation without warmth? What is left over at all if I abstract from the object or content of sensations and from the activities of the ego? How can I, for example, ascribe the sensation or the activity of seeing to the ego, and how can I accommodate it in psychology and define it if I take it in abstraction from its object—the light? Seeing is, first of all, nothing but the sensation or perception of light and the sensation of being affected by light; the eye is the "light sense." Seeing without light is as much as breathing without air; to see is to partake of light.

Now it is true that one can also turn the ego into a universal principle of deduction, albeit in contradiction to the meaning which, since Fichte, we associate with the concept or, at any rate, the word "ego." However, this can be done only under the condition that one discovers and demonstrates a non-ego in the ego itself; and not only a non-ego but differences and oppositions in general, for it is absolutely impossible to achieve anything meaningful with the unimaginative and monotonous litany of the eternal $I = I$. The ego from which a musical note emerges is totally different from the ego that produces a logical category, a moral or juridical law. But that would mean that psychology is the only science that precedes all other sciences, and is the first and the general science whose aim is none other than to follow the ego through all its inflections in order to deduce intrinsically different principles from the different relations in which the ego is involved. In that case, it is wholly inadequate and inadmissible to make psychology—as Reiff does—into a particular science and to deduce from it only abstract sciences of logic and metaphysics. But the original and the most essential antithesis, an antithesis necessarily connected with the ego, is the body, the flesh. The conflict between the spirit and the body alone is the highest metaphysical principle; it is the secret of creation and the ground on which the world rests. Indeed, the flesh or, if you prefer, the body has not only a natural-historical or empirico-psychological meaning, but essentially a speculative, a metaphysical one. For what else is the body if not the passivity of the ego? And how are you going to deduce even the will and the sensation from the ego without a passive principle? The will cannot be conceived without something striving against it; and in all sensation, however spiritual, there is no more activity than passivity, no more spirit than flesh, no more ego than non-ego.

The Necessity of a
Reform of Philosophy

There is a qualitative difference between a new philosophy that falls into a common epoch with earlier philosophies and one that belongs to an entirely new phase in the history of mankind. To be more specific, there is a fundamental distinction involved between a philosophy that owes its existence to a philosophical need, as, for example, the philosophy of Fichte in relation to that of Kant, and one that corresponds to a need of mankind. In short, there is a world of difference between a philosophy that is related to mankind only indirectly by virtue of its belonging to the history of philosophy and one that is directly the history of mankind.

The question therefore arises whether a transformation, a reform, or a regeneration of philosophy is called for. If so, how can or how must it be? Is this change to take place in the spirit and in the meaning of philosophy as it has existed until now, or is the change to have a new meaning? Do we have to look for a philosophy similar to the one we have had so far or for an essentially different one? The ultimate question, upon which also the preceding ones depend, is: Do we find ourselves on the threshold of a new age, of a new period in the history of mankind, or are we still in the same old rut? Are we to retain man in his old form, making only certain indispensable modifications that have become necessary due to the march of time? If we approach this question solely from a philosophical stand-point, then our understanding of its scope would be too narrow. We would then be treating it on the level of ordinary scholastic bickerings. Nothing would be more superfluous.

The only true and necessary change in philosophy can be one that harks to the need of the age as well as that of mankind. In times when a world-historical view of things is in decline, the needs of men become contradictory. Some feel the need to preserve the old and reject the new; others feel the need to translate the new into practice. On which side does the true need lie? Only on the side that represents the need of the future, that is, the anticipated future; on the side on which the onward movement is located. The need to preserve the old is only an artificially produced reaction. The Hegelian philosophy was an arbitrary combination of the different existing systems, of so many half-truths that had no positive power for want of absolute negativity. Only he who has the courage to be absolutely negative has also the power to create something new.

The historical epochs of mankind are distinguished from each other on the basis of religious changes. The origins of a historical movement can be understood only to the extent to which they are discovered in the heart of man. The heart is not a form of religion which could also exist in the heart; it is the very essence of religion. The question therefore is: Has a religious revolution already occurred within us? And the answer is, yes! We have no heart, we have no religion any more. Christianity has been negated, and negated even by those who still seem to cling to it. One is only reluctant to let it be known that it has been negated. Not willing to admit this out of political reasons, one would rather make a secret of it, and so one deceives oneself both intentionally and unintentionally. Indeed, one even parades the negation of Christianity as Christianity itself, thus turning it into a mere name. The practical negation of Christianity has gone so far that one casts aside all positive guidelines, that one does not even require the symbolic books, the Church Fathers, or the Bible as the measure of that which is to be called Christian—as if a religion could continue to be what it is even in the absence of a definite criterion of what constitutes its essence, as if it could go on being what it is without a focal point, without a definite principle. The principle now is the preservation of religion under the form of its negation. What, after all, is Christianity? If we no longer possess a Testament, how are we to know the will and the message of its founder? This can only mean that Christianity has really ceased to exist. Such phenomena are nothing but the manifestations of the inner decay, of the decline and fall of Christianity.

Christianity is no longer able to respond to the needs of either the theoretical or the practical man. Nor is it any longer capable of satisfying our mind or our heart, for we have now discovered other interests for our heart than the eternal heavenly bliss.

All philosophy until now falls into the epoch of the downfall of Christianity or into the epoch of its negation—an epoch that aimed, rather, to establish it. The Hegelian philosophy only concealed the negation of Christianity behind the contradiction between conception and thought, behind the contradiction between the emerging and the fully emerged Christianity—that is, it negated Christianity while positing it. It claimed that the emerging Christianity was necessary because of its liberating role. However, a religion preserves itself only so long as it is preserved in its original meaning and intention. In the beginning all religion is fire, energy, and truth; at its origins all religion is uncompromising and absolutely rigorous. With the progress of time, however, it loses its verve, grows lax, becomes indifferent and untrue to itself and falls victim to habit. In order to explain—or conceal—this discrepancy in practice, this discrepancy between religion and its deterioration, one either invokes the original tradition or points to the modifications effected in the old Book of Law. So the Jews. As for the Christians, they solve the problem by imputing a meaning to their holy documents that positively contradicts them.

Christianity stands negated—in the mind as well as in
the heart, in science as well as in life, in art as well as in
industry—stands thoroughly, irretrievably and irrevocably
negated, because men have now appropriated to themselves all that is true, human, and anti-holy, thus denuding
Christianity of all its oppositional force. So far, the negation was an unconscious one. Only now is it being consciously willed and directly intended, the more so because
Christianity has associated itself with forces inhibiting the
basic drive of contemporary mankind—political freedom.
This conscious negation inaugurates a new age and establishes the necessity for a new and open-hearted philosophy
which has ceased to be Christian; indeed, is definitely un-
Christian.

Philosophy steps into the place that religion had occupied. This means, however, that a totally different philosophy replaces all previous philosophy. The hitherto prevailing philosophy cannot replace religion for, given its
nature, it was devoid of religion. It left the peculiar essence
of religion lying outside itself and vindicated only the form
of thought. Should philosophy be able to replace religion,
it must, qua philosophy, become religion. This means that
it must, in a way suited to its own nature, incorporate the
essence of religion or the advantage that religion possesses
over philosophy.

The necessity for an essentially different philosophy is
also borne out by the fact that the type of philosophy that
has so far existed now lies perfected before us. Anything
similar to it would therefore be redundant, and whatever
is produced in its spirit, no matter how divergent it may
be in its particular qualities, is bound to be superfluous.
Yes, the personal God may be conceived and demonstrated
in this or that way—we have heard enough and we do not
want to know anything more about it. We just don't want
any more theology.

The essential differences within philosophy are the essential differences within mankind. The place of belief has
been taken by unbelief and that of the Bible by reason.
Similarly, religion and the Church have been replaced by

politics, the heaven by the earth, prayer by work, hell by material need, and the Christian by man. Those who are not divided between a lord in heaven and a lord on earth—that is, those who embrace reality with undivided soul—are quite different from those who live in discord. That which is the result of the mediating process of thought in philosophy is immediate certainty for us. Accordingly, we need a principle that conforms to this immediacy. If man has now taken over the place of the Christian in practice, then in theory, too, the human essence must take over the place of the divine. In short, we must concentrate into one ultimate principle, one ultimate word what we wish to be. Only thus can we sanctify our life and determine its direction. Only thus can we free ourselves from the contradiction that is at present poisoning our innermost being—the contradiction between our life and thought on the one hand, and a religion that is fundamentally opposed to them on the other. For religious we must once again become if politics is to be our religion. But this can be achieved only if we possess the highest point of reference within ourselves as the condition for making politics our religion.

There can be an instinctive transformation of politics into religion, but what we need is a distinctively ultimate ground for such a transformation, an official principle. This principle, negatively expressed, is nothing other than atheism, or in other words, the renunciation of a God who is other than man.

Religion, in the ordinary sense of the word, plays so minimal a role in holding the state together that it should rather be regarded as its dissolution. According to religion, God is the Father, Sustainer, Provider, Guardian, Protector, Regent, and Lord of the world-monarchy. Consequently, man does not stand in need of man, and for everything he is supposed to derive from himself or other men, he is actually directly indebted to God. He depends on God rather than on man; his gratitude is due to God rather than to man. On this account, man is only accidentally related to man. But if we explain the reality of the state from the point of view of the subject, we would realize that the reason why men come together is precisely that they do not believe in any god, that they negate their religious belief unconsciously, involuntarily, and in practice. Not the belief in God, but rather the doubt concerning him is the actual cause underlying the foundation of states. From the point of view of the subject, it is the belief in man as the God of man that explains the origin of the state.

Within the state, the powers of man differentiate and unfold themselves in order, through this differentiation and synthesis, to constitute an infinite being; for the multitude of men and the multitude of forces form one single power. The state comprehends all realities and is man's providence for him. Within the state, one represents the other, one is complementary to the other—what I am not able to do or know, someone else is. I am not alone and delivered up to the hazards of the power of nature but I am together with others; I am surrounded by a universal being; I am part of a whole. The true state is the unlimited, infinite, true, perfect, and divine man. It is primarily the state in which man emerges as man; the state in which the man who relates himself to himself is the self-determining, the absolute man.

The state represents the reality, just as it does the practical refutation of religious belief. Even in our day, the believer in need of help seeks it from men. Yet, he is contented with "God's blessing," which he expects to be present everywhere. However, whether he succeeds or not depends not so much on human activity as on favorable circumstances, often on chance. But "God's blessing" is only the blue haze that veils the practical atheism of the unbelieving believer.

It is therefore this practical atheism that provides the states with what holds them together; human beings come together in the state because here they are without God, because the state is their god, which is why it can justifiably claim for itself the divine predicate of "majesty." The practical atheism, which so far has only unconsciously been the ground and cohesive force of the state, has now dawned upon our consciousness. The reason why contemporary man is turning to politics is that he has found out that the religion of Christianity is poison to his political energy.

What knowledge is to the consciousness of the thinking man, instinct is to that of the practical man. But the practical instinct of mankind is a political one; that is, it is an instinct for an active participation in the affairs of the state, an instinct demanding the abolition of political hierarchy and the unreason of the people. It is an instinct demanding the negation of political catholicism. The Age of Reformation destroyed religious catholicism, but the modern era has put political catholicism in its place. What the Reformation aimed to achieve in the field of religion, one aims to achieve now in the field of politics.

Just as the transformation of God into reason did not dissolve but only transubstantiated Him, so in the same way Protestantism transubstantiated the Pope into the king. Now we have to do with the political Popedom; the reasons for the necessity of the king are not different from those for the necessity of the Pope.

The so-called Modern Age is in reality the Protestant Middle Ages; it has kept alive the Roman Church with its half negations and half measures; it has preserved universities in their old form. With the dissolution of Protestant Christianity, which as religious power and truth has hitherto determined the spirit, we now enter upon a new age. The spirit of this age, or that of the future, is realism. If we conceive a being different from man as the highest being and principle, the condition for knowing that being would still involve the necessity to abstract from man. In this way we shall never be able to achieve direct unity with ourselves, with the world, with reality; our relationship with the world would still be mediated through a different, a tertiary instance; we would always have a product in front of us instead of the producer; we would still have a beyond even if inside rather than outside us; we would always find ourselves within a dichotomy between theory and practice, and would have one being in our head, another in our heart—that is, the Absolute Spirit in our head and Man in our heart or in actual life—we would have thought, which is not concrete being, on the one side, and being, which is neither noumenon nor thought, on the other. Each step in life takes us outside philosophy; each philosophical thought takes us outside life.

The Pope, the head of the Church, is as good a man as I, and the king is as good a man as we all. Therefore, he cannot unrestrictedly do whatever he pleases; he does not stand above the state or above the community. A Protestant is a religious republican. That is why Protestantism naturally leads to political republicanism once its religious content has disappeared; that is, has been exposed, unveiled. Once we have abolished the Protestant dichotomy between heaven where we are masters, and earth where we are slaves—that is, once we have recognized the earth as our destination—Protestantism will soon lead us towards a republican state. If in earlier times the republican state joined hands with Protestantism, it was, of course, by accident—even if not without significance—because Protestantism promises only religious freedom; to be both a republican and a Protestant was, therefore, a contradiction. Only after abolishing Christianity will you acquire, so to speak, the right to constitute a republican state, for in Christian religion you have your republic in heaven and you do not need one here. On the contrary: You must be a slave here, otherwise heaven is superfluous.

Preliminary Theses on the Reform of Philosophy (1842)

The secret of *theology* is *anthropology*, but *theology* itself is the secret of *speculative philosophy*, which thus turns out to be *speculative* theology. As such, it distinguishes itself from *ordinary* theology by the fact that it places the divine being back into this world—ordinary theology projects it into the beyond out of fear and ignorance; in contrast to ordinary theology, it *actualizes, determines,* and *realizes* the Divine Being.

Spinoza is actually the initiator of modern speculative philosophy; *Schelling,* its restorer; and *Hegel,* its consummator.

"Pantheism" is the *necessary consequence* of theology (or of theism); it is *consequent* theology. *"Atheism"* is the *necessary consequence* of *"Pantheism"*; it is consequent *"Pantheism."* *

Christianity is the *contradiction* of *polytheism* and *monotheism.*

Pantheism is *monotheism* with the *predicate* of polythe-

* These *theological* designations are being used here in the sense of *trivial* nicknames.

ism; i.e., pantheism makes the independent beings of polytheism into predicates or attributes of the one independent being. Thus Spinoza, taking thought as the sum of all thinking things and matter as the sum of all extended things, turned them into the attributes of substance; i.e., of God. God is a thinking thing; God is an extended thing.

The philosophy of identity distinguished itself from that of Spinoza only by the fact that it infused into Spinoza's substance—this dead and phlegmatic thing—the Spirit of idealism. Hegel, in particular, turned self-activity, the power of self-differentiation, and self-consciousness into the attribute of the substance. The paradoxical statement of Hegel—"the consciousness of God is God's self-consciousness"—rests on *the same foundation* as the paradoxical statement of Spinoza—"the extension or matter is an attribute of substance"—and has no other meaning than self-consciousness is an attribute of the substance or of God; God is Ego. The consciousness that the theist ascribes to God in contradistinction to the real consciousness is only an idea without reality. But the statement of Spinoza—"matter is the *attribute* of substance"—says nothing more than this, that matter is substantial divine essence. Similarly, the statement of Hegel says nothing more than consciousness is divine essence.

The method of the reformative critique of *speculative philosophy* as such does not differ from that already used in the *Philosophy of Religion*. We need only turn the *predicate* into the *subject* and thus as *subject* into *object* and *principle*—that is, only *reverse* speculative philosophy. In this way, we have the unconcealed, pure, and untarnished truth.

"Atheism" is reversed "Pantheism."

Pantheism is the *negation of theology from the standpoint of theology*.

Just as according to Spinoza (*Ethics,* Part I. Definition 3 and Proposition 10) the attribute or the predicate of substance is the substance itself, so according to Hegel the *predicate* of the Absolute—that is, of the subject in general —is the *subject itself*. The Absolute, according to Hegel, is Being, Essence, or Concept (Spirit or Self-consciousness). The Absolute, conceived only as being, is, however, *nothing other than* being; the Absolute, in so far as it is thought of under this or that determination or category, loses itself *completely* in this category or determination, so that apart from it, it is a mere name. But, nevertheless, the Absolute *as subject* still constitutes that which lies at the base; the *true* subject or *that* through which the Absolute is not just a name but is *something*, is *determination*, and still has the meaning of a mere predicate, exactly like the predicate in Spinoza.

The Absolute or the Infinite of speculative philosophy, looked at psychologically, is nothing other than that which is not determined, the indeterminate; namely, the abstraction from all that is determinate and posited as a being that is on the one hand distinct from this abstraction and on the other hand identified with it. Historically considered, it is, however, nothing other than the old theological-metaphysical being or un-being which is *not* finite, *not* human, *not* material, *not* determinate, and *not* created— the world-antecedent nothingness posited as *Deed*.

The Hegelian Logic is *theology* that has been turned into *reason* and *presence;* it is theology turned into *logic. Just as the Divine Being of theology is the ideal or abstract embodiment of all realities, i.e., of all determinations, of all finitudes, so, too, it is the same with the Logic.* All that exists on earth finds itself back in the heaven of theology; likewise, *all that is in nature reappears in the heaven of the divine Logic*—quality, quantity, measure, essence, chemism, mechanism, and organism. In theology, we have everything *twice over,* first in abstracto and then in concreto; similarly, we have everything *twice over* in the Hegelian philosophy—as the object of logic, and then, again, as the object of the philosophy of nature and of the Spirit.

The essence of theology is the *transcendent;* i.e., the essence of man posited outside man. The essence of Hegel's *Logic* is *transcendent* thought; i.e., the thought of man *posited outside man.*

Just as theology *dichotomizes* and *externalizes* man in order to then identify his externalized essence with him, so similarly Hegel *pluralizes* and splits up the *simple, self-identical essence* of nature and man in order later to bring together forcibly what he has separated forcibly.

Metaphysics or logic is a *real* and *immanent science* only when it is *not separated* from the so-called *subjective spirit.* Metaphysics is *esoteric psychology.* What arbitrariness, what an act of violence it is to regard quality on its own account or sensation on its own account, to cleave both apart into two sciences, as if quality could be anything without sensation, and sensation anything without quality.

The *Absolute Spirit* of Hegel is none other than *abstract* spirit, i.e., *finite* spirit that has been separated from itself; just as the infinite being of theology is none other than the abstract *finite being.*

The Absolute Spirit according to Hegel reveals or realizes itself in art, religion, and philosophy. This simply means that the *spirit of art, religion, and philosophy is the Absolute Spirit.* But one cannot separate art and religion from human feeling, imagination, and perception, nor can one separate philosophy from thought. In short, one cannot separate the Absolute Spirit from the Subjective Spirit, or from the essence of man, without being thrown back to the standpoint of theology, without being deluded into regarding the Absolute Spirit as being *another* spirit that is distinct from the being of man, i.e., without making us accept the illusion of a ghost of ourselves existing outside ourselves.

The Absolute Spirit is the "deceased spirit" of theology that, as a *specter,* haunts the Hegelian philosophy.

Theology is *belief in ghosts.* Ordinary theology has its ghosts in the sensuous imagination, but *speculative* theology has its ghosts in non-sensuous abstraction.

To abstract means to posit the *essence* of nature *outside nature,* the *essence* of man *outside man,* the *essence* of thought *outside the act of thinking.* The Hegelian philosophy has alienated man *from himself* in so far as its whole system is based on these acts of abstraction. Although it again identifies what it separates, it does so only in a *separate* and *mediated* way. The Hegelian philosophy lacks *immediate unity, immediate certainty, immediate truth.*

The direct, crystal-clear, and undeceptive identification of the essence of man—which has been taken away from him through abstraction—*with* man, cannot be effected through a positive approach; it can only be derived from the Hegelian philosophy as its *negation;* it can only be *apprehended* at all if it is apprehended *as the total negation* of speculative philosophy, although it is the *truth* of this philosophy. It is true that everything is contained in Hegel's philosophy, but always together with its *negation,* its *opposite.*

The *obvious* proof that the Absolute Spirit is the so-called finite, subjective spirit, or, in other words, that the latter cannot be separated from the former, is *art.* Art is

born out of the feeling that the life of this world is the true
life, that the *finite* is the *infinite;* it is born out of enthusiasm for a *definite* and *real* being as the *highest* and the
Divine Being. *Christian monotheism does not* contain
within itself the principle of an *artistic* and *scientific culture.* Only *polytheism,* so-called *idolatry,* is the *source of
art and science.*

The Greeks raised themselves to the perfection of the
plastic arts only through the fact that to them the human
form was *absolutely* and *unhesitatingly* the highest form—
the form of divinity. The Christians were able to create
poetry only at the point where they *practically negated
Christian theology* and worshiped the *female principle*
as the *divine* principle. As artists and poets, the Christians
found themselves in contradiction to the essence of their
religion as they conceived it and as it constituted the *object*
of their consciousness. Petrarch *regretted,* from the point
of view of religion, the poems in which he had deified his
Laura. Why do the Christians not have, as do the pagans,
works of art adequate to their religious ideas? Why do
they not have a fully satisfying image of Christ? Because
the religious art of the Christians founders on the fatal
contradiction between their *consciousness* and *truth.* The
essence of the Christian religion is, in truth, human essence; in the consciousness of the Christians it is, however,
a *different,* a *non-*human essence. Christ is supposed to be
both man and not man; he is an ambiguity. Art, however,
can represent only the true and the *unequivocal.*

The decisive consciousness—a consciousness that has become flesh and blood—that the human is the divine and
the finite the infinite is the source of a new poetry and
art which will excede all previous poetry and art in energy,
depth, and fire. The belief in the beyond is an absolutely
unpoetical belief. Pain is the source of poetry. Only he
who experiences the loss of a finite being as an infinite loss
is capable of burning with lyrical fire. Only the painful
stimulus of the memory of that which is *no more* is the

first artist, the first idealist in man. But belief in the beyond turns every pain into mere appearance, into untruth.

A philosophy that derives the finite from the infinite and the determinate from the indeterminate *can never find its way to a true positing of the finite and the determinate.* That the finite is derived from the infinite means that the infinite, or the indeterminate, is determined, and hence *negated;* it is admitted that the infinite is *nothing without determination—that is, without finiteness*—and that it is the *finite* posited as the *reality* of the infinite. However, the negative un-being, this nuisance of the absolute, still remains the underlying principle; the posited finiteness has, therefore, to be abolished again and again. The *finite* is the *negation* of the infinite, and, again, the *infinite* is the *negation* of the finite. The philosophy of the absolute is a *contradiction.*

Just as in theology, *man* is the *truth* and *reality* of God —for all predicates that realize God as God, or make God into a *real* being, predicates such as power, wisdom, goodness, love, even infinity and personality, which have as their condition the *distinction* from the finite, are posited first *in* and *with* man—likewise in speculative philosophy the *finite* is the *truth* of the infinite.

The truth of the finite is expressed by Absolute Philosophy only in an *indirect, inverted* way. If the infinite *has any meaning,* if it has *truth* and *reality* only when it is *determinate*—i.e., when it is posited not as infinite but as *finite*—then indeed the *finite* is the *infinite* in truth.

The task of true philosophy is not to cognize the infinite as the finite, but as the *non*-finite; i.e., as the infinite. In other words, not to posit the finite in the infinite, but to posit the infinite in the finite.

The beginning of philosophy is neither God nor the Absolute, nor is it as being the *predicate* of the Absolute or of the Idea; rather the beginning of philosophy is the finite,† the determinate, and the *real*. The infinite cannot possibly be conceived without the finite. Can you think of quality and define it without thinking of a definite quality?

It is, therefore, not the indeterminate, but the determinate that comes first, since *determinate* quality is nothing but *real* quality; real quality precedes the quality which is imagined.

The *subjective* origin and course of philosophy is also its *objective* course and origin. Before you think quality, you already feel quality. *Suffering* precedes thinking.

The infinite is the *true essence* of the finite—the true finite. The *true* speculation or philosophy is nothing but what is *truly and universally empirical*.

The infinite in religion and philosophy is, and never was anything different from, a finite or a determinate of some kind, but *mystified;* that is, it was a finite or a determinate with the *postulate* of being nothing finite and nothing determinate. Speculative philosophy has made itself guilty of the *same error* as theology; it has made the determinations of reality or finiteness into the determinations and predicates of the infinite through the *negation* of determinateness.

† I am using the term "finite" throughout in the sense of Absolute Philosophy to which, in so far as it occupies the standpoint of the Absolute, the real appears as unreal and worthless, because it holds the unreal and the indeterminate to be the real. However, the finite and the worthless appear to it also as real when they are not viewed from the standpoint of the Absolute. This contradiction is conspicuous in the early philosophy of Schelling, but it also lies at the base of Hegelian philosophy.

Honesty and uprightness are useful for all things—and that also applies to philosophy. Philosophy is, however, only honest and upright when it concedes the finiteness of its speculative infinity—when it concedes, e.g., that the mystery of nature in God is nothing but the mystery of human nature, that the *night* which it posits in God in order to produce out of it the light of consciousness is nothing but its own *dark, instinctual* feeling of the reality and indispensability of matter.

The course taken so far by all speculative philosophy from the abstract to the concrete, from the ideal to the real, is an inverted one. This way never leads one to the *true* and *objective reality,* but only to the *realization of one's own abstractions* and, precisely because of this, never to the true *freedom* of the Spirit; for *only the perception of things and beings in their objective reality can make man free and devoid of all prejudices.* The transition from the ideal to the real has its place only in practical philosophy.

Philosophy is the knowledge of *what* is. To think and know things and being *as* they are—that is the highest law, the highest task of philosophy.

To speak of what is *as* it is, or in other words, to speak *truly* of the true, *appears superficial;* to speak of what is *as it is not,* or in other words, to speak of the true in an *untrue, inverted* way, *appears* to be *profound.*

Truthfulness, simplicity, and *determinateness* are the formal characteristics of real philosophy.

Being, with which philosophy begins, cannot be separated from consciousness any more than consciousness can be separated from being. Just as the reality of feeling is

162 THE FIERY BROOK

quality and, inversely, feeling the reality of quality, so also
is being the reality of consciousness, but also equally consciousness the reality of being—only consciousness is *real*
being. The *real* unity of spirit and nature is consciousness
alone.

All the determinations, forms, categories, or however
one would like to put it that speculative philosophy has
cast off from the Absolute and banished into the realm of
the finite and the empirical contain within themselves precisely the *true essence* of the finite; i.e., the true infinite—
the *true and ultimate mysteries* of philosophy.

Space and *time* are the forms of existence of all beings.
Only existence in space and time is *existence*. The negation
of space and time is always only the *negation of their
limits, not of their being*. A non-temporal feeling, a non-
temporal will, a non-temporal thought, a non-temporal
being are all absurdities. He who is absolutely timeless has
also no time, no urge to will and to think.

The negation of space and time in metaphysics, in the
being of things, has the most pernicious practical consequences. Only he who *everywhere* occupies the standpoint
of space and time has also *good sense* and *practical understanding* in life. Space and time are the primary criteria
of praxis. A people that banishes time from its metaphysics
and deifies the eternal—i.e., *abstract* and time-detached existence—excludes, in consequence, time from its politics,
and worships the anti-historical principle of stability which
is against right and reason.

Speculative philosophy has turned into a form, or into
an attribute of the Absolute, the *development* which it has
detached from time. This detachment of development from
time is, however, truly a masterpiece of *speculative arbitrariness* and the conclusive proof of the fact that the
speculative philosophers have done with their Absolute ex-

actly what theologians have done with their God who possesses all emotions of men *without having emotion,* loves *without love,* and is angry *without anger.* Development without time amounts to development without development. The proposition that the Absolute Being unfolds itself is, moreover, true and rational only the *other way round.* It must, therefore, be formulated thus: Only a being that develops and unfolds itself in time is an absolute; i.e., a *true* and *actual* being.

Space and time are the forms of manifestation of the real infinite.

Where there is *no limit, no time,* and *no need, there is also no quality, no energy, no spirit, no fire,* and *no love.* Only that being which *suffers from need* (*notleidend*) is the *necessary* (*notwendig*) being. Existence *without need* is *superfluous* existence. Whatever is absolutely free from needs has no need of existence. Whether it is or is not is indifferent—indifferent to itself and indifferent to others. A being without need is a being without *ground.* Only that which can *suffer* deserves to exist. Only that being which *abounds in pain is the divine being.* A being *without suffering* is a being *without* being. A being without suffering is nothing but a being *without sensuousness, without matter.*

A philosophy that has no *passive principle* in it, a philosophy that speculates over existence *without time and duration,* over quality *without feeling,* over being *without being,* over life *without life*—i.e., without flesh and blood—such a philosophy, like the philosophy of the absolute, above all, has, due *necessarily* to its *one-sidedness,* the empirical as its opposite. Spinoza has no doubt made matter into an attribute of substance, but he does not take matter to be a principle of suffering. For Spinoza, matter is the attribute of substance precisely because it *does not* suffer, because it is unique, indivisible, and infinite, because it has the same determinations as its *opposite* attribute of thought; in short, because it is an *abstract* matter, matter *without matter,* just as essence in Hegel's *Logic* is the essence of nature and man, but *without essence, without nature,* and *without man.*

The philosopher must take into the *text* of philosophy that aspect of man which *does not* philosophize, but, rather, is *opposed* to philosophy and abstract thinking, or in other words, that which in Hegel has been reduced to a mere *footnote.* Only thus can philosophy become a *universal, free from contradictions, irrefutable,* and *irresistible power.* Philosophy has to begin then not so much *with itself* as with its own *antithesis;* i.e., with *non-philosophy.* This being which is distinguished from thought, which is unphilosophical, this absolutely *anti-scholastic* being in us is the principle of *sensualism.*

The essential tools and organs of philosophy are: the *head,* which is the source of activity, freedom, metaphysical infinity, and idealism, and the *heart,* which is the source of suffering, finiteness, needs, and sensualism. Or theoretically expressed: thought and sense perception, for *thought* is the *need* of the *head,* and sense perception, the *sense,* is the *need* of the *heart.* Thought is the principle of the schools; i.e., of the system; perception, the *principle of life.* When perceiving through the senses, I am *determined* by the object; when thinking, it is I who *determines* the object; in thought I am *ego,* in perception, *non-ego.* Only out of the *negation* of thought, out of *being determined* by the object, out of *passion,* out of the source of all pleasure and need is born true, objective thought, and true, objective philosophy. Perception gives being that is *immediately identical with existence;* thought gives being that is *mediated* through the *distinction* and *separation* from existence. *Life* and *truth* are, therefore, only to be found where essence is united with existence, thought with sense-perception, activity with passivity, and the *scholastic ponderousness of German metaphysics* with the *anti-scholastic, sanguine principle of French sensualism and materialism.*

What applies to philosophy, applies to the philosopher, and vice versa; the qualities of the philosopher, i.e., the *subjective conditions* and *elements* of philosophy, are also their *objective* conditions and elements. The true philosopher who is identical with life and man must be of Franco-German parentage. Do not be frightened, you chaste Germans, by this mixture. The *Acta Philosophorum* already spelled out this idea in the year 1716. "If we compare the *Germans* and the *French* with each other and ascertain that the latter have more agility in their temperament, and the former more weightiness, so one could justly say that the *temperamentum gallico-germanicum* is best suited for philosophy, or a child who had a *French* father and a *German* mother would (*caeteris paribus*) be endowed with a good *ingenium philosophicum.*" Quite right; only we must make the mother French and the father German. The *heart*—the feminine principle, the *sense* of the finite, and the seat of materialism—is of *French disposition;* the *head*—the masculine principle and the seat of idealism—of German. The heart makes revolutions, the head reforms; the head brings things into existence, the heart sets them in *motion.* But only where there is movement, upsurge, passion, blood, and sensuousness is there also *spirit.* It was the *esprit* of a Leibniz, his sanguine *materialistic*-idealistic principle, that first pulled the Germans out of their philosophical pedantry and scholasticism.

In philosophy, the heart was hitherto regarded as the breastwork of theology. However, it is precisely the heart that is the positively *anti-theological* principle; in terms of theology it is the unbelieving, atheistic principle in man. For it believes in *nothing* except *itself;* it believes only in the unshakable, divine, and absolute reality of its *own* being. But the *head,* which *does not* understand the heart, transforms—since it is its business to separate and differentiate subject and object—the very being of the heart into a being that is *distinguished* from the heart; that is, *objective* and *external*. To be sure, the heart needs *another* being, but only one that is its own kind—i.e., not distinguished from the heart—and one that does not contradict the heart. Theology *denies* the *truth* of the *heart* or the *truth* of the *religious emotion*. The religious emotion, the heart, says, for example: God suffers. Theology, however, says: God does not suffer. That is, the heart denies the difference between God and man, but theology affirms it.

Theism rests on the *dichotomy* of the *head* and the *heart;* pantheism is the resolution of this dichotomy, but *within* dichotomy, for it makes the Divine Being immanent only as a *transcendent* being; anthropotheism is *without such dichotomy*. Anthropotheism is the heart raised to intellect; it speaks through the head in terms of the intellect only what the heart speaks in its own way. Religion is only emotion, feeling, heart, and love; i.e., the negation and *dissolution of God* in man. The new philosophy as the *negation of theology*, which denies the truth of religious emotion, is therefore a positing of religion. Anthropotheism is religion conscious of itself; it is religion that *understands itself*. Theology, on the other hand *negates* religion *under the appearance of positing* it.

Schelling and *Hegel* are opposites. Hegel represents the masculine principle of self-autonomy and self-activity; in short, the idealist principle. Schelling represents the feminine principle of receptivity and impressionability; in short, the materialist principle—he first imbibed Fichte, then Plato and Spinoza, and finally Böhme. Hegel lacks sense perception, Schelling the power of thought and the power to determine. Schelling is a thinker only of the *general;* when it comes to tackling the particular and the determinate, he lapses into the somnambulism of imagination. In Schelling, rationalism is only appearance; irrationalism the *truth*. The extent of Hegel's achievement is only an *abstract,* irrational principle; that of Schelling only a *mystical* and *imaginary* existence and reality that are opposed to a rational principle. Hegel compensates his lack of realism through robustly sensuous words; Schelling through fine words—Hegel expressed the uncommon in a common way, whereas Schelling expressed the common in an uncommon way. Hegel turns *things* into *mere thoughts,* whereas Schelling turns mere thoughts—for example, the aseity of God—into *things*. Hegel deludes thinking heads, Schelling only *unthinking* ones. Hegel turns unreason into reason; Schelling, conversely, reason into unreason. Schelling's is a philosophy in the element of dream; Hegel's in that of the concept. Schelling negates abstract thought through *fantasy;* Hegel through *abstract thought*. Hegel, as the *self-negation* of negative thought, or as the culmination of the old philosophy, is the negative beginning of the new philosophy. Schelling's is old philosophy *with the illusion and pretense* of being the new realistic philosophy.

The Hegelian philosophy is the resolution of the contradiction between thinking and being as, in particular, expressed by Kant; but, *nota bene,* the resolution of the contradiction still remains *within the contradiction;* i.e., within *one* element—*thought*. *Thought* is *being* in Hegel; i.e., *thought* is the *subject, being* the *predicate*. The *Logic* is thought in the element of thought, or thought thinking itself; it is thought as *subject without predicate,* or thought that is *subject* and *at the same time its own predicate*. But thought in the element of thought is still abstract; it therefore has to realize and externalize itself. This realized and externalized thought is nature, the real in general—being. But what is the truly real in this real? Thought! That is why it soon casts off from itself the predicate of reality in order to constitute a state without predicates as its true being. But this is exactly why Hegel remained unable to arrive at *being as being;* i.e., at free, independent being that is felicitous in itself. Hegel conceived objects only as the *predicates* of thought thinking itself. The admitted contradiction between the existing and conceived religion in Hegel's philosophy of religion is possible only because here, too, as elsewhere, thought is turned into the subject, but the object; i.e., religion, only into a mere *predicate* of thought.

He who clings to Hegelian philosophy also clings to theology. The Hegelian doctrine that nature or reality is posited by the Idea, is the *rational expression* of the theological doctrine that nature, the material being, has been created by God, the non-material; i.e., abstract, being. At the end of the *Logic,* the absolute Idea even comes to a nebulous "decision" to document with its own hands its descent from the theological heaven.

The Hegelian philosophy is the last refuge and the last rational mainstay of theology. Just as once the Catholic theologians became *de facto* Aristotelians in order to combat Protestantism, so now the Protestant theologians must *de jure* become *Hegelians* in order to combat "atheism."

The true relationship of thought to being is this only: *Being* is the *subject, thought* the *predicate.* Thought comes from being, but being does not come from thought. Being comes from itself and is through itself; being is given only through being; being has its ground within itself because only being is meaning, reason, necessity, and truth; in short, it is all in all. Being *is* because not-being is no being; i.e., nothing or *nonsense.*

The essence of being *as being* is the essence of nature. The temporal genesis applies only to the forms, not to the essence of nature.

Being is derived from thought only where the *true unity* of thought and being is *rent asunder,* where one, through abstraction, first takes away from being its *soul* and *essence* and then finds in this abstracted essence the *meaning* and *ground* of being thus emptied. Similarly, the world is, and must be, derived from God where one arbitrarily separates the essence of the world from the world.

He who directs his speculation towards finding a particular realistic principle of philosophy, like the so-called positive philosophers,

> is like an *animal,* on a *barren heath*
> driven by an *evil spirit* in a circle round and round
> and all about lies *beautiful, grazing ground.*

This beautiful, green grazing ground is nature and man, for both belong together. Behold nature, behold man! Here, before your eyes, are the mysteries of philosophy.

Nature is *being* that is *not distinguished* from *existence;* man is *being* that *distinguishes itself* from existence. The being that does not distinguish is the ground of the being that distinguishes; nature is, therefore, the ground of man.

The new and the only positive philosophy is the *negation of all scholastic philosophy,* although it contains the truth of the latter; it is the negation of philosophy as an *abstract, particular,* i.e., *scholastic,* quality; it has no *shibboleth,* no *particular* language, no *particular* name, no *particular* principle; it is *the thinking man* himself, i.e., man who *is* and *knows himself* as the self-conscious essence of nature, history, states, and religion; it is man who *is* and *knows himself* to be the *real* (not imaginary), absolute identity of all oppositions and contradictions, of all active and passive, mental and sensuous, political and social, qualities; it is man who *knows* that the *pantheistic* being, which the speculative philosophers or rather theologians have *separated* from and objectified as an abstract being, is nothing but *his own indeterminate* being, but one that is capable of *infinite determinations.*

The new philosophy is the *negation of rationalism* as much as *mysticism;* of *pantheism* as much as *personalism;* of *atheism* as much as *theism;* it is the *unity of all these antithetical truths as an absolutely independent and pure truth.*

The new philosophy has already expressed itself as the philosophy of religion both positively and negatively in equal measure. One need only make the conclusions of its analysis into premises in order to recognize the principles of a positive philosophy. The new philosophy, however, does not court the favor of the public. Certain of itself, it scorns to *appear* as what it is; but precisely for that reason, it must be for our age—in whose most essential interests, appearance passes for essence, illusion for reality, and the name for the thing itself—that which it *is not.* That is the way opposites complement each other! Where *nothing* stands for *something* and *lies* for *truth,* it is only consistent that *something* must stand for *nothing* and *truth* for lies. And in a situation in which one undertakes the outrageous and unprecedented attempt to base philosophy exclusively on the *favor* and *opinion* of the *newspaper public*—and ironically at the very moment when philosophy is involved in a decisive and universal act of *self-disillusion*—in such a situation one can only seek, in an honest and Christian fashion, to *refute* philosophical works by publicly *slandering* them in the *Augsburger Allgemeine Zeitung.* O, how honorable and moral, indeed, are public affairs in Germany!

A new principle always makes its appearance with a new name; i.e., it elevates a name from a low, unprivileged station to the princely station—transforms it into the designation for the highest. If one were to *translate* the name of the new philosophy—the name "man"—by *"self-consciousness,"* one would interpret the new philosophy in terms of the old and hence return it to the old standpoint;

for the self-consciousness of the old philosophy *as divorced from man* is an *abstraction without reality*. Man *is* self-consciousness.

———————

According to language, the name "man" is indeed a particular one, but according to truth it is the name of all names. The predicate "many-named" duly belongs to man; whatever man names or expresses, he always expresses his own essence. Language is, therefore, the criterion of judging how high or low the degree of the cultural development of mankind is. The name "God" is but the name for what man regards as the highest force and the highest being, i.e., for the highest feeling and the highest thought.

———————

The word "man" commonly means only man with his needs, sensations, and opinions; it means man as person in distinction from man as mind; above all it means man as distinguished from his general public qualities on the whole, or man as distinguished from, say, the artist, thinker, writer, judge, etc.—as if it were not a *characteristic* and *essential quality of man* to be a judge and so on; as if man were *outside his own being* in art, science etc. Speculative philosophy has, theoretically, fixed the separation of the essential qualities of man from man, thus deifying purely abstract qualities as independent beings. The Hegelian *Philosophy of Right* (§ 190), for example, has this: "In right, what we have before us is the *person;* in the sphere of morality, the *subject;* in the family, the familymember; in civil society as a whole, the burgher (as bourgeois). Here at the standpoint of needs what we have before us is the composite *idea* which we call *man.* It is thus here for the first time, and indeed properly only here, that we speak of man in this sense." In *this* sense: We speak in truth only and always of *one* and the *same* being; i.e., of man, even if we do so in a different sense and in a different quality, when we speak of the burgher, the subject, the family member, and the person.

———————

All speculation concerning right, will, freedom, and personality without regard to man; i.e., outside of or even above man, is speculation *without unity, necessity, substance, ground,* and *reality.* Man is the existence of freedom, the existence of personality, and the existence of right. Only man is the *ground and base* of the Fichtean Ego, the *ground and base* of the Leibnizian Monad, and the *ground and base* of the Absolute.

All science must be grounded in *nature.* A doctrine remains a *hypothesis* as long as it has not found its *natural basis.* This is true particularly of the *doctrine of freedom.* Only the new philosophy will succeed in *naturalizing* freedom which was hitherto an *anti-hypothesis,* a *supernatural hypothesis.*

Philosophy must again unite itself with natural science, and *natural science with philosophy.* This unity, based on mutual need, on inner necessity, will be more durable, more felicitous and more fruitful than the previous *mésalliance* between philosophy and theology.

Man is the fundamental being of the state. The state is the realized, developed, and explicit totality of the human being. In the state, the essential qualities or activities of man are realized in particular estates (Ständen), but in the person of the head of state they are again resolved into an identity. It is the function of the head of state to represent all estates without distinction; to him, they are all equally necessary and equally entitled before him. The head of state represents universal man.

The Christian religion has linked the name of man with the name of God in the one name "God-man." It has, in other words, raised the name of man to an attribute of the highest being. The new philosophy has, in keeping with the truth, turned this attribute into substance, the predicate into the subject. The new philosophy is *the idea realized—the truth* of Christianity. But precisely because it contains within itself the *essence* of Christianity, it abandons the *name* of Christianity. Christianity has expressed the truth only *in contradiction to the truth*. The pure and unadulterated truth without contradiction is a *new truth*—a *new, autonomous deed* of mankind.

Principles of the Philosophy of the Future

PREFACE

These *Principles* are the continuation and further substantiation of my *Theses on the Reform of Philosophy,* which was banned by the unbounded despotism of German censorship. As intended in the first draft, these *Principles* were to take the form of an elaborate book; but, while preparing the final version, I was for some mysterious reason myself seized by the spirit of German censorship and inflicted upon the manuscript a barbaric curtailment. What escaped this indiscreet censorship saw itself reduced to the following few sheets of paper.

I called them *Principles of the Philosophy of the Future* because the present—a time of tricky illusions and hoggish prejudices—is incapable of understanding, let alone appreciating, the simple truths from which these *Principles* are derived: Their very simplicity makes them incomprehensible to the present age.

The *Philosophy of the Future* addresses itself to the task of leading philosophy from the realm of "detached souls" back into the realm of embodied, living souls; of compelling philosophy to come down from its divine and self-sufficient blissfulness in thought and open its eyes to human misery. To this end, it needs nothing more than human understanding and human speech. But to think, speak, and act in a genuinely human way is to be the privilege only of future generations. At present, the task is not to invent a theory of man, but to pull man out of the mire in which he is bogged down. These *Principles* are the fruit of engaging in such clean, yet sour work. Their task was to derive the necessity of a philosophy of man, that is, anthropology, from the Philosophy of the Absolute, that is, theology, in order thus to establish a critique of human philosophy through a critique of divine philosophy. A close familiarity with modern philosophy must therefore be presupposed as a condition for their appreciation.

The consequences of these *Principles* cannot remain unnoticed.

Bruckberg
July 9, 1843

Principles of the Philosophy of the Future

1

The task of the modern era was the realization and humanization of God—the transformation and dissolution of theology into anthropology.

2

The *religious* or *practical* form of this humanization was Protestantism. *The* God who is man, that is to say the human God, Christ, this and only this is the God of Protestantism. Unlike Catholicism, Protestantism is no longer concerned with what God is in himself, but only with what he is for man; hence, it knows no speculative or contemplative tendency like Catholicism. It has ceased to be *theology*—it is essentially *Christology; that is, religious anthropology.*

3

However, Protestantism negated God-in-himself or God as God—for only God-in-himself is, strictly speaking, God —*only in practice;* theoretically, it left him intact. He *exists;* however, not for man; that is, the *religious* man. He is a transcendent being or a being that will one day become an object *for man* up there in heaven. But that which is *other-worldly* to religion, is *this-worldly* to phi-

losophy; what does not constitute an object for the former,
does so precisely for the latter.

4

The *rational* or *theoretical* assimilation and dissolution
of the God who is other-worldly to religion, and hence
not given to it as an object, is the speculative philosophy.

5

The *essence* of speculative philosophy is nothing other
than the *rationalized, realized, actualized essence of God*.
The speculative philosophy is the *true, consistent, rational*
theology.

6

Taken as an *intelligible* (*geistig*) or an *abstract* being,
that is, regarded *neither* as human *nor* as sensuous, but
rather as one that is an *object for and accessible only to
reason or intelligence*, God qua God is *nothing but the
essence of reason* itself. But, *basing* themselves *rather on
imagination, ordinary theology* and *Theism* regard him as
an independent being existing separately from reason. Under these circumstances, it is an inner, a sacred *necessity*
that the essence of reason as distinguished from reason itself be at last *identified with it* and the divine being thus
be apprehended, realized, *as the essence* of reason. It is
on this necessity that *the great historical significance of
speculative philosophy* rests. The proof of the proposition
that the divine essence is the essence of reason or intelligence lies in the fact that the *determinations* or *qualities*
of God, in so far as they are *rational* or *intelligible* and
not *determinations* of *sensuousness* or *imagination*, are,
in fact, *qualities of reason*.

"*God* is *the infinite being* or *the being without any
limitations whatsoever*." But what cannot be a limit or
boundary on God can also not be a limit or boundary on
reason. If, for example, God is elevated above all limitations of sensuousness, so, too, is reason. He who cannot

conceive of any entity except as sensuous, that is, he whose reason is limited by sensuousness, can only have a God who is limited by sensuousness. Reason, which conceives God as an infinite being, conceives, in point of fact, *its own* infinity in God. What is divine to reason is also truly *rational* to it, or in other words, it is a being that perfectly corresponds to and satisfies it. That, however, in which a being finds satisfaction, is nothing but the being *in which it encounters itself as its own object.* He who finds satisfaction in a philosopher is himself of a philosophical nature. That he is of this nature is precisely what he and others encounter in this satisfaction. Reason "does not, however, pause at the finite, sensuous things; it finds satisfaction in the infinite being alone"—that is to say, the essence of reason is disclosed to us primarily in the infinite being.

"God is the necessary being." But his necessity rests on the ground that he is a *rational, intelligent* being. The ground for what the world or matter is does not lie in the world or matter itself, for it is completely indifferent to whether it is or is not, or to why it is so and not otherwise.* Hence, it must necessarily presuppose another being as its cause, a being that is *intelligent* and *self-conscious* and acts according to reasons and goals. For if this being were to be conceived of as lacking intelligence, the question as to its own ground must arise again. The necessity of the primary and the highest being rests, therefore, on the presupposition that the *intellect* alone is the being that is *primary, highest, necessary,* and *true.* Just as the truth and reality of metaphysical or ontotheological determinations depend on their reducibility to psychological or rather anthropological determinations, so the necessity of the divine being in the old metaphysics or ontotheology has meaning, truth, and reality only in the

* It is quite obvious that here, as in all sections where the problem is to deal with, and present the development of, historical phenomena, I do not speak and argue from my point of view, but rather let each phenomenon speak for itself. This applies also to my treatment of theism here.

psychological or anthropological characterization of God
as an intelligent being. The necessary being is one that it
is necessary to think of, that must be affirmed absolutely
and which it is simply impossible to deny or annul, but
only to the extent to which it is a *thinking* being *itself.*
Thus, it is its own necessity and reality which reason demonstrates in the necessary being.

"*God is unconditional, general—'God* is not this or that
particular thing'—*immutable, eternal, or timeless being.*"
But absoluteness, immutability, eternality, and generality
are, according to the judgment of metaphysical theology
itself, also qualities of the truths or laws of reason, and
hence the qualities of reason itself; for what else are these
immutable, general, absolute, and universally valid truths
of reason if not expressions of the essence of reason itself?

"*God is the independent, autonomous being not requir-
ing any other being in order to exist, hence subsisting entirely by and through itself.*" But even this abstract, metaphysical characterization has meaning and reality only as
a definition of the essence of intelligence and, as such, it
states only that God is a thinking and intelligent being or,
vice versa, that the thinking being is the divine being; for
only a *sensuous* being will need some other being outside
itself in order to exist. I need air to breathe, water to
drink, light to be able to see, plants and animals to eat,
but nothing—not directly at any rate—in order to think. I
cannot conceive of a breathing being without air, nor of a
seeing being without light, but I can conceive of a thinking being as existing in complete isolation. A breathing
being is *necessarily* referred to a being outside itself, that
is to say, it has the *essential* object, through which it is
what it is, *outside itself;* but the thinking being is *referred
only to itself,* is its own object, carries its essence within
itself and is what it is only through itself.

7

That which is *object* in *theism* is subject in *speculative
philosophy.* That which is only the conceived and *imag-*

ined essence of reason in theism, is the *thinking* essence of reason itself in speculative philosophy.

The theist represents to himself God as a *personal* being *existing outside reason* and man; as a subject, he thinks God as an object. He conceives God as a being, i.e., as an *intelligible, non-sensuous* being with regard to his idea of it, but as a *sensuous* being with respect to its actual *existence* or its *truth;* for the *essential characteristic* of an objective existence; i.e., of an existence outside thought or perception, is *sensuousness.* He distinguishes God from himself in the same sense in which he distinguishes the sensuous objects and beings from himself as existing outside himself; in short, he thinks God from the *standpoint of sensuousness.* In contrast to this, the speculative theologian or philosopher thinks of God from the *standpoint of thought;* that is why the distracting idea of a sensuous being does not interpose itself between him and God; and, thus unhindered, he identifies the objective, conceived being with the *subjective,* thinking being.

The inner necessity by which God is turned from an *object* of man into his *subject, into his thinking ego,* can be demonstrated more specifically in the following way: God is an object of man and of man alone and not of the animal. However, *what* a being is can be known only through its *object;* the object to which a being is necessarily related is nothing but its own *manifest* being. Thus, the object of the herbivorous animals is the plant; it is, however, precisely through their object that these are distinguished from other animals, the carnivorous ones. Similarly, the object of the eye is light and not sound or smell, and it is through this object that the eye reveals its essence to us. It therefore comes down to the same thing whether someone cannot see or has no eyes. That is also why we name things in life with respect to their objects. The eye is the "light organ." He who cultivates land is a land cultivator (peasant); someone else, the object of whose activity is hunting, is a hunter; he who catches fish is a fisher, and so forth. Now, if God is an object of man —and he is indeed that necessarily and essentially—the es-

sence of this object expresses nothing but man's own essence. Imagine to yourself that a thinking being on some
planet, or even on a comet, happened to glance at a few
paragraphs of Christian dogmatics dealing with the being
of God. What would this being infer from these paragraphs? Perhaps the existence of a God in the sense of
Christian dogmatics? No. Its inference would be that the
earth, too, is inhabited by thinking beings; in their definitions of God, it would discover only the definitions of their
own essence. For example, in the definition "God is spirit,"
it would only see the proof and expression of their own
spirit; in short, it would infer the essence and the qualities
of the subject from those of the object. And with complete justification, because in the case of *this particular*
object the distinction between what the object is in itself
and what it is for man dissolves itself. This distinction is
valid only in the case of an object which is given in immediate sense perception and which, precisely for that
reason, is also given to other beings besides man. Light is
there not only for man; it also affects animals, plants, and
inorganic substances; it is a being of a general nature. In
order to know what light is, we therefore observe not
only the impressions and effects it makes upon ourselves,
but also upon beings different from us. Hence, in this context, the distinction between the object *in itself* and the
object *for us,* that is, between the object in reality and the
object in our thought and imagination is necessary and
objectively founded. God, however, is an object *only* for
man. Animals and stars praise God *only in a human sense.*
It belongs therefore to the essence of God himself that he
is not an object of any other being except man, that he
is a specifically human object, that he is a secret of man.
But, if God is an object *only* for man, what does his essence disclose to us? Nothing but the essence of man. He
whose object is the highest being is himself the highest
being. The more man is the object of animals, the higher
they must rank, and the closer must their approximation
be to man. An animal whose object was man qua man,
that is, man in his specific human nature, would itself be a

man and no longer simply an animal. Only equal beings are equal objects for one another; that is, beings as they are *in themselves*. Now, it is true that theism, too, knows the identity of the divine and the human essence, but this identity forms its object only as *sensuous* identity, only as *similarity* or *affinity*, because, even if it grounds the essence of God in the spirit, it conceives God as a sensuous being existing outside man. Affinity expresses the same thing as identity; but concurrently connected with it is the sensuous idea that the related beings are two independents; that is, sensuous, beings existing apart from each other.

8

Ordinary theology turns the *standpoint* of *man* into the *standpoint of God;* by contrast, the *speculative* theology turns the *standpoint of God* into the *standpoint of man, or rather into that of the thinker.*

For ordinary theology, God is an object just like any other sensuous object; but, at the same time, he is also a subject for it, and, indeed, just like the human subject. God creates things that are apart from *himself;* he is referred back to himself in a reflexive self-relationship and is related to other things existing apart from him; he both loves and contemplates himself simultaneously with other beings. In short, man makes his thoughts, even his feelings, the thoughts and feelings of God; his own essence and standpoint are made the essence and standpoint of God. Speculative theology, however, reverses this.

In ordinary theology, God is thus a *contradiction with himself,* for he is supposed to be a *non*-human, a *super*-human being, and yet with respect to all his determinations, he is in truth only a human being. In speculative theology or philosophy on the other hand, God is in *contradiction to man;* he is supposed to be the essence of man —at any rate of reason—but he is in truth a non-human, a super-human, that is, an abstract being. In ordinary theology, the super-human God is only an edifying phrase, a mere idea, a toy of fantasy; in speculative philosophy, on

the other hand, he is truth, bitter seriousness. The acute
contradiction experienced by speculative philosophy arose
from the fact that it turned God, who in theism is merely
a being of fantasy, an indefinite, nebulous and remote
being, into a definite and encounterable being, thus destroying the illusory magic which a distant being has in
the blue haze of the imagination. No wonder then that the
theists have been vexed by the circumstance that although
Hegel's *Logic* understands itself as the presentation of
God in his eternal, world-antecedent essence, it nevertheless deals—for example, in the doctrine of magnitude—with
extensive and intensive quantity, fractions, powers, pro-
portions, etc. How, they exclaimed in horror, can this
God be our God? And yet, what else is this God if not the
God of theism who has been drawn out of the fog of the
imagination and brought into the light of the determining
thought; the God of theism who has created and ordered
everything according to measure, number and weight
taken, so to speak, by his word? If God has ordered and
created everything according to number and measure; that
is, if measure and number, before they assumed reality
in things existing apart from God, were contained in the
intelligence and, hence, in the essence of God—and there
is no difference between God's intelligence and his essence
—does not, then, mathematics, too, belong to the mysteries
of theology? But of course there is a world of difference
between what something appears to be in the imagination
and what it is in truth and reality. No wonder then that
the one and the same thing appears as two completely
different things to those who rely only on appearance.

9

The *essential qualities or predicates of the Divine Being* are the *essential qualities or predicates of speculative
philosophy.*

10

God is pure spirit, pure essence, pure activity—*actus
purus*—without passions, without predicates imposed from

outside, without sensuousness, without matter. The speculative philosophy is this *pure spirit, this pure activity realized as an act of thought—the absolute being as absolute thought.*

Just as once the abstraction from all that is sensuous and material was the necessary condition of theology, so it was also the necessary condition of speculative philosophy, the only difference being that the abstraction of theology was itself a sensuous abstraction (or ascetics) because its object, although arrived at through abstraction, was nevertheless conceived as a sensuous being, whereas the abstraction of speculative philosophy is only spiritual and ideated, having only a scientific or theoretical, but no practical, meaning. The beginning of Cartesian philosophy —namely, the abstraction from sensuousness and matter— is also the beginning of modern speculative philosophy. But Descartes and Leibniz regarded this abstraction only as a subjective condition for cognizing the non-material being of God; they conceived the non-materiality of God as an *objective* quality *independent* of abstraction and thought. Theirs was still the standpoint of theism, that is to say, they considered the non-material being as the *object* and not as the *subject;* i.e., the *active principle,* the real *essence* of philosophy itself. It is of course true that God in both Descartes and Leibniz is the principle of philosophy, but only as an *object distinguished* from thought and hence a principle only in a general sense and only in imagination, but not in reality and truth. God is only the *first* and the *general* cause of matter, movement, and activity; the particular movements and activities, the definite and concrete material things are, however, considered and cognized independently of God. Leibniz and Descartes are idealists only in a general sense, but when it comes to particular things they are materialists. God is the only consistent, perfect, and true idealist because he alone perceives things in complete freedom from darkness or, in the sense of Leibniz's philosophy, without the mediation of the senses and the imagination; he is pure intellect, that is, pure in the sense of being separated from all sen-

suousness and materiality; for him, material things are
therefore pure creatures of the intellect, pure thoughts;
for him, matter does not exist at all because its possibility
is anchored only in dark, that is, sensuous, perceptions.
And yet man, according to Leibniz, carries within himself
a good portion of idealism, for how else would it be possible for him to conceive a non-material being without
possessing a non-material faculty and, consequently, non-
material perceptions? In addition to the senses and the
imagination, man possesses intellect and the intellect is
precisely a non-material, a *pure* being because it thinks;
the human intellect, however, is not *quite* as pure as the
divine intellect or the Divine Being because it lacks pure
infinity and extension. Man, or rather this man Leibniz,
is therefore only a *partial,* a *semi-idealist,* whereas *God*
alone is *a complete idealist,* "the *Perfect Philosopher"* as
Wolff expressly calls him. This means that God is the idea
underlying the absolute idealism of the later speculative
philosophy, but only in its completed form and only as
unfolded in all its details. For what after all is the intellect
and what, in general, the essence of God? Nothing other
than the intellect and nothing other than the essence of
man, though severed from the determinations that, at a
given time, constitute the limitations of man, no matter
whether real or imaginary. He whose intellect is not at
odds with his senses, he who does not take the senses to
be a limitation, also does not take the intellect without
the senses to be the highest, the true intellect. What else
is the idea of a thing if not its essence having been purged
of the limitations and obscurations to which it is subject
on account of its coexistence with other things in reality?
Thus, according to Leibniz, the limitation of the human
intellect arises out of the fact that it is burdened with materialism, that is to say, with dark perceptions; and these
dark perceptions spring only from the circumstance that
the being of man is interrelated with other beings, that it
finds itself in the context of the world. This relatedness,
however, does not apply to the essence of the intellect;
rather, it is in contradiction to it, because the intellect

in itself; that is, according to its idea, is something non-material or something which is *for itself*—an isolated being. And this idea, this intellect, purged of all materialistic perceptions is precisely the divine intellect. But what was just an *idea* with Leibniz became *truth* and *reality* in later philosophy. *The absolute idealism* is nothing but the *realized divine intellect* of Leibnizian theism, nothing but pure intellect which has been systematically unfolded, which strips all things of their sensuousness turning them into pure entities of intellect and thought, and which, unhampered by anything alien, is occupied with itself alone as the essence of all essences.

11

God is a thinking being; but the objects that he thinks and encompasses in himself are, like his own intellect, *not distinguished from his being,* so that in thinking other things he thinks only himself and thus persists in an *uninterrupted unity with himself.* But this *unity* of the *thinking and the thought* is precisely the *secret of speculative philosophy.*

Thus, for example, in the *Logic* of Hegel the objects of thought are not distinguished from the essence of thought. Here thought exists in an uninterrupted unity with itself; the objects of thought are only the determinations of thought itself, that is, they have nothing in themselves that would resist their complete dissolution in thought. But that which is the essence of *Logic* is also the essence of God. God is a spiritual and an abstract being; but he is at the same time both the essence of all beings and that which encompasses all beings so as to form a unity with his abstract essence. But what are these beings that are identical with an abstract and spiritual being? They are themselves abstract beings—*thoughts.* As things are in God, so they are not outside God; they are just as distinguished from the real things as the things constituting the object of *Logic* are from those given as the objects of real perception. To what, therefore, is the distinction between the divine and the metaphysical thought reducible? Only to the one imaginary distinction—that between imaginary and *real* thought.

12

The difference between *God's knowledge* or *thought,* which *precedes* and *creates* all things as their *archetype,* and *man's knowledge,* which *follows* things *as their copy,* is nothing but the *difference* between *a priori,* or speculative, and a *posteriori,* or *empirical knowledge.*

Although theism looks upon God as a thinking or spiritual being, it regards him at the same time as a *sensuous being.* Hence, it directly links *sensuous* and *material* effects with the thought and will of God—effects that are in contradiction to the essence of thought and will, expressing nothing more than the power of nature. Such a *material* effect—hence merely an expression of sensuous power—is above all the creation or bringing forth of the real material world. Speculative theology, on the other hand, transforms this sensuous activity which contradicts the essence of thought into a logical or theoretical activity; the material creation of the object into a speculative creation out of the Notion. In theism, the world is a temporal product of God—the world exists for several million years, but God's existence antedates this; in speculative theology, on the other hand, the world or nature comes *after* God only according to rank or significance; the accident presupposes the substance, and nature presupposes logic according to the notion and not according to sensuous existence and, hence, not according to time.

Theism, however, attributes to God not only speculative but also *sensuous* and *empirical* knowledge understood in its highest perfection. But just as God's pre-worldly and object-antecedent knowledge has found its realization, truth, and reality in the *a priori* knowledge of speculative philosophy, so too has the *sensuous knowledge* of God found its realization, truth, and reality in the empirical sciences of the modern era. The most perfect and, hence, divine, sensuous knowledge is therefore nothing but the most sensuous of all knowledge, the knowledge of the

tiniest minutiae and of the most inconspicuous details—
"God is omniscient," says St. Thomas Aquinas, "because
he knows even the most particular things"—*the* knowledge
that does not just indiscriminately put the hair on the
human head together into a tuft, but counts and knows
each one of it, hair for hair. But this divine knowledge,
which is only a matter of imagination and fantasy in theology, became the *rational* and *real* knowledge of the
natural sciences produced through the telescope and mi-
croscope. Natural science has counted the stars in the sky,
the ova in the spawn of fish and butterflies, and the dots
on the wings of the insects in order to distinguish one
from the other; alone in the caterpillar of the willow moth,
it has anatomically demonstrated the existence of 288
muscles in the head, 1,647 in the body, and 2,186 in the
stomach and intestines. What more can one ask? We have
here a clear example of the truth that man's idea of God
is the idea of the human individual of his own species,
that God as the totality of all realities and perfections is
nothing other than the totality of the qualities of the species compendiously put together in him for the benefit of
the limited individual, but actually dispersed among men
and realizing themselves in the course of world history.
In terms of its quantitative scope, the field of the natural
sciences is too vast for any single individual to traverse.
Who will be able to count the stars in the sky and at the
same time the muscles and nerves in the body of the caterpillar? Lyonet lost his sight over the anatomy of the willow
caterpillar. Who is able to observe simultaneously both the
differences of height and depth on the moon and at the
same time observe the differences of the innumerable am-
monites and terebrates? But what one man cannot accomplish and does not know, can be accomplished and
known by all men collectively. Thus, the divine knowledge
that knows each particular thing simultaneously has its
reality in the knowledge of the species.

What is true of the Divine Omniscience is true also of
the Divine Omnipresence which has equally realized itself in man. While one man heeds what is going on on

the moon or Uranus, someone else observes Venus, or
the entrails of the caterpillar, or some other place never
penetrated by the human eye under the erstwhile reign
of an omniscient and omnipresent God. Indeed, while man
observes this star from the standpoint of Europe, he also
observes it simultaneously from the standpoint of America.
What is absolutely impossible for *one* man alone to achieve
is possible for two. But God is present in all places at one
and the same time and knows everything simultaneously
and completely. Of course. But it must be noted that this
omniscience and omnipresence exists only in the imagination and fantasy, and we must not lose sight of the important distinction between the merely imagined and the
real things we have already mentioned several times. In
the imagination, to be sure, one can survey the 4,059
muscles of a caterpillar in one glance, but in reality, where
they exist apart from one another, they can be viewed
only one at a time. Thus, the limited individual can also
conceive in his imagination the whole extent of human
knowledge as limited, but if he really wanted to make it
his own, he would never reach the point where it ends.
Take just one science—say history—as an example, and try
in thought to "dissolve" world history into the history of
the individual countries, these into the history of individual
provinces, these again into the chronicles of towns, and
the chronicles, finally, into family histories and biogra-
phies. Would it ever be possible for one single man to
arrive at the point where he could exclaim: "Here, at
this point, I stand at the end of the historical knowledge
of mankind!" In the same way, our life span—both the
past as well as the possible future—appears to us in the
imagination as extraordinarily short, no matter how long
we extend it; and we feel compelled to make good this
evanescent brevity by an infinite and unending life after
death. But how long in reality does a day, or just an hour,
last! Whence this difference? From the following: Time
in the imagination is *empty* time, that is, a nothing between
the beginning and the termination of our reckoning of
it; the real life span is, however, fulfilled time where

mountains of difficulties of all kinds lie midway between the now and the then.

13

The beginning of speculative philosophy, in so far as it is a beginning without any presuppositions whatsoever, is nothing else than the beginning without presuppositions, or the aseity of the Divine Being. Theology distinguishes between active and reposing qualities of God. Philosophy, however, transforms even the qualities of repose into active ones; the whole being of God into activity—human activity. This is also true of what was mentioned at the beginning of this paragraph. Philosophy presupposes nothing; this can only mean that it *abstracts* from all that is immediately or sensuously given, or from all objects distinguished from thought. In short, it abstracts from all wherefrom it is possible to abstract without ceasing to think, and it makes this act of abstraction from all objects its own beginning. However, what else is the absolute being if not the being for which nothing is to be presupposed and to which no object other than itself is either given or necessary? What else is it if not the being that has been subtracted from all objects—from all things distinct and distinguishable from it—and, therefore, becomes an object for man precisely through abstracting from these things? Wherefrom God is free, therefrom you must also free yourself if you want to reach God; and you make yourself really free when you present yourself with the idea of God. In consequence, if you think God without presupposing any other being or object, you yourself think without presupposing any external object; the quality that you attribute to God is a quality of your own thought. However, what is *activity* in man is *being* in God or that which is imagined as such. What, hence, is the Fichtean Ego which says, "I simply am because I am," and what is the pure and presuppositionless thought of Hegel if not the Divine Being of the old theology and metaphysics which has been transformed into the *actual, active,* and *thinking* being of man?

14

Speculative philosophy as the realization of God is the *positing* of God, and *at the same time* his *cancellation or negation; theism and at the same time atheism:* for God—in the sense of theology—is God only as long as he is taken to be a being distinguished from and independent of the being of man as well as of nature. *The* theism that as the positing of God is simultaneously his negation or, conversely, as the negation of God equally his affirmation, is *pantheism.* Theological theism—that is, theism properly speaking—is nothing other than *imaginary* pantheism which itself is nothing other than real and true theism.

What separates theism from pantheism is only the imaginary representation of God as a personal being. All the determinations of God—and these must be predicated of him, otherwise he would be nothing and not at all the object of the imagination—are determinations of reality, either of nature or of man or those common to both, and hence *pantheistic* determinations; for that which does not distinguish God from the being of nature or of man is pantheism. God is distinguished from the world, from the totality of nature and mankind, only with respect to his personality or existence, but not with respect to his determinations or to his essence; that is, he is only *imagined to be* but is *in truth not a different being.* Theism is the contradiction of appearance and essence, imagination and truth, whereas pantheism is the unity of both—pantheism is the *naked* truth of theism. All the conceptions of theism, if taken seriously, carried out, and realized, must necessarily lead to pantheism. Pantheism is *consistent* theism. Theism holds God to be the cause, indeed, to be the living, personal cause, to be the creator of the world; God has brought forth the world by his will. But the will alone does not suffice. If the will is there, the intellect must also be there; *what* one wills is a matter of the intellect. There can be no object without the intellect. The things that God created existed therefore *in* God prior to their creation; that is, existed in him as the objects of his intellect, or as intellectual entities. As theology has it, the intellect of God is the comprehensive unity of all things and essences. Whence could they have sprung if not out of nothing? And what difference does it make whether you think of this nothingness in your imagination as independent or transpose it into God? But God contains everything or is everything *in an ideational way;* that is, in the way of the imagination. This ideational pantheism, however, leads necessarily to the real or concrete; for it is not far from the intellect of God to his being and from his being to his reality. How should it be possible to separate the intellect from the being, and the being from the reality or existence of God? If things are in the intellect of God, how could they be outside of his being? If they result from his intellect, why not then also from his being? And if in God his being is directly identical with his reality, if the existence of God cannot be divorced from the concept of God, how then could the conception of the object and the real object be separated in God's conception of things?

How, therefore, could *the* difference that constitutes only the nature of the finite and non-divine intellect, namely, the difference between the object as given in the imagination and as existing apart from it, occur in God? But once we have no objects whatsoever left *outside the intellect of God,* we soon will have nothing whatsoever left *outside his being* and finally nothing *outside his existence.* All objects *are* in God and, indeed, actually and in truth, not only in the imagination; for where they exist only in the imagination of God as well as of man, that is, where they are in God only in an ideal, or rather imaginary way, they exist at the same time outside the imagination, outside God. But given that we have no objects and no world outside God, we would also no longer have God outside the world; that is, God taken not only as an ideal or as imagined, but also as a real being. In *one* word, we thus have Spinozism or pantheism. Theism conceives God only as a purely non-material being. But to determine God as non-material is nothing different from determining matter

as a nonentity, as a monstrosity, for only God is the measure of what is real; only God is Being, truth, and essence;
only that which is true of God and in God, that alone *is;*
what is negated of God, that also does not exist. To derive
matter from God means, therefore, nothing but to want
to establish its being through its non-being; for to derive
means to establish something by indicating its ground.
God made matter. But how, why, and out of what? Theism does not provide an answer to these questions. Matter
for theism is a purely *inexplicable* existence; this means
that it is the *limit,* the *end* of theology on which it founders
in life as well as in thought. How can I then extract out
of theology itself its negation and end without discarding
it? How can I expect any explanatory principle or information from theology when its wisdom falters? How can
I extract the affirmation of matter from a negation of matter and world which constitutes the essence of theology?
How can I, despite the God of theology, produce the proposition *"matter exists"* out of the proposition "matter does
not exist?" How else but through mere fiction? Material
objects can be derived from God only if *God himself is
determined as a material being.* Only thus can God become the *real* cause of the world and not merely be an
imagined and fictitious cause. He who is not ashamed to
make shoes, should also not be ashamed to be and be
called a cobbler. Hans Sachs was indeed both a cobbler
and a poet. But the shoes were the work of his hands
whereas the poems were that of his head. As the effect, so
the cause. But matter is *not* God; it is rather the finite, the
non-divine, that is, that which negates God—the unconditional adherents and worshipers of matter are atheists.
Hence, pantheism unites atheism with theism, the *negation* of God with God; *God* is a *material* or, in Spinoza's
language, an *extended* being.

15

Pantheism is *theological atheism* or *theological materialism;* it is *the negation of theology* while itself confined
to the *standpoint of theology,* for it turns matter, the ne-

gation of God, into a predicate or an *attribute of the Divine Being*. But he who turns matter into an attribute of God, declares matter to be a *divine being*. The realization of God must in principle *presuppose godliness;* that is, the *truth* and *essentiality of the real*. The *deification of the real,* of *that which exists materially*—materialism, empiricism, realism, and humanism—or the *negation* of theology, is the *essence* of the modern era. Pantheism is therefore nothing more than *the essence of the modern era* elevated into the *divine essence,* into a *religio-philosophical principle.*

Empiricism or realism—meaning thereby the so-called sciences of the real, but in particular the natural science —negates theology, albeit not theoretically but only practically, namely, *through the actual deed* in so far as the realist makes the negation of God, or at least that which is *not* God, into the *essential* business of his life and the *essential* object of his activity. However, he who devotes his mind and heart exclusively to that which is material and sensuous *actually* denies the transsensuous its reality; for only that which constitutes an object of the real and concrete activity is real, at least for man. "What I don't know doesn't affect me." To say that it is not possible to know anything of the supersensuous is only an excuse. One ceases to know anything about God and divine things only when one does not *want* to know anything about them. How much did one know about God, about the devils or angels as long as these supersensuous beings were still objects of a *real* faith? To be *interested* in something is to have the *talent* for it. The medieval mystics and scholastics had no talent and aptitude for natural science only because they had no interest in nature. Where the sense for something is not lacking, there also the senses and organs do not lack. If the heart is open to something, the mind will not be closed to it. Thus, the reason why mankind in the modern era lost the organs for the supersensuous world and its secrets is because it also lost the sense for them together with the belief in them; because its essential tendency was anti-Christian and anti-theological; that is, anthropological, cosmic, realistic, and materialistic.* Spinoza hit the nail on the head with his paradoxical proposition: God is an extended, that is, material being. He found, at least for his time, the true philosophical expression for the materialistic tendency of the modern era; he legitimated and sanctioned it: God himself is a materialist. Spinoza's philosophy was religion; he himself was an amazing man. Unlike so many others, Spinoza's materialism did not stand in contradiction to the notion of a non-material and anti-materialistic God who also quite consistently imposes on man the duty to give himself up only to *anti-materialistic, heavenly tendencies* and *concerns;* for God is nothing other than the archetypal and ideal image of man; *what* God is and *how* he is, is what man *ought* to be or *wants* to be, or at least hopes to be in the future. But only where theory does not belie practice, and practice theory, is there character, truth, and religion. Spinoza is the Moses of modern free-thinkers and materialists.

16

Pantheism is the *negation* of *theoretical,* and *empiricism* the negation of *practical,* theology. Pantheism negates the *principle,* whereas empiricism negates the *consequences* of theology.

Pantheism makes God into a present, real, and material being; empiricism—to which rationalism also belongs—makes God into an absent, remote, unreal, and negative being. Empiricism does not deny God existence, but denies him all positive determinations, because their content is supposed to be only finite and empirical; the infinite cannot, therefore, be an object for man. But the more determinations I deny to a being, the more do I cut it off from myself, and the less power and influence do I con-

---

* In the context of the present work, the differences between materialism, empiricism, realism, and humanism are, of course, irrelevant.

cede to it over me, the freer do I make myself of it. The more qualities I possess, the more I am for others, and the greater is the extent of my influence and effects. And the *more* one *is,* the more one is *known* to others. Hence, each negation of an attribute of God is a partial atheism, a sphere of godlessness. To the extent to which I take away an attribute of God, to the same extent do I take away his being. If, for example, sympathy and mercy are not attributes of God, then I am alone with myself in my suffering; God *is not there* as my comforter. If God is the negation of all that is finite, then, in consequence, the finite is the negation of God. Only if God thinks of me—so concludes the religious man—have I reason and cause to think of him; only in his being-for-me lies the ground of my being-for-him. In truth, therefore, the theological being is no longer anything to empiricism, at least nothing real; but empiricism does not transpose this non-being into the object, but only *into itself,* into its *knowledge.* It does not deny God being, a being that is a dead or indifferent being, but it denies him the being which proves itself *as being;* namely, as effective and tangible being that cuts into life. It affirms God, but *negates all the consequences* which *necessarily* follow from this affirmation. It rejects and abandons theology, although not out of theoretical grounds, but out of *aversion* and *disinclination* for the objects of theology; that is, out of a vague feeling for its unreality. Theology is nothing, thinks the empiricist; but he adds to this, *"for me,"* that is, his judgment is a subjective, a *pathological* one; for he does not have the freedom, nor the desire and the calling, to drag the objects of theology before the forum of reason. This is the calling of philosophy. The concern of modern philosophy was therefore none other than to elevate *the pathological judgment of empiricism—theology is nothing—*to a *theoretical* and *objective* judgment, to transform the indirect, unconscious, and negative negation of theology into a direct, positive, and conscious negation. How ridiculous it is, therefore, to want to suppress the "atheism" of philosophy without at the same time suppressing the atheism of empiricism! How

ridiculous it is to persecute the theoretical negation of
Christianity and to ignore the actual refutations of Christianity with which the modern era is replete! How ridiculous it is to hold that with the *awareness* of the sympton
of evil, the cause of evil is also eliminated! How ridiculous
indeed! And yet, how rich is history in such mockeries!
They repeat themselves in all critical periods. And no wonder! We are always accommodating to whatever has happened in the past and acknowledge the necessity of all the
changes and revolutions that have occurred, but we resist
with all the means at our disposal to take the same attitude
to the *present* situation. Out of shortsightedness and com-
placency, we except the present from the rule.

17

The elevation of matter into a divine being is directly
and at the same time the elevation of *reason* into a *divine
being*. What the theist negates of God by means of the
imagination and out of his *emotional need* and his yearn-
ing for unlimited bliss, the pantheist affirms of God out of
his *rational need*. Matter is an essential object for reason.
If there was no matter, reason would have no *stimulus* and
no *material* for thought and, hence, no content. One *cannot give up* matter without *giving up reason;* one *cannot
acknowledge matter without acknowledging reason.* Materialists are rationalists. But pantheism affirms reason as
a divine being only *indirectly;* namely, only by turning
God from a being mediated through the imagination—and
this is what he is in theism as a personal being—into an
object of reason, or a rational being. The direct apotheosis
of reason is *idealism*. Pantheism *necessarily* leads to idealism. Idealism is related to pantheism in the same way as
pantheism is related to theism.

As the object, so the subject. According to Descartes, the
being of physical things, the body or *substance,* is the object of reason alone and not of the senses. But precisely
because of this, the being of the perceiving subject, that
is, of man, is not the senses, but reason. It is only to being
that being is given as object. For Plato, the objects of

opinion are only transient things; but for that matter opinion itself is transient and changing knowledge—mere opinion. The being of music is the highest being to the musician and, consequently, the sense of hearing, the highest organ; he would sooner lose his eyes than his ears. The natural scientist, on the contrary, would sooner part with his ears than with his eyes because his objective being is light. To elevate sound to godliness is to deify the ear. Hence, if I, like the pantheist, say the deity or, what amounts to the same thing, the absolute being or absolute truth *is an object for and of reason alone,* then I declare God to be a rational thing or a rational being, and in so doing I indirectly express only the absolute truth and reality of reason. Hence, it is necessary for reason to turn *to itself* with a view to *reverse* this *inverted* self-recognition, to declare itself directly to be the absolute truth and to become, without the intervention of any intermediary object, its own object as the absolute truth. The pantheist says the same thing as the idealist, except that the former expresses objectively and realistically what the latter expresses only subjectively or idealistically. The pantheist has his *idealism in the object:* Nothing exists apart from substance, apart from God, and all things are only determinations of God. The idealist has his *pantheism* in the *ego:* Nothing exists apart from the ego, and all things are what they are only as objects of the ego. But all the same, idealism is the truth of pantheism; for God or substance is only the object of reason, of the ego, or of the thinking being. If I believe in and conceive of no God at all, then I have no God. He *exists for me only through me,* and only through reason does he exist for reason. The *a priori,* or the *initial* being is therefore not the being that is *thought,* but the *thinking* being; *not the object, but the subject.* With the same necessity with which natural science turned from the light back to the eye, philosophy turned from the objects of thought back to the thinking ego. What is light—as the shining and illuminating being, as the object of optics—without the eye? Nothing. And thus far goes natural science. But what—asks philosophy further—

is the eye without consciousness? Equally nothing: It is
identical whether I see *without consciousness* or I do *not*
see. Only the consciousness of seeing is the reality of seeing or actual seeing. But why do you believe that something exists apart from you? Because you see, hear and
feel something. This something is therefore a *real* something, a *real object,* only in so far as it is *an object of consciousness,* and hence, consciousness is the absolute reality
or actuality—the measure of all existence. All that exists,
exists only in so far as it exists for consciousness, that is,
in so far as it is *conscious;* for only consciousness is *being.*
Thus does the essence of theology realize itself in idealism; namely, the essence of God in the ego and in consciousness. Nothing can exist, and nothing can be thought
of, without God; this means, in the context of idealism,
that all that exists, be it an actual or a possible object,
exists only as the object of consciousness. To be is to be
an object; that is, being presupposes consciousness. Things,
the world in general, are the work and the product of
God as an absolute being. *This absolute being* is, however, an ego, a *conscious* and *thinking* being, which means
that the world is, as Descartes admirably puts it from the
standpoint of theism, an *Ens rationis divinae,* a thought-
thing, a phantom of God. But in theism and theology, this
thought-thing itself is again only a vague idea. If we therefore realize this idea, if we, so to say, translate into practice what in theism is only theory, then we have the world
as a product of the ego (Fichte) or—at least as it appears
to us and as we perceive it—as a work or product of our
perception and understanding (Kant). "Nature is derived
from the laws of the possibility of experience in general.
. . . The understanding does not obtain its laws (*a priori*)
from nature, but rather prescribes them to it." The Kantian idealism, in which things conform to the intellect and
not the intellect to things, is therefore nothing other than
the realization of the theological conception of the divine
intellect which is not determined by things, but, on the
contrary, determines them. How absurd it is, therefore, to
acknowledge idealism in heaven—that is, the idealism of

the imagination, as a divine truth—but reject the idealism on earth—that is, the idealism of reason—as a human error! Should you deny idealism, then you must also deny God! God alone is the originator of idealism. If you do not like the consequences, then you also should not like the principle! Idealism is nothing but *rational* or rationalized theism. But the Kantian idealism is still a limited idealism—*idealism* situated on *the standpoint of empiricism*. According to what has been discussed above, God is for empiricism only a being in the imagination, or in theory—in the ordinary, bad sense—but not in practice and truth; a thing in itself, but no longer a thing for empiricism, for as far as empiricism is concerned, only real and empirical things are things for it. Since matter is the only material for its thinking, it is left without any *material to construct* God. God exists, but he is *for us* a *tabula rasa,* an empty being, a mere thought. God, as we imagine and think of him, is our own ego, our own reason, and our own being; but *this* God is only an *appearance of us and for us, and not God in himself.* Kant is the embodiment of an idealism that is still shackled by theism. It often happens that in actual practice we have long ago freed ourselves from a particular thing, a doctrine, or an idea, but we are far from being free from it in the mind. It has ceased to have any truth for *our actual being*—perhaps it never had—but it still continues to be a theoretical truth; that is, a limit on our mind. The mind is always the last to become free, because it takes things more thoroughly. Theoretical freedom is, at least in many things, the last freedom. How many are republicans in their heart and in their attitude, but in their minds cannot reach beyond monarchy; their republican heart founders on the objections and difficulties raised by the intellect. This is also the case with Kant's theism. Kant has realized and at the same time negated theology within the sphere of morality, and the divine being within the sphere of *the will.* For Kant, the will is the true, original, absolute, and self-initiating being. In other words, Kant actually bestows on the will what are the predicates of the divinity; the only significance his theism can have, therefore, is that of a theoretical limit. Fichte is a Kant who has been liberated from the limit of theism—the "Messiah of speculative reason." Fichte's is the Kantian idealism, *but an idealism nonetheless.* Only from the standpoint of empiricism can, according to Fichte, there be a God distinguished from and existing apart from us. But in truth, from the standpoint of idealism the thing in itself, God—for God is, properly speaking, the thing in itself—is only the ego *in itself;* that is, the ego that is distinct from the individual and empirical ego. Outside the ego, there is no God: "Our religion is reason." But the Fichtean idealism is only the negation and realization of abstract and formal theism, of monotheism, and not of religious, material, content-replete theism, not of trinitarianism, whose realization is the *"absolute,"* or Hegelian idealism. Or in other words, Fichte has realized the God of pantheism only *in so far as* he is a *thinking* being, but not in so far as he is an extended and material being. Fichte embodies theistic, whereas Hegel embodies pantheistic, idealism.

18

Modern philosophy has realized and superseded the Divine Being which is severed and distinguished from sensuousness, the world, and man, but *only in thought, only in reason,* and indeed in a reason that is *equally severed and distinguished from sensuousness, the world, and man.* That is to say, modern philosophy has proved only *the divinity of the intellect;* it recognized only the abstract *intellect* as the *divine and absolute being. Descartes' definition of himself as mind*—"my being consists *solely of the fact that I think"*—is *modern philosophy's definition of itself.* The *will* in both the Kantian and the Fichtean idealism is itself a *pure being of the intellect,* and sense perception, which Schelling, in opposition to Fichte, connected with the intellect, is mere fantasy; it is not the truth and hence does not come into consideration.

Modern philosophy proceeded from theology; it is itself

nothing else but theology dissolved and transformed into philosophy. The abstract and transcendent being of God could therefore be realized and superseded *only in an abstract and transcendent way*. In order to transform God into reason, reason itself had to assume the quality of an abstract, divine being. The senses, says Descartes, do not yield true reality, nor being, nor certainty; only the intellect separated from all sensuousness delivers the truth. Where does this dichotomy between the intellect and the senses come from? It comes only from theology. God is not a sensuous being; rather, he is the negation of all sensuous determinations and is known only through abstraction from the senses. But he is God; that is, the *truest, the most real, the most certain* being. Whence should the truth enter into the senses, the born atheists? God is the being in which existence cannot be separated from essence and concept; God is the being that cannot be thought of in any other way except as existing. Descartes transforms this objective being into a subjective one and the ontological proof into a psychological one; he transforms the proposition, "because God is thinkable, therefore he exists," into the proposition, "I think, therefore I am." Just as in God, being cannot be separated from being thought, so in me—as I am essentially mind—being cannot be separated from thought; and just as this inseparability is constitutive of the essence in the former, so also is it in the latter. A being—no matter whether in itself or for me—that *exists only to the extent that it is thought of,* and only to the extent that it forms the object of abstraction from all sensuousness, necessarily realizes and subjectifies itself in a being that *exists only to the extent that it thinks* and whose essence is abstract thought.

19

The *culmination* of modern philosophy is the *Hegelian* philosophy. The *historical necessity* and *justification* of the new philosophy must therefore be derived mainly from a *critique of Hegel's.*

20

According to its historical point of departure, the new philosophy has *the same* task and position in relation to the *hitherto existing philosophy* as *the latter* had in relation to theology. The new philosophy is the *realization* of the Hegelian philosophy or of all preceding philosophy, but a realization which is simultaneously the *negation,* and indeed the negation *without contradiction* of this philosophy.

21

The *contradiction* of the modern philosophy, especially of pantheism, consists of the fact that it is the *negation of theology from the standpoint of theology* or *the* negation of theology which itself is *again theology;* this contradiction *especially characterizes the Hegelian philosophy.*

For modern philosophy, and hence also for Hegel, the non-material being or being as a pure object of the intellect, as a pure being of the intellect, is the only true and Absolute Being, that is, God. Even matter, which Spinoza turns into an attribute of the divine substance, is a metaphysical thing, a pure being of the intellect, for the essential determination of matter as distinguished from the intellect and the activity of thinking—that it is a passive being—is taken away from it. But Hegel differs from earlier philosophy by the fact that he determines the relationship of the material sensuous being to the non-material being differently. The earlier philosophers and theologians held the true divine being to be detached and liberated from nature; that is, from sensuousness or matter. They situated the toil of abstraction and self-liberation from the sensuous *in themselves* in order to arrive at that which *in itself is free* from the sensuous. To this condition of *being free,* they ascribed the blissfulness of the divine, and to this self-liberation, the virtue of the human essence. Hegel, on the other hand, turned this subjective activity into the *self-activity* of the Divine Being. Even God must subject himself to this toil, and must, like pagan heroes, win his divinity through virtue. Only in this way does the freedom of the Absolute from matter, which is, besides, only a precondition and a conception, become reality and truth. This self-liberation from matter, however, can be posited in God only if matter, too, is posited in him. But how can it be posited in him? Only in this way that he himself posits it. But in God there is only God. Hence, the only way to do this is that he posits *himself* as matter, as non-God; that is, as his otherness. In this way, matter is not an antithesis of the ego and the spirit, preceding them, as it were, in an incomprehensible way; it is the *self-alienation* of the Spirit. Thus, matter itself acquires spirit and intellect; it is taken over into the absolute essence as a moment in its life, formation, and development. But then, matter is again posited as an *untrue* being resembling nothingness in so far as only the being that restores itself out of this alienation, that is, that sheds matter and sensuousness off from itself, is pronounced to be the perfect being in its true form. The natural, material, and sensuous—and indeed, the sensuous, not in the vulgar and moral, but in the metaphysical sense—are therefore even here *something to be negated,* like nature which in theology has been poisoned by the original sin. Indeed, the sensuous is incorporated into reason, the ego, and the spirit, but it is something irrational, a note of discord within reason; it is *the non-ego* in the *ego,* that is, that which *negates* it. For example in Schelling nature in God is the non-divine in God; it is in God and yet outside him; the same is true of the body in the philosophy of Descartes which, although connected with me, that is, with the spirit, is nevertheless external, and does not belong to me, that is, to my essence; it is of no consequence, therefore, whether it is or is not connected with me. Matter will remain *in contradiction* to what is presupposed by philosophy as the true being.

Matter is indeed posited in God, that is, posited as God, and to posit matter as God is as much as saying, "There is no God," or as much as abolishing theology and recog-

nizing the truth of materialism. But the fact remains that
the truth of theology is at the same time taken for granted.
Atheism, the negation of theology, is therefore negated
again; this means that theology is restored through philosophy. God is *God* only through the fact that he overcomes and negates matter; that is, the negation of God.
And according to Hegel, it is only the negation of the negation that constitutes the true positing. And so in the
end, we are back to whence we had started—in the lap of
Christian theology. Thus, already in the most central principle of Hegel's philosophy we come across the principle
and conclusion of his philosophy of religion to the effect
that philosophy, far from abolishing the dogmas of theology, only restores and mediates them through the negation of rationalism. The secret of Hegel's dialectic lies
ultimately in this alone, that it negates theology through
philosophy in order then to negate philosophy through
theology. Both the beginning and the end are constituted
by theology; philosophy stands in the middle as the negation of the first positedness, but the negation of the negation is again theology. At first everything is overthrown,
but then everything is reinstated in its old place, as in
Descartes. The Hegelian philosophy is the last grand attempt to restore a lost and defunct Christianity through
philosophy, and, of course, as is characteristic of the modern era, by *identifying* the *negation* of Christianity *with
Christianity itself*. The much-extolled speculative identity
of spirit and matter, of the infinite and the finite, of the
divine and the human is nothing more than the wretched
contradiction of the modern era having reached its zenith
in metaphysics. It is the identity of belief and unbelief,
theology and philosophy, religion and atheism, Christianity
and paganism. This contradiction escapes the eye and is
obfuscated in Hegel only through the fact that the negation of God, or atheism, is turned by him into an objective determination of God; God is determined as a *process,* and atheism as a moment within this process. But a
belief that has been reconstructed out of unbelief is as little true belief—because it is always afflicted with its antith-

esis—as the God who has been reconstructed out of his
negation is a true God; he is rather a self-contradictory,
an atheistic God.

22

Just as the Divine Being is nothing other than the being
of man freed from the limits of nature, so is the essence of
absolute idealism nothing other than *the essence of subjective idealism freed from the limits, and, indeed, rational
limits of subjectivity,* that is, from *sensuousness or objectivity* as such. The Hegelian philosophy can therefore be
directly derived from the Kantian and Fichtean idealism.

Kant says: "If we regard, as is reasonable, the objects
of the senses as *mere phenomena,* then we thereby concede at the same time that underlying them there is a
thing in itself, even if we do not know its nature excepting
its phenomenal form; that is, the way our senses are effected by this unknown something. Hence, by virtue of the
fact that it is susceptible to the phenomena, the intellect
concedes at the same time the existence *of the things in
themselves,* and to that extent we can say that the idea of
such entities which underlie the phenomena, that is, the
idea of *pure intellectual entities,* is not only permissible
but also *inevitable.*" The objects of the senses, of experience, are for the intellect, therefore, *mere phenomena
and not the truth;* they do not satisfy the intellect, or in
other words, they *do not correspond to its essence.* Consequently, the intellect is not at all limited in its essence by
sensuousness; otherwise, it would take the sensuous things
not to be phenomena but the naked truth. What does not
satisfy me also does not limit and restrict me. Yet the beings of the intellect should not be real objects for the intellect! The Kantian philosophy is the contradiction of
subject and *object, essence* and *existence, thinking* and
being. In it, essence falls into the sphere of the intellect
and existence into that of the senses. *Existence without
essence is mere appearance*—these are sensuous things;
essence without existence is mere thought—these are entities of the intellect and noumena; they are thought of but

they lack existence—at least for us—and objectivity; they
are things in themselves, the *true* things; only they are not
real things, and consequently not objects for the intellect,
that is, they can neither be determined nor known by the
intellect. But what a contradiction to separate the truth
from reality and reality from the truth! If we therefore
eliminate this contradiction, we have the philosophy of
identity in which the *objects of the intellect,* that is, the
objects that are true because they are thought are also the
real objects, in which the essence and constitution of the
objects of the intellect correspond to the essence and constitution of the intellect or of the subject, and where the
subject is no longer limited and conditioned by something
existing apart from it and contradicting its essence. But
the subject which has nothing more outside itself and consequently no more limits within itself, is no longer a "finite" subject—no longer *the* ego to which an object is counterposed; it is the Absolute Being whose theological or
popular expression is the word "God." Although it is the
same subject and the same ego as in subjective idealism, it
is nevertheless *without limits—the ego* which therefore no
longer seems to be an ego, that is, a subjective being, and
for that reason is no longer *called* ego.

23

The Hegelian philosophy is *inverted,* that is, *theological,*
idealism, just as the *Spinozist* philosophy is *theological
materialism.* It posited the *essence* of the ego *outside* the
ego, that is, in separation from it, and it objectified the
ego as substance, as God. But in so doing, it expressed—
indirectly and in a *reverse* order—*the divinity of the ego,*
thus making it, as Spinoza makes matter, into an attribute
or form of the divine substance, meaning that *man's consciousness of God* is God's own self-consciousness. That
means that the being belongs to God and knowing to man.
But the being of God, according to Hegel, is actually nothing other than the being of thought, or thought *abstracted
from the ego, that is, the thinker.* The Hegelian philosophy
has turned thought, that is, the *subjective being*—this, how-

ever, conceived without subject, that is, conceived as a being *different* from it—into the *Divine* and *Absolute* Being.

The secret of "absolute" philosophy is therefore the secret of theology. Just as theology turns the determinations of man into those of God in that it robs these determinations of the specificity through which they are what they are, so, too, does the absolute philosophy. "To think rationally is to be expected of anybody; in order to think of reason as *absolute,* that is, in order to arrive at the standpoint which I demand, it is necessary to *abstract from thought.* For him, who makes this *abstraction,* reason immediately ceases to be something *subjective,* as it is taken to be by most people; indeed, it itself can no longer be thought of as *something objective,* because *something objective* or *something conceived* is possible *only in opposition* to something that thinks, a *complete abstraction* from that which is the case here; thus, through this *abstraction,* reason becomes the true *in-itself* which is situated just at the point where there is no difference between the subjective and the objective." Thus Schelling. But the same applies to Hegel as well, the essence of whose *Logic* is thought denuded of its determinateness through which it is thought or the activity of subjectivity. The third part of the *Logic* is, and it is even expressly called, the *Subjective Logic,* and yet the forms of subjectivity which constitute its object *are not supposed to be subjective.* The concept, the judgment, the conclusion, indeed even the individual forms of conclusion and judgment such as the problematic or assertive judgment, are not our concepts, judgments, and conclusions; no, they are objective forms existing absolutely and in and for themselves. This is how Absolute Philosophy externalizes and alienates from man his own being and his own activity! Hence, the violence and torture that it inflicts on our mind. We are required not to think as our own that which is our own; we are called upon to abstract from the determinateness through which something is what it is, that is, we are supposed to think of it *without sense* and take it in the *non-sense* of

the absolute. *Non-sense* is the highest essence of theology
—of ordinary as well as of speculative theology.

Hegel's disapprobative remark about the philosophy of
Fichte to the effect that everyone believes to have the
ego in himself, that everyone is reminded of himself and
yet does not find the ego in himself is true of speculative
philosophy in general. It takes almost everything in a sense
in which it is no longer recognizable to anyone. And the
source of this evil is, of course, theology. The Divine and
Absolute Being must distinguish itself from finite, that is,
real being. But we have no determinations for the Absolute except the determinations of real things, be they
natural or human things. How do these determinations
become the determinations of the absolute? Only in a way
in which they are taken not in their real sense, but in another, that is, a completely opposite, sense. Everything
that exists within the finite, exists also in the Absolute; but
the way it exists within the finite is *completely different*
from the way it exists in the Absolute, where altogether
different laws operate than those among us; what is pure
non-sense with us is reason and wisdom there. Hence, the
boundless arbitrariness of speculation when it uses the
name of a thing, without at the same time recognizing the
concept which is linked with it. Speculation excuses this
arbitrariness by claiming that the names it chooses from
the language to serve as its own concepts are only re-
motely similar to them because "ordinary consciousness"
connects them with its own ideas; thus, it shifts the blame
to the language. But the fault lies in the matter, in the
principle of speculation itself. The contradiction that exists
between the idea and the concept of speculation, between
its name and its subject-matter, is nothing other than the
old theological contradiction between the determinations
of the divine and the human being; when applied to man,
these determinations are taken in a proper and real sense,
but when applied to God, they are taken only in a sym-
bolical or analogical sense. Of course, philosophy need not
bother about the ideas which vulgar usage or misuse as-

sociates with a name; but it must bind itself to the determined nature of things whose signs names are.

24

The identity of thinking and being which is the *central point* in the *philosophy of identity* is nothing other than a *necessary consequence* and *unfolding* of the *concept of God* as the being whose concept or essence contains existence. Speculative philosophy has only *generalized* and made into an attribute of thought or of the *concept in general* what theology made into an *exclusive attribute of the concept of God*. The identity of thinking and being is therefore only an expression for the *divinity of reason*— the expression thereof that thought or *reason* is the absolute being or the *comprehensive unity of all truth* and reality, that there is *no antithesis* of reason, that rather reason is everything just as, in strict theology, God is everything; that is, all that essentially and truly is. But a being that is *not distinguished* from thought, that is, a being that is only a *predicate* or determination of reason, or only a *conceived* and *abstract* being, is, in truth, *no* being at all. The identity of thinking and being expresses, therefore, only the *identity* of *thought with itself.* This means that absolute thought is *unable to cleave itself from itself, that it cannot step out of itself to be able to reach being.* Being remains something of the Beyond. Absolute philosophy has, to be sure, turned *the other world of theology* into *the world of here and now* for us, but for that matter it has turned *the this-sidedness of the real world* into an over-beyond.

The thought of speculative or absolute philosophy determines being distinct *from itself* as the activity of mediation, *as that which is immediate, as that which is unmediated. For thought*—at least for the thought which we are discussing—being is nothing more than this.

Thought posits being as counterposed to itself, but still *within itself;* it thereby immediately and without difficulty eliminates the opposition between being and itself; for being, as the antithesis of thought *within thought,* is nothing itself but thought. If being is nothing more than that which is unmediated, if unmediatedness alone constitutes its distinction from thought, how easy it is then to demonstrate that the determination of unmediatedness, namely, being, belongs to thought as well! If the essence of being is constituted by what is merely a *determination of thought,* how should being be distinguished from thought?

25

The proof that something *is* has no other meaning than that it is *not just something thought.* This proof *cannot,* however, be derived *from thought itself.* Should *being* accrue to an object of thought, it must accrue to thought itself.

Kant's example of the difference between a hundred dollars in the imagination and a hundred dollars in reality, which he employs for the purpose of designating the difference between thought and being—Hegel derides it—while dwelling on his critique of the ontological proof, is essentially quite correct. For the dollars of the imagination I have only in my *head,* whereas the dollars of reality I have in my *hand;* the former exist only *for me,* but the latter also *for others;* they can be felt and seen. Only that which exists at the same time for me and others, whereon I and others agree, which is not merely mine, but is also *common to all, really* exists.

In thought as such I find myself in identity with myself; and I am absolute master; nothing here contradicts me; here I am judge and litigant at the same time, and consequently, here there is no critical difference between the object and my thoughts about it. But if it is a question exclusively of the *being* of an object, then I cannot look only to myself for advice, but rather must hear witnesses *other than myself.* These witnesses that are distinguished from me as a thinking being are the senses. Being is something in which not only I but also others, and above all the *object* itself, *participate. Being* means *being a subject, being for itself.* And indeed, it is far from being the same thing whether I am a subject or only an object, whether I am a being for myself or only a being for another being; that is, only a thought. Where I am a mere object of imagination and hence no longer myself, where I am like a man after death, there I have to take everything lying down; there anyone can turn a portrait of mine into a true caricature without my being able to protest against it. But if I still exist, then I can put a spoke in his wheel, then I can make him feel and prove to him that between what I am in his idea of me and what I am in reality; that is, that there is a world of difference between what I am as an object for him and what I am as a subject. In thought, I am an absolute subject; I let everything exist only as my object or predicate; that is, as object or predicate of myself as a thinking being. I am intolerant. In relation to the activity of my senses, I am, on the other hand, a liberal; I let the object be what I myself am—a subject, a *real* and *self-activating* being. Only sense and only sense perception give me something as *subject*.

26

A being that *only* thinks and *thinks abstractly, has no idea at all of what being, existence,* and *reality* are. *Thought is bounded by being; being qua being is not an object of philosophy, at least not of abstract and absolute philosophy.* Speculative philosophy *itself expresses this* indirectly in so far as it *equates being with non-being, that is, nothing.* But nothing *cannot be an object of thought.*

Being *in the sense in which it is an object of speculative thought* is that which is purely and simply unmediated, that is, undetermined; in other words, there is *nothing to distinguish and nothing to think of in being.* In its own estimation, however, speculative thought is the measure of all reality; it declares as something only that wherein it finds itself active and which provides it with its material. Consequently, being in and for itself is nothing for abstract thought because it is nothing in relation to thought; that is nothing for thought. It is *devoid of thought.* Precisely because of this, being, as drawn by speculative philosophy into its sphere and vindicated as a concept, is a pure specter that stands in absolute contradiction to real being and to what man understands by being. For what man understands *by being*—aptly and according to reason— is *existence, being-for-itself, reality, actuality*, and *objectivity*. All these determinations or names express one and the same thing, but from different points of view. Being in thought, being *without* objectivity, *without* reality, *without* being for itself, is of course nothing; *in terms of this nothing, however, I only express the nothingness of my own abstraction.*

27

Being in *Hegel's Logic* is the *being of the old metaphysics* which is predicated of all things *without distinction* because of its underlying assumption that *all things agree in that they are*. But this *undifferentiated being* is only an *abstract idea* or an *idea without reality*. *Being is as differentiated as things themselves.*

For example, a metaphysical theory from the school of Wolff maintains that God, world, man, table, book, and so forth agree with one another in that they are. And Christian Thomasius says: "Being is everywhere the same; only essence is as manifold as things." This being which is everywhere the same, this undifferentiated and contentless being, is also the being of Hegel's *Logic*. Hegel himself observes that the polemic against the identity of being and nothing arises only out of the fact that a definite content is subsumed under being. But precisely the consciousness of being is always and necessarily linked with *definite* contents. If I abstract from the *content* of being and indeed from all content—for whatever is, is a content of being—then naturally I am left with nothing more than the idea of nothing. And hence, when Hegel reproaches vulgar consciousness for subsuming under being something that does not belong to being, that is, to being as the object of *Logic*, then it is rather he himself who must be reproached for subsuming a groundless abstraction under what man's consciousness justifiably and in keeping with the dictates of reason understands by being. Being is *not a general concept that can be separated from things. It is one with that which is.* It is thinkable only as mediated, that is, only through the predicates which constitute the essence of a thing. Being is wherein essence posits itself. *That which is my essence is my being.* The being of the fish is its being in water, and from this being you cannot separate its essence. Language already identifies being and essence. Only in human life does it happen, but even here only in abnormal and unfortunate cases, that being is separated from essence; only here does it happen that a man's essence is not where his being is, but also that because of this separation a man is not truly with his soul where he really is with his body. *You are* only *where* your heart is. But all beings, excepting cases contrary to nature, are glad to be where and what they are; this means that their essence is not separated from their being and their being is not separated from their essence. Consequently, you cannot postulate being as simply self-identical, distinct from essence that varies. The notion of being *resulting from a removal of* all *essential qualities* from things is only *your notion* of being—a fabricated, invented being, a being *without the essence* of Being.

28

The *Hegelian philosophy has remained unable to overcome the contradiction of thought and being.* The *Being with which the Phenomenology* begins stands no less than *the Being with which the Logic begins in the most direct contradiction to real being.*

This contradiction manifests itself in the *Phenomenology* in the form of the "this" and the "general"; for the particular belongs to being, but the general to thought. Now, in the *Phenomenology,* one kind of "this" flows into another kind of "this" in a way indistinguishable for thought. But what an enormous difference there is between a "this" that is the object of abstract thought and a "this" that is the object of reality! *This wife, for example, is my wife,* and *this* house is *my* house, although every one speaks, as I do, of his house and his wife, as this house and this wife. The indifference and indistinguish-

ability of the logical "this" is here interrupted and annulled by our sense for the right. Were we to accept the
logical "this" in natural law, we would immediately arrive at a community of goods and wives where there is no
difference between this one and that one and where every
man possesses every woman; we would then come upon a
situation where all right has been abolished, for right is
grounded only on the reality of the distinction between this
and that.

We have before us in the beginning of the *Phenomenology* nothing but the contradiction between the *word,*
which is general, and the object, which is always particular. And the thought, which depends only on the word,
will remain unable to overcome this contradiction. But
being that is *spoken* or *thought* is just as far from being
real being as the word is from being the object. Were one
to reply that being in Hegel is treated not from the practical, as here, but from the theoretical standpoint, then it
must be reciprocated that the practical standpoint is precisely what is needed here. *The question of being is indeed
a practical question;* it is a question in which our being
participates—a question of life and death. And if we stick
to our being when it comes to law, then we will also not
want the *Logic* to take it away from us. Even the *Logic*
must recognize our being, unless it would rather per-
sist in its contradiction with real being. Besides, the practical standpoint—the standpoint of eating and drinking—is
adopted even by the *Phenomenology* in refuting the truth
of sensuous, that is, particular, being. But here, too, I owe
my existence by no means to the verbal or the logical bread
—to the bread in itself—but always only to *this* bread, the
"non-verbal." Being, grounded as it is altogether on such
non-verbalities, is therefore itself something non-verbal.
Indeed, it is that which cannot be verbalized. Where
words cease, life begins and being reveals its secret. If,
therefore, non-verbality is the same as irrationality, then
all existence is irrational because it is always and forever
only *this* existence. But irrational it is not. Existence has
meaning and reason in itself, without being verbalized.

29

Thought that *"seeks to reach beyond its other"*—and the "other of thought" is being—is *thought that oversteps its natural boundaries.* This reaching beyond its other on the part of thought means that it *claims for itself that which does not properly belong to thought but to being.* That which belongs to *being* is *particularity* and *individuality,* whereas that which belongs to *thought* is *generality.* Thought thus lays claim to particularity; it makes the negation of generality, that is, *particularity,* which is the essential form of sensuousness, *into a moment of thought.* In this way, "abstract" thought or abstract concept, which has being *outside itself,* becomes a "concrete" concept.

But how does it come about that man encroaches upon that which is the property of being? Through theology. In God, being is immediately connected with essence or the concept; particularity, or the form of existence, with generality. *The "concrete concept" is God transformed into concept.* But how does man arrive from "abstract" to "concrete" or absolute thought; how from philosophy to theology? The answer to this question has already been provided by history in the transition from ancient pagan philosophy to the so-called *neo-Platonic* philosophy; for neo-Platonic philosophy differs from ancient philosophy only in that the former is theology, whereas the latter is philosophy. Ancient philosophy had reason, the "idea" for its constitutive principle; but "the idea was not posited by Plato and Aristotle as the all-containing." Ancient philosophy left something existing outside thought—a residue, as it were, that could not be dissolved in thought. The image of this being existing outside thought is *matter*—the substratum of reality. Reason came up against its own *limit* in matter. Ancient philosophy still moved within the distinction between thought and being; for it, thought, mind, or the idea was not yet the *all-encompassing; that is, the only, exclusive, and absolute reality.* The ancient philosophers were men *whose wisdom still had reference to the world;* they were physiologists, politicians, zoologists;

they were, in short, *anthropologists,* not theologians, or at
least only partly theologians. Precisely for that reason, of
course, they could not but be partial; that is, limited and
defective anthropologists. To the neo-Platonists, on the
other hand, matter or the real material world in general
is no longer binding and real. Fatherland, family, worldly
ties, and goods in general, which the ancient Peripatetic
philosophy still regarded as belonging to man's happiness
—all this is nothing for the neo-Platonic sage. To him,
death is even better than corporeal life; he holds the body
as not belonging to his essence; he translocates blissfulness exclusively in the soul while he detaches himself completely from all corporeal, in short, external things. But
where man has nothing left outside himself, there he seeks
and finds *everything within himself;* there he puts the
imaginary and intelligible world in place of the real world
so that the former contains everything that is there in the
latter, but only in an *abstract* and *imagined* way. Even
matter is to be found in the immaterial world of the neo-
Platonists, but only as something ideated, conceived, and
imaginary. And where man has no longer a being that is
given outside himself, there he sets up a being in his
thought, which, although *an ideated entity,* has nevertheless the *qualities of a real entity,* which *as a non-sensuous
entity is at the same time a sensuous being,* and which *as
a theoretical* object is at the same time a *practical* object.
This being is *God*—the highest good of the neo-Platonists.
Only in *being* does man feel satisfied. He therefore overcomes the lack of a real being by substituting an ideated
being for it, that is, he now ascribes the essence of the
relinquished or lost reality to his conceptions and thoughts;
his conception is *no longer* a conception, but the *object*
itself; the image is *no longer* an image but the thing itself;
reality is now idea and thought. Precisely because he no
longer relates himself as a subject to a real world as his
object, *his conceptions* become for him *objects, beings,
spirits,* and *gods.* The more abstract he is, and the more
negative his attitude is toward the real and the sensuous,
the more *sensuous* he is *in his abstractions.* God, the One,

the highest object and being arrived at by abstracting from all plurality and diversity, that is, from all sensuousness, is known by contact and direct presence (παρουσία). Indeed, what is the highest, the One, is known equally through *non-cognition* and *ignorance* like that which is the lowest—matter. This means that being that is only ideated and abstract, that is, only *non*-sensuous and *super*-sensuous, is at the same time a *sensuous* and really existing being.

Just as by decorporealizing himself or by negating the *body*—the *rational limit* of subjectivity—man lapses into a fantastic and transcendent practice, surrounding himself with *corporealized* appearances of spirits and gods; that is, *practically* eliminating the distinction between imagination and sense perception. So also does the *difference between thought and being, subjective and objective, sensuous and non-sensuous, theoretically* disappear when *matter* has no *reality* for him and is *consequently not a boundary* limiting the thinking reason; that is, when reason—the intellectual being, or *the essence of subjectivity in general*—is *in its boundlessness the sole and absolute being* for him. Thought negates everything, but only in order to posit everything in itself. It *no longer has a boundary in anything that exists outside* itself, but precisely thereby it itself steps *out of its immanent* and *natural limits*. In this way reason, the idea, becomes *concrete;* this means that *what should flow from sense perception is made the property of thought* and *what is the function and concern of the senses, of sensibility and of life,* becomes the function and concern of *thought.* This is how the *concrete* is turned into a *predicate* of thought, and being into a mere *determination of thought;* for the proposition *"the concept is concrete"* is *identical with the proposition "being is a determination of thought."* What is imagination and fantasy with the neo-Platonists, Hegel has merely transformed into the concept, or in other words, rationalized. Hegel is not the "German or Christian Aristotle"; he is the German *Proclus. "Absolute philosophy"* is the *reborn Alexandrian philosophy.* According to Hegel's explicit characterization, it is not the Aristotelian nor the ancient pagan philosophy in general, but that of the Alexandrian school that is absolute (although still resting on abstraction from concrete self-consciousness) and Christian philosophy (albeit mixed with pagan ingredients).

It should be further remarked that neo-Platonic theology shows particularly clearly that an object corresponds to its subject and vice versa; that consequently the object of theology is nothing other than the objectified essence of the subject; that is, of man. To the neo-Platonists, God at his highest is the simple, the one, the simple indeterminable and uniform; he is not a being, but rather above being, for being is still something determined due to the fact that it is being; he is not a concept, nor is he intellect, but rather without and above the intellect, for the intellect, too, is something determined by virtue of being intellect; and where there is intellect, there is also distinction and dichotomization into the thinker and the thought, an activity that cannot take place in that which is absolutely simple. But that which is objectively the highest being for the neo-Platonist, is also subjectively the highest being for him; that which he posits as being in the object, in God, he posits in himself as activity and striving. Having ceased to be distinction, having ceased to be intellect and self, is and means being God. But what God *is,* is precisely what the neo-Platonist strives to *become;* the goal of his activity is to cease "being self, intellect, and reason." Ecstasy or rapture is the highest psychological state that, according to the neo-Platonist, man can achieve. This state, objectified as being, is the Divine Being. Thus, God results from man, but conversely, man does not result from God, at least not originally. This is also shown particularly clearly in the neo-Platonists' characterization of God as the being who does not stand in need of anything—the blissful being. For in what else has this being without pain and without needs its ground and origin if not in the pain and needs of man? The idea and feeling of blissfulness disappear with the affliction of need and pain. Only contrasted to wretchedness does blissfulness have any reality.

Only in the misery of man lies the birthplace of God.
Only from man does God derive all his determinations;
God *is* what man *desires* to be; namely, his own essence
and goal imagined as an actual being. Herein, too, lies the
distinguishing factor separating the neo-Platonists from
the Stoics, the Epicureans, and the Skeptics. Existence
without passion, bliss, independence from need, freedom,
and autonomy were also the goals of these philosophers,
but only as virtues of man; this means that these goals
were based on the *truth of the concrete and real man.*
Freedom and bliss were supposed to belong to this subject
as its predicates. Hence, with the neo-Platonists—although
they still regarded pagan virtues as true—these predicates
became subject; that is, human adjectives were turned into
something substantial, into an actually existing being—
hence the distinction between the neo-Platonist and Christian theology which transferred man's bliss, perfection, or
likeness to God into the beyond. Precisely through this,
real man became a mere abstraction lacking flesh and
blood, an allegorical figure of the divine being. Plotinus,
at least on the evidence of his biographers, was ashamed
to have a body.

30

The understanding that only the *concrete* concept, that
is, *the* concept that contains within itself the nature of the
real, is the *true* concept, expresses the recognition of the
truth of that which is concrete and real. But because from
the very outset the concept, that is, *the essence of thought,
is also presupposed as the absolute and as the only true
essence,* the real can be recognized only indirectly—only
as the necessary and essential adjective of the concept.
Hegel is a *realist,* but a *purely idealistic* realist, or rather
an abstract realist; namely, a realist abstracting from all
reality. He *negates* thought—that is, abstract thought—but
he does so *while remaining within abstractive thought*
with the result that his negation of abstraction still remains
abstraction. Only "that which is" is the object of philosophy according to Hegel; however, this "is" is again

only something *abstract,* only something *conceived.* Hegel
is a thinker who *surpasses* himself in thought. His aim is
to capture the thing itself, but only in the *thought* of the
thing; he wants to be *outside* of thought, but still remaining *within thought*—hence the difficulty in grasping the
concrete concept.

31

The recognition of the *light of reality* within the *darkness of abstraction* is a *contradiction*—both the affirmation
and the negation of the real at one and the same time. The
new philosophy, which thinks the *concrete not* in an abstract but a concrete way, which acknowledges the real
in its reality—that is, in a way corresponding to the being
of the real as true, which elevates it into the *principle*
and *object* of philosophy—is consequently the *truth* of the
Hegelian philosophy, indeed of *modern philosophy as a
whole.*

To look at it more closely, the historical necessity, or
the genesis of the new philosophy from the old, results as
follows. According to Hegel, the concrete concept, the
idea, exists at first only in an abstract way, only in the
element of thought—the rationalized God of theology *before the creation of the world.* But the manner in which
God expresses, manifests, and realizes himself, the manner in which he becomes worldly, is the same as that in
which the idea realizes itself: Hegel's philosophy is the
history of theology transformed into a logical process. But
if the realization of the idea takes us into the realm of
realism, if the *truth* of the idea is that it *really* is, that it
exists, then we have indeed raised *existence* into the *criterion of truth: True* is what *really* exists. The only question then is: What really exists? Is it alone that which is
thought? That which is the object of thought and intellect? But we shall never in this way get beyond the idea
in abstracto. The Platonic idea, too, is the object of
thought; the heavenly hereafter, too, is an inner object—
the object of belief and imagination. If the reality of
thought is reality *as thought,* it is itself only thought, and

we are forever imprisoned in the *identity of thought with itself,* in idealism—an idealism that differs from subjective idealism only in so far as it encompasses the whole of reality, subsuming it under the predicates of thought. Hence, should the reality of thought be a matter of *real seriousness* to us, something other than thought must accrue to it: It must, as *realized thought,* be *other* than what it is as *unrealized, pure thought*—the object not only of thought, but also of *non*-thought. That thought realizes itself means simply that it *negates* itself, ceases to be mere thought. Now what is this non-thought, this something different from thought? It is the sensuous. That thought realizes itself means, accordingly, that it makes itself the *object of the senses.* Thus, the reality of the Idea is *sensuousness;* but reality is also the *truth* of the Idea—hence sensuousness is the truth of the Idea. But in this way we have at the same time made sensuousness the predicate, and the Idea or thought, the subject. The only question is, why does the Idea take on sensuousness? Why does it *cease* to be *true* when it is *not real or sensuous?* Is not its truth thus made dependent on sensuousness? Are not significance and value thus being conceded to the sensuous as such; that is, apart from its being the reality of the Idea? If taken by itself, sensuousness is nothing, why is it needed by the Idea? If value and content are bestowed upon sensuousness by the Idea, sensuousness is pure luxury and trumpery—only an illusion which thought practices upon itself. But it is not so. The demand that the Idea realize itself, that it assume sensuousness arises from the fact that sensuous reality is *unconsciously held to be the truth which is both prior to and independent of thought.* Thought proves its truth by taking recourse to sensuousness; how could this be possible if sensuousness was not *unconsciously* held to be the truth? But since one *consciously* proceeds from the truth of thought, the truth of sensuousness is acknowledged only in retrospect whereby sensuousness is reduced merely to an attribute of the Idea. But this is a contradiction; for sensuousness is an attribute and yet it lends truth to thought; that is, it is both essential and inessential, both substance and accident. The only way out of this contradiction is to regard sensuous reality as *its own subject;* to give it an absolutely independent, divine, and primary significance, not one derived from the Idea.

32

Taken in its reality or regarded as *real,* the real is the object of the senses—the *sensuous.* Truth, reality, and sensuousness are one and the same thing. Only a sensuous being is a *true* and *real* being. Only through the senses is an object given *in the true sense,* not through thought *for itself.* The object given by and identical with ideation is merely thought.

An object, i.e., a real object, is given to me only if a being is given to me in a way that it affects me, only if my own activity—when I proceed from the standpoint of thought—experiences the activity of another being as a *limit* or boundary to itself. The concept of the object is originally nothing else but the concept of another *I*—everything appears to man in childhood as a freely and arbitrarily acting being—which means that in principle the concept of the *object* is mediated through the concept of You, the *objective ego.* To use the language of Fichte, an object or an alter ego is given not to the ego, but to the non-ego in me; for only where I am transformed from an ego into a You—that is, where I am passive—does the idea of an activity *existing outside myself,* the idea of objectivity, really originate. But it is only through the senses that the ego is also non-ego.

A question characteristic of earlier abstract philosophy is the following: How can different independent entities or substances act upon one another, for example, the body upon the soul or ego? In so far as this question was an abstraction from sensuousness, in so far as the supposedly interacting substances were abstract entities, purely intellectual creatures, philosophy was unable to resolve it. The mystery of their interaction can be solved only by sensuousness. Only sensuous beings act upon one another.

I am I—for myself—and at the same time You—for others. But I am You only in so far as I am a sensuous being. But the abstract intellect isolates being-for-self as substance, ego, or God; it can, therefore, only arbitrarily connect being-for-others with being-for-self, for the necessity for this connection is sensuousness alone. But then it is precisely sensuousness from which the abstract intellect abstracts. What I think in isolation from sensuousness is what I think without and outside all connections. Hence the question: How can I think the unconnected to be at the same time connected?

33

The new philosophy looks upon *being*—being as given to us not only as thinking, but also as really existing being —*as the object of being*, as *its own* object. Being as the object of being—and *this* alone is truly, and deserves the name of, being—is sensuous being; that is, the being involved in sense perception, feeling, and love. Or in other words, being is a *secret* underlying sense perception, feeling, and love.

Only in feeling and love has the demonstrative *this*— this person, this thing, that is, the particular—absolute value; only then is the *finite infinite:* In this and this alone does the infinite depth, divinity, and truth of love consist. In love alone resides the truth and reality of the God who counts the hairs on your head. The Christian God himself is only an abstraction from human love and an image of it. And since the demonstrative *this* owes its absolute value to love alone, it is only in love—not in abstract thought— that the secret of being is revealed. Love is passion, and passion alone is the distinctive mark of existence. Only that which is an object of passion, exists—whether as reality or possibility. Abstract thought, which is devoid of feeling and passion, abolishes *the distinction between being and non-being;* non-existent for thought, this distinction is a reality for love. To love is nothing else than to become aware of this distinction. It is a matter of complete indifference to someone who loves nothing whether something

exists or not, and be that what it may. But just as being as
distinguished from non-being is given to me through love
or feeling in general, so is everything else that is other
than me given to me through love. Pain is a loud protest
against identifying the subjective with the objective. The
pain of love means that what is in the mind is not given
in reality, or in other words, the subjective is here the objective, the concept itself the object. But this is precisely
what ought not to be, what is a contradiction, an untruth,
a misfortune—hence, the desire for that true state of affairs in which the subjective and the objective are not
identical. Even physical pain clearly expresses this distinction. The pain of hunger means that there is nothing objective inside the stomach, that the stomach is, so to speak,
its own object, that its empty walls grind against each other
instead of grinding some content. Human feelings have,
therefore, no empirical or anthropological significance in
the sense of the old transcendental philosophy; they have,
rather, an ontological and metaphysical significance: Feelings, everyday feelings, contain the deepest and highest
truths. Thus, for example, love is the true *ontological* demonstration of the existence of objects apart from our head:
There is no other proof of being except love or feeling in
general. Only that whose *being brings you joy* and whose
not-being, pain, has existence. The difference between subject and object, being and non-being is as *happy* a difference as it is *painful.*

34

The new philosophy bases itself on the *truth of love,* on
the *truth of feeling.* In love, in feeling in general, *every
human being confesses to the truth of the new philosophy.*
As far as its basis is concerned, the new philosophy is
nothing but *the essence of feeling raised to consciousness*
—it only *affirms in the form and through the medium of
reason what every man*—every *real* man—*admits in his
heart.* It is the heart made aware of itself as reason. The
heart demands *real* and *sensuous objects, real and sensuous beings.*

35

The *old* philosophy maintained that that which *could not be thought of also did not exist;* the *new* philosophy maintains that that which is not loved or *cannot be loved does not exist.* But that which cannot be loved can also not be adored. That which is the *object of religion* can alone be the object of philosophy.

Love is not only objectively but also subjectively the criterion of being, the criterion of truth and reality. *Where there is no love there is also no truth.* And only he who *loves* something *is* also something—*to be nothing* and *to love nothing* is one and the same thing. The more one is, the more one loves, and vice versa.

36

The old philosophy had its point of departure in the proposition: I am an abstract, a merely thinking being to which the body does not belong. The new philosophy proceeds from the principle: I am a real and sensuous *being; indeed, the whole of my body is my ego, my being itself.* The old philosopher, therefore, thought in a *constant contradiction to and conflict with the senses* in order to avoid sensuous conceptions, or in order not to pollute abstract concepts. In contrast, the new philosopher thinks *in peace and harmony with the senses.* The old philosophy conceded the truth of sensuousness *only in a concealed way,* only in terms of the *concept,* only *unconsciously* and *unwillingly,* only because it had to. This is borne out even by its concept of God as the being who encompasses all other beings within himself, for he was held to be distinct from a merely conceived being; that is, he was held to be existing outside the mind, outside thought—a really objective, sensuous being. In contrast, the new philosophy *joyfully* and *consciously* recognizes the truth of sensuousness: It is a *sensuous* philosophy with an *open heart.*

37

The philosophy of the modern era was in search of something *immediately certain*. Hence, it rejected the *baseless* thought of the Scholastics and grounded philosophy on *self-consciousness*. That is, it posited the *thinking* being, the *ego*, the *self-conscious mind* in place of the merely conceived being or in place of God, the highest and ultimate being of all Scholastic philosophy; for a being who thinks is infinitely closer to a thinking being, infinitely more actual and certain than a being who is only conceived. Doubtful is the existence of God, doubtful is in fact anything I could think of; but indubitable is that I am, I who think and doubt. Yet this self-consciousness in modern philosophy is again something that is only conceived, only mediated through abstraction, and hence something that can be doubted. *Indubitable* and *immediately certain* is only that which is *the object of the senses, of perception and feeling.*

38

True and *divine* is only that which *requires no proof*, that which is *certain immediately through itself*, that which *speaks immediately for itself* and carries the affirmation of its being within itself; in short, that which is *purely and simply unquestionable, indubitable, and as clear as the sun.* But only the sensuous is as clear as the sun. When sensuousness begins all doubts and quarrels cease. The secret of *immediate* knowledge is *sensuousness*.

All is mediated, says the Hegelian philosophy. But something is *true* only when it is no longer mediated; that is, when it is immediate. Thus, new historical epochs originate only when something, having so far existed in the mediated form of conception, becomes the object of immediate and sensuous certainty; that is, only when something—erstwhile only thought—becomes a *truth*. To make out of mediation a divine necessity or an essential quality of truth is mere scholasticism. The necessity of mediation is only a *limited* one; it is necessary only where a *wrong presupposition* is involved; where a different truth or doctrine, contradicting an established one which is still held to be valid and respected, arises. A truth that *mediates itself* is a truth that still has its opposite clinging to it. The opposite is taken as the starting point, but is later on discarded. Now, if it is all along something to be discarded or negated, why should I then proceed from it rather than from its negation? Let us illustrate this by an example. God as God is an abstract being; he particularizes, determines, or realizes himself in the world and in man. This is what makes him concrete and hereby is his abstract being negated. But why should I not proceed directly from the concrete? Why, after all, should that which owes its truth and certainty only to itself not stand higher than that whose certainty depends on the nothingness of its opposite? Who would, therefore, give mediation the status of necessity or make a principle of truth out of it? Only he who is still imprisoned in that which is to be negated; only he who is still *in conflict and strife with himself;* only he who has *not yet fully made up his mind* —in short, only he who regards truth as a matter of talent, of a particular, albeit outstanding faculty, but not of genius, not of the whole man. Genius is immediate sensuous knowledge. Talent is merely head, but genius is flesh and blood. That which is only an object of thought for talent is an object of the senses for genius.

39

The old absolute philosophy drove away the senses into the region of appearance and finitude; and yet contradicting itself, it determined the *absolute,* the *divine* as an *object* of *art.* But an object of art is—in a mediated form in the spoken, in an unmediated form in the plastic arts—an object of vision, hearing, and feeling. Not only is the finite and phenomenal being, but also the divine, the true being, an object of the senses—*the senses are the organs of the absolute.* Art "presents the truth by means of the sensuous"—properly understood and expressed, this means that *art presents the truth of the sensuous.*

40

What applies to art, applies to *religion*. The *essence of the Christian religion* is not ideation but *sensuous perception*—the form and *organ of the highest and divine being*. But if sensuous perception is taken to be the *organ of the Divine and True Being*, the *Divine Being is expressed and acknowledged as a sensuous being, just as the sensuous is expressed and acknowledged as the Divine Being; for subject and object correspond to each other*.

"And the word became flesh and dwelt among us, and we *saw* its glory." Only for later generations is the object of the Christian religion an object of conception and fantasy; but this goes together with a restoration of the original sensuous perception. In Heaven, Christ or God is the object of *immediate sensuous* perception; there he turns from an *object of conception and thought*—that is, from a *spiritual being* which he is for us here—into a *sensuous, feelable, visible being*. And—remembering that the goal corresponds to the origin—this is, therefore, the essence of Christianity. Speculative philosophy has, therefore, grasped and presented art and religion not in the true light, not in the light of reality, but only in the twilight of reflection in so far as in keeping with its principle—abstraction from sensuousness—it dissolved sensuousness into the formal determinateness of art and religion: Art is God *in* the formal determinateness of sensuous perception, whereas religion is God *in* that of conception. But that which appears to reflection as a mere form is in truth essence. Where God appears and is worshiped *in* the fire, there it is that fire is in actual truth worshiped as God. God *in* the fire is nothing else than the being of fire which is so striking to men because of its effects and qualities; *God in man* is nothing else than *the being of man*. And, similarly, that which art represents in the form of sensuousness is nothing else than *the very essence of sensuousness that is inseparable from this form*.

41

It is not only "external" things that are objects of the senses. *Man,* too, is *given to himself only through the senses;* only as a sensuous object is he an object for himself. The *identity* of *subject and object*—in self-consciousness only an abstract thought—has the character of *truth* and reality only in *man's sensuous perception of* man.

We feel not only stones and wood, not only flesh and bones, but also feelings when we press the hands or lips of a feeling being; we perceive through our ears not only the murmur of water and the rustle of leaves, but also the soulful voice of love and wisdom; we see not only mirror-like surfaces and specters of color, but we also gaze into the gaze of man. Hence, not only that which is external, but also that which is internal, not only flesh, but also spirit, not only things, but also the *ego* is an object of the senses. All is therefore capable of being perceived through the senses, even if only in a mediated and not immediate way, even if not with the help of crude and vulgar senses, but only through those that are cultivated; even if not with the eyes of the anatomist and the chemist, but only with those of the philosopher. Empiricism is therefore perfectly justified in regarding ideas as originating from the senses; but what it forgets is that the most essential sensuous object for man is *man himself;* that only in man's glimpse of man does the spark of consciousness and intellect spring. And this goes to show that idealism is right in so far as it sees the origin of ideas *in* man; but it is wrong in so far as it derives these ideas from man understood as an isolated being, as mere soul existing for himself; in one word, it is wrong when it derives the ideas from an ego that is not given in the context of its togetherness with a perceptibly given You. Ideas spring only from conversation and communication. Not alone but only within a dual relationship does one have concepts and reason in general. It takes two human beings to give birth to a man, to physical as well as spiritual man; the together-

ness of man with man is the first principle and the criterion of truth and universality. Even the certitude of those
things that exist outside me is given to me through the
certitude of the existence of other men besides myself.
That which is seen by me alone is open to question, but
that which is seen also by another person is certain.

42

The *distinction* between *essence* and *appearance, cause*
and *effect, substance* and *accident, necessity* and *contingency, speculative* and *empirical* does not mean that there
are two different realms or worlds—the supersensuous
world which is essence, and the sensuous world which is
appearance; rather, *this distinction is internal to sensuousness itself.* Let us take an example from the natural sciences. In Linne's system of plants the first groups are determined according to the number of filaments. But in the
eleventh group where twelve to twenty stamens occur—
and more so in the group of twenty stamens and polysta-
mens—the numerical determinations become irrelevant;
counting is of no use any more. Here in one and the same
area we have, therefore, before us the difference between
definite and indefinite, necessary and indifferent, rational
and irrational multiplicity. This means that we *need not go
beyond sensuousness* to arrive, *in the sense of the Absolute Philosophy*, at the *limit of the merely sensuous and
empirical;* all we have to do is *not separate the intellect
from the senses* in order to find the supersensuous—spirit
and reason—*within the sensuous.*

43

The *sensuous* is *not* the *immediate* in the sense of speculative philosophy; i.e., *in the sense* in which it is the *profane*, the *readily obvious*, the *thoughtless*, the *self-evident.*
According to speculative philosophy the immediate sensuous perception comes *later* than conception and fantasy.
Man's *first* conception is itself only a conception based on
imagination and fantasy. The task of philosophy and science consists, therefore, *not* in *turning away* from *sensu-*

ous—i.e., *real* things—but in *turning towards* them—*not* in transforming *objects* into *thoughts* and ideas, but in making *visible*—i.e., *objective*—*what is invisible to common eyes.*

In the beginning men see things *as they appear to them,* not as they are. What they see in things is not they themselves, but their own ideas about them; they transpose their own being into things, and do not distinguish between an object and the idea of it. To the subjective and uncultivated man, imagined reality is *closer* than actually perceived reality, for in perceiving it he is compelled to move out of himself, but in imagining it he *remains inside himself.* And just as it is with imagination, so it is with thought. Initially and for far longer, men occupy themselves with heavenly, with divine things rather than with earthly things; that is, initially and for far longer they occupy themselves with things *translated into thoughts* rather than with *things in the original,* with things in their *own innate* language. Only in the modern era has mankind—as once in Greece after a foregoing era of the oriental dreamworld—found its way back to a *sensuous;* i.e., *unadulterated and objective* perception of the sensuous or the real. But with this, it has also found its way *back to itself,* for a man who occupies himself only with creatures of the imagination and abstract thought is himself only an abstract or fantastic, not a *real,* not a truly human being. The reality of man depends on the reality of his objects. If you *have* nothing, you *are* nothing.

44

Space and *time* are not *mere forms of appearance:* They are *essential conditions, rational forms, and laws of being as well as of thought.* "Here-being" is the being that comes first, the being that is the first to be determined. *Here* I am —that is the first sign of a *real* and *living* being. The index finger shows the way from nothingness to being. Saying *here* is the first boundary, the first demarcation. I am here, you are there; in between there is a distance separating us; this is what makes it possible for both of us to exist without jeopardizing each other; there is enough room. The sun is not where Mercury is, and Mercury is not where Venus is; the eye is not where the ear is, and so on. Where there is no space, there is also no place for *any system*. The *first determination of reason* upon which every other determination rests is to *situate* things. Although space immediately presupposes its differentiation into places, the organizing work of nature begins with a distribution of locations. Only in space does reason orient itself. The first question asked by awakening consciousness, the first question of practical wisdom is: Where am I? The first virtue that we inculcate in the child, the raw material of man, is that of being limited by space and time, and the first difference that we teach it is the difference of place, the difference between what is proper and what is improper. What the distinction of place means is indifferent to the unfinished man; like the fool, he does everything at all places without distinction. Fools, therefore, achieve reason when they recover the sense for time and place. To put different things in different places, to allot different places to things that differ in quality—that is the condition for all economy including even that of the mind. Not to put in the text what belongs to the footnotes, not to put at the beginning what is to be put at the end, in short, spatial differentiation and limitation belong also to the wisdom of the writer.

It is true that we are speaking here of a definite kind of place; but even so the question is nothing else than that of the determination of place. And I cannot separate place from space were I to grasp space in its *reality*. The concept of space arises in me when I ask: Where? This question as to where is universal and applies to every place without distinction; and yet it is particular. As the positing of the particular "where" is simultaneously a positing of the universal "where," so the universality of space is posited with the particularity of place. But precisely for that reason the general concept of space can be a real and concrete concept only if it includes the particularity of place. Hegel attributes to space—as to nature in general—a *negative* determination. Nevertheless, "here-being" is positive. I am *not* there *because* I *am here*—this not-being-there is therefore only a consequence of the positive and emphatic here-being. The separation of here from there is by no means a limit in itself; only your imagination regards it as such. That they are separate is something that *ought to be* the case, something that does not contradict but corresponds to reason. But this separation is a negative determination in Hegel because it is a separation of that which *ought not to be* separate—because the logical concept, understood as absolute self-identity, is what Hegel regards as the truth; space is to him the *negation* of the Idea, of reason, and hence the only means by which reason can be put back into the Idea is to *negate* it (the Idea). But far from being the negation of reason, space is the first sphere of reason, for it is space that makes room for the idea, for reason. Where there are no spatial distinctions, there are also no logical distinctions. Or vice versa— should we depart, like Hegel, from Logic to space—where there is no distinction, there is no space. Distinctions in thought arise out of the activity of distinguishing; whatever arises out of the activity of distinguishing is spatially set apart. Spatial distinctions are, therefore, the *truth* of logical distinctions. But only that which exists separately can also be thought as forming a sequence. *Real* thought is thought in time and space. Even the negation of time and space (duration) must fall *within* time and space themselves. Only in order to *gain time* and *space,* do we wish to save them.

45

Things in thought should not be different from what they are in reality. What is *separate in reality* should *not* be *identical in thought.* To *exclude* thinking or ideas—the intellectual world of the neo-Platonists—from *the laws of reality* is the *privilege* of *theological capriciousness.* The *laws of reality* are also the *laws of thought.*

46

The *immediate unity of opposite* determinations is *possible* and *valid* only in *abstraction*. In *reality*, contradictory statements are always linked by means of an intermediary concept. This intermediary concept is the *object* to which those statements refer; it is their *subject*.

Nothing is therefore easier than to demonstrate the unity of opposite predicates; all one needs is to abstract from the object underlying the predicates or from the subject of these predicates. Once the object has thus vanished, the boundary between the opposites also vanishes; having no ground to stand on and nothing to hold on to, they immediately collapse and lose themselves in indistinction. If, for example, I regard being only as such, that is, if I abstract from every determination whatsoever, being will be the same for me as nothing. Determinateness is indeed the only difference or boundary between being and nothing. If I disregard *that which* is, what then is this mere "is" about? But what applies to *this* particular case of opposites and their identity applies to all other opposites in speculative philosophy.

47

The only means by which *opposite* or *contradictory determinations* are *united* in one and the same being in a way corresponding to reality is in *time*.

This is true at least in the case of living beings. Only here, for example in man, does the contradiction appear that I am now filled and swayed by this determination—this particular feeling, this particular intention—and now by another, opposite determination. Only where one idea ousts another, where one feeling drives the other out, where nothing is finally settled, where no lasting determination emerges, where the soul continually alternates between opposite states—there alone does the soul find itself in the hellish pain of contradiction. Were I to unite contradictory determinations within myself, the result would be their mutual neutralization and loss of character, not unlike the opposite elements of a chemical process which lose their difference in a neutral product. But the pain of contradiction consists precisely in the fact that I passionately am and want to be at the present moment what I equally emphatically am not and do not want to be in the following, in the fact that positing and negating follow each other, both opposing each other and *each, with the exclusion of the other,* affecting me with all its determinateness and sharpness.

48

The *real* can be *presented* in *thought not as a whole* but only *in parts.* This distinction is normal; it lies in the nature of thought whose essence is generality as distinct from reality whose essence is individuality. That in spite of this distinction no *formal contradiction* may arise between *thought* and *reality* can be achieved only if thought does not proceed *in a straight line* or *within its self-identity, but is interrupted by sensuous perception.* Only that thought which is *determined* and *rectified* by *sensuous perception* is *real objective* thought—the thought of *objective truth.*

The most important thing to realize is that absolute thought, that is, thought which is isolated and cut off from sensuousness, *cannot get beyond formal identity—the identity of thought with itself;* for although thought or concept is determined as the unity of opposite determinations, the fact remains that these determinations are themselves only abstractions, thought-determinations—hence, always repetitions of the self-identity of thought, only *multipla* of identity as the absolutely true point of departure. The Other as counterposed to the Idea, but posited by the Idea itself, is not truly and in reality distinguished from it, not allowed to exist outside the Idea, or if it is, then only *pro forma,* only in appearance to demonstrate the liberality of the Idea; for the *Other* of the Idea is *itself Idea* with the only difference that it does not yet have the form of the idea, that it is not yet posited and realized as such. Thought *confined to itself* is thus unable to arrive at anything positively distinct from and opposed to itself; for that very

reason it also has no other criterion of truth except that
something does not contradict the Idea or thought—only a
formal, subjective criterion that is not in a position to decide whether the truth of thought is also the truth of reality.
The criterion which alone can decide this question is
sensuous perception. One should always hear the opponent.
And sensuous perception is precisely the *antagonist* of
thought. Sensuous perception takes things in a *broad* sense,
but thought takes them in the *narrowest* sense; perception
leaves things in their *unlimited freedom,* but thought imposes on them *laws* that are only too often *despotic;* perception introduces clarity into the head, but without
determining or *deciding* anything; thought performs a determining function, but it also often makes the mind narrow; perception in itself has no *principles* and thought in
itself has no *life;* the rule is the *way of thought* and *exception* to the rule is *that of perception.* Hence, just as true
perception is perception determined by thought, so true
thought is the thought that has been enlarged and opened
up by perception so as to correspond to the essence of reality. The thought that is identical, and exists in an uninterrupted continuity, with itself, lets the world circle, in
contradiction to reality, around itself as its center; but the
thought that is *interrupted* through the observation as to
the irregularity of this movement, or through the anomaly
of perception, transforms this circular movement into an
elliptical one in accordance with the truth. The *circle* is the
symbol, the coat of arms of *speculative* philosophy, of the
thought that has *only itself* to support itself. The Hegelian
philosophy, too, as we know, is a circle of circles, although
in relation to the planets it declares—and led to this by
empirical evidence—the circular course to be "the course
of a *defectively regular* movement"; in contrast to the circle, the *ellipse* is the symbol, the coat of arms of *sensuous*
philosophy, of thought that is based on *perception.*

49

Only those determinations are productive of *real*
knowledge which *determine the object by the object itself;*

that is, *by its own individual* determinations but *not* those
that are *general,* as for example the logico-metaphysical
determinations that, being applicable to *all objects without
distinction, determine no object.*

Hegel was therefore quite justified in transforming the
logico-metaphysical determinations from determinations of
objects into independent determinations—namely, into the
determinations of the Concept—quite justified in turning
them from predicates—this is what they were in the old
metaphysics—into subjects, thus attributing to metaphysics
or logic the significance of a self-sufficient divine knowledge. But it is a contradiction when these logico-
metaphysical shadows are made, in the concrete sciences
in exactly the same way as in the old metaphysics, into
the determinations of real things—something that is naturally possible only in so far as either the concrete determinations—that is, those that are appropriate because of their
derivation from the object—are connected with the logico-
metaphysical determinations, or the object is reduced to
wholly *abstract* determinations in which it is *no longer
recognizable.*

50

*The real in its reality and totality, the object of the new
philosophy,* is the object also of a *real* and *total* being. The
new philosophy therefore regards as its *epistemological
principle,* as its *subject, not the ego, not the absolute*—i.e.,
abstract spirit, *in short, not reason for itself alone*—but the
real and the *whole being of man. Man* alone is the *reality,*
the *subject* of *reason.* It is man who thinks, not the ego,
not reason. The new philosophy does not depend on the
divinity; i.e., the truth of reason for itself alone. Rather, it
depends on the *divinity; i.e., the truth of the whole man.*
Or, to put it more appropriately, the new philosophy is
certainly based on reason as well, but on a reason whose
being is the same as the *being of man;* that is, it is based
not on an empty, colorless, nameless reason, but on a reason that is *of the very blood of man.* If the motto of the old
philosophy was: "The rational alone is the true and real,"

the motto of the new philosophy is: "The *human* alone
is the *true* and *real*," for the human alone is the rational;
man is the measure of reason.

51

The *unity* of *thought* and *being* has *meaning* and *truth*
only if *man* is comprehended as the *basis and subject of
this unity.* Only a *real being* cognizes *real things;* only
where thought is not its own subject but the *predicate* of a
real being is it *not separated from being.* The unity of
thought and being is therefore not formal, meaning that
being as a determination does not belong to *thought in and
for itself;* rather, this unity depends on the *object,* the *content* of thought.

From this arises the following categorical imperative:
Desire not to be a philosopher if being a philosopher
means being different to man; do not be anything more
than a *thinking man;* think not as a thinker, that is, not as
one confined to a faculty which is *isolated* in so far as it
is *torn away* from the totality of the real being of man;
think as a *living, real* being, in which capacity you are
exposed to the vivifying and refreshing waves of the ocean
of the world; think as one who exists, as one who is *in the
world* and is part of the world, not as one in the vacuum
of abstraction, not as a solitary monad, not as an absolute
monarch, not as an unconcerned, extra-worldly God; only
then can you be sure that being and thought are united in
all your thinking. How should thought as the activity of a
real being not grasp real things and entities? Only when
thought is cut off from man and confined to itself do em-
barrassing, fruitless, and, from the standpoint of an
isolated thought, unresolvable questions arise: How does
thought reach being, reach the object? For *confined to
itself,* that is, posited *outside man,* thought is outside all
ties and connections with the world. You elevate yourself
to an object only in so far as you lower yourself so as to
be an object for others. You think only because *your
thoughts* themselves can be thought, and they are true only
if they pass the test of objectivity, that is, when someone

else, to whom they are given as objects, acknowledges them as such. You see because you are yourself a visible being, you feel because you are yourself a feelable being. Only to an open mind does the world stand open, and the *openings of the mind* are only the senses. But the thought that exists in isolation, that is *enclosed in itself,* is *detached from the senses, cut off from man,* is *outside* man—that thought is *absolute subject* which cannot or ought not to be an object for others. But precisely for that reason, and despite all efforts, it is *forever unable to cross over to the object, to being;* it is like a head separated from the body, which must remain unable to seize hold of an object because it lacks the means, the organs to do so.

52

The new philosophy is the *complete* and *absolute dissolution of theology into anthropology,* a dissolution *in which all contradictions have been overcome;* for the new philosophy is the dissolution of theology not only in reason —this was effected by the old philosophy—but also in the *heart;* in short, in the *whole* and *real* being of man. In this regard, it is only the *necessary outcome* of the old philosophy; for that which was once dissolved in reason must dissolve itself in *life,* in the *heart,* in the *blood* of man; but as a *new* and *independent* truth, the new philosophy is also the truth of the old philosophy, for only *a truth that has become flesh and blood is the truth.* The old philosophy *necessarily* relapsed into theology, for that which is sublated only *in reason,* only in the concept, still has an *antithesis* in the *heart.* The new philosophy, on the other hand, *cannot suffer such a relapse* because there is nothing to relapse into; that which is dead in both body and soul cannot return even as a ghost.

53

It is *by no means only through thinking that man is distinguished from the animal.* Rather, his *whole being* constitutes *his distinction from* the *animal.* It is true that he who does not think is not a man; but this is so not be-

cause thinking is the cause, but only because it is a *necessary consequence* and *quality* of man's being.

Hence, here too we need not go beyond the realm of
sensuousness in order to recognize man as a being superior
to animals. Man is not a particular being like the animal;
rather, he is a *universal* being; he is therefore not a
limited and unfree but an unlimited and free being, for
universality, being without limit, and freedom are inseparable. And this freedom is not the property of just one
special faculty, say, the will, nor does this universality re-
side in a special faculty of thinking called reason; this freedom, this universality applies to the *whole* being of man.
The senses of the animal are certainly keener than those
of man, but they are so only in relation to certain things
that are necessarily linked with the needs of the animal;
and they are keener precisely because of the determination
that they are limited by being exclusively directed towards
some definite objects. Man does not possess the sense of
smell of a hunting dog or a raven, but because his sense
of smell encompasses all kinds of smell, it is free and also
indifferent to particular smells. But where a sense is elevated above the limits of particularity and above being tied
down to needs, it is elevated to an *independent,* to a *theoretical* significance and dignity—*universal* sense is *intellect,*
and *universal* sensuousness is *intellectuality.* Even the lowest senses—smell and taste—are elevated in man to intellectual and scientific activities. The smell and taste of things
are objects of natural science. Indeed, even the *stomach*
of man, no matter how contemptuously we look down
upon it, is something *human* and not animal because it is
universal; that is, not limited to certain kinds of food. That
is why man is free from that ferocious voracity with which
the animal hurls itself on its prey. Leave a man his head,
but give him the stomach of a lion or a horse, and he will
certainly cease to be a man. A limited stomach is compatible only with a limited, that is, animal sense. Man's moral
and rational relationship to his stomach consists therefore
in his according it a human and not a beastly treatment.
He who thinks that what is important to mankind is

stomach, and that stomach is something animal, also authorizes man to be bestial in his eating.

54

The new philosophy makes *man, together with nature as the basis of man,* the *exclusive, universal,* and *highest object* of philosophy; it makes *anthropology, together with physiology,* the *universal science.*

55

Art, religion, philosophy, and *science* are only expressions or manifestations of the *true being of man.* A man is truly and perfectly man only when he possesses an *aesthetic* or *artistic, religious* or *moral, philosophical* or *scientific* sense. And only he who *excludes from himself nothing that is essentially human* is, strictly speaking, man. *Homo sum, humani nihil a me alienum puto*—this sentence, taken in its *universal* and *highest meaning,* is the *motto* of the *new philosophy.*

56

The *philosophy of Absolute Identity* has *completely mislocated the standpoint of truth.* The *natural standpoint* of man, the standpoint of the *distinction* between *"I"* and *"You,"* between *subject* and *object* is the *true,* the *absolute* standpoint and, hence, also the *standpoint of philosophy.*

57

The *true unity of head and heart* does not consist in wiping out or covering up their difference, but rather in the recognition that *the essential object of the heart* is also *the essential object of the head,* or in the identity of the *object.* The new philosophy, which makes the essential and highest object of the heart—man—also the essential and highest object of the intellect, lays the foundation of a rational unity of head and heart, of thought and life.

58

Truth does not exist in thought, nor in cognition confined to itself. *Truth is only the totality of man's life and being.*

59

The single man *in isolation* possesses in himself the *essence* of man neither as a *moral* nor as a *thinking* being. The *essence* of man is contained only in the community, in the *unity of man with man*—a unity, however, that rests on the *reality* of the *distinction* between "I" and "You."

60

Solitude means being *finite* and *limited*, *community* means being *free* and *infinite*. For *himself* alone, man is just man (in the ordinary sense); but man *with* man—*the unity of "I" and "You"*—that is *God*.

61

The *absolute* philosopher said, or at least thought of himself—naturally as a *thinker* and not as a man—*"La vérité c'est moi,"* in a way analogous to the absolute monarch claiming, *"L'Etat c'est moi,"* or the absolute God claiming, *"L'être c'est moi."* The human philosopher, on the other hand, says: *Even in thought, even as a philosopher, I am a man in togetherness with men.*

62

The *true* dialectic is *not a monologue of the solitary thinker with himself;* it is a *dialogue between "I" and "You."*

63

The *Trinity* was the *highest mystery,* the *central point* of the *absolute philosophy* and *religion.* But the secret of the Trinity, as demonstrated historically and philosophically in the *Essence of Christianity,* is the secret of *com-*

munal and *social life*—the secret of the *necessity of a "You" for an "I."* It is the truth that *no being whatsoever,* be it man or God and be it called "spirit" or "I," can be a *true, perfect,* and *absolute* being *in isolation,* that the *truth* and *perfection* are only the *union* and *unity* of beings that are similar in essence. Hence, the highest and ultimate principle of philosophy is *the unity of man with man.* All essential relationships—the principles of various sciences— are only *different kinds and modes of this unity.*

64

The old philosophy possesses a *double truth;* first, its *own* truth—*philosophy*—which is not concerned with man, and second, the truth *for man*—*religion.* The new philosophy as the philosophy of man, on the other hand, is also essentially the *philosophy for man;* it has, without in the least compromising the dignity and autonomy of theory— indeed it is in perfect harmony with it—essentially a *practical* tendency, and is practical in the highest sense. The new philosophy takes the place of religion; it has within itself the *essence* of religion; in truth, it is *itself religion.*

65

All attempts undertaken so far to reform philosophy are not very different from the old philosophy to the extent that they are *species* belonging to the same *genus.* The most indispensable condition for a really new—i.e., independent—philosophy corresponding to the need of mankind and of the future is, however, that it distinguish itself *in essence* from the old philosophy.

Preface to the Second Edition of the *Essence of Christianity*

The foolish and perfidious judgments passed on this work since its first publication have not surprised me in the least, for I did not expect, or could I have reasonably expected, anything to the contrary. With this work, I have in any case spoiled my chances with both God and the world. I have had the "wicked audacity" to spell out as early as in the Preface that "Christianity, too, has had its classical age and that only that which is true, great, and classic deserves to be an object of thought; however, that which is untrue, small, or unclassic is better dealt with by the forum of satire and comedy; and that I have therefore put myself back into those times when the bride of Christ was still a virtuous and immaculate virgin, when she had not yet braided the roses and myrtles of the pagan Venus into her heavenly bridegroom's crown of thorns; when, although poor in earthly treasures, she was nevertheless more than rich and more than felicitous in the enjoyment of the secrets of a supernatural love. Only thus, that is, only after extricating Christianity from its reduction to a dissolute, characterless, comfortable, belletristic, coquettish, Epicurean Christianity could I turn to it as an object worthy of thought." So this wicked audacity of mine consists in pulling the true Christianity—glossed over and disowned by pseudo-Christians—out of the darkness of the past and placing it in the light of day, although not with

what would have been the laudable and sensible intention
to present it as the *non plus ultra* of human mind and
heart. Far from it; the underlying "foolish" and "dia-
bolical" intention was to reduce Christianity to a higher,
more general principle. No wonder then, that as a consequence of my wicked audacity I have understandably become the curse of modern Christians, especially theologians. Further, I have attacked speculative philosophy at
its most vulnerable point, at its *point d'honneur,* in that I
relentlessly destroyed the apparent harmony which it had
construed between itself and religion by demonstrating
that in order to establish this harmony it in fact robbed
religion of its true and essential content. In doing so, I
had also dealt a fatal blow to the so-called positive philosophy in as much as I demonstrated that the origin of its
idol was man, that flesh and blood belonged essentially to
personality. Through this extraordinary work of mine I
have thus gravely offended the whole pack of ordinary
schoolmen. Further, through an extremely unpolitical—unfortunately—yet, intellectually and morally speaking, necessary enlightenment concerning the obscure essence of
religion, I have brought upon myself the displeasure of
politicians—just as much of those who use religion as a
political weapon to suppress and repress people as of those
to whom religion is politically completely indifferent and
who, although acceptable as friends in the spheres of politics and industry, are nevertheless enemies of light and
freedom. Finally, I am guilty of committing a dreadful
and unpardonable offence against the current code of decency simply because of the uncompromising language I
employ in my effort to call everything unceremoniously
by the name it deserves.

The normal and current tone of the times, the tone of
"polite society," the neutral, anemic tone of conventional
illusions and untruths is the tone in which not only political matters—this is quite obvious—but also religious and
scientific matters, that is, the evils of the age, are discussed.
Semblance is the essence of the age; semblance, our science. Under these circumstances, he who speaks the truth

is impertinent, uncivilized; and since uncivilized, therefore also immoral. To our age, truth is therefore synonymous with immorality. What is moral, indeed even authorized and condoned, is the hypocritical denial of Christianity disguised as its affirmation. A morally upright denial of Christianity, that is a denial that makes no bones about its being a denial, is, however, immoral and decried. Moral is, on the other hand, that game of capriciousness with Christianity that lets one basic article of faith lapse in reality, but lets another seemingly stand. After all, Luther has said that he who overthrows one article of faith overthrows all the others, at least in principle. Immoral, again, is the earnest and innerly necessitated desire to abandon Christianity, but moral, the jarring halfness rather than a self-certain and determined wholeness. Similarly, moral is what is an abominable contradiction, but immoral is all rigorous consistency; moral, again, is all mediocrity because it is unable to tackle and get down to the bottom of anything, yet immoral is all genius because it makes a clean slate and does not rest until it has exhausted all the possibilities contained in an object. In short, the lie is moral because it skirts or conceals the evil of the truth or, what is now the same thing, the truth about the evil.

In our age, however, truth is not only immoral, but also unscientific; it is the limit of science. Just as the German maritime commerce on the Rhine stretches *jusques à la mer,* so the freedom of German science stretches *jusques à la verité.* Whenever it reaches the truth, whenever it becomes the truth, science ceases to be science and becomes an object for the police—the police are the boundary between truth and science. Truth is man and not reason *in abstracto;* it is life and not thought that remains confined to paper, the element in which it finds and unfolds its existence. Hence, those thoughts that pass straight from the pen into the blood or from reason into the heart of man are no longer scientific truths, because science is essentially a harmless—but also useless—toy tool of a reason turned lazy; it consists in being occupied with things that are indifferent to life and man; or even granting that it does not occupy itself with indifferent things, the fact remains that it is so useless an activity that no one will bother with it. These days, the necessary qualifications for a genuine, commendable, and "kosher" scholar—at least for a scholar whose science necessarily brings him in contact with delicate questions of the age—are a confused head, inactive heart, unconcern for truth, and spiritlessness—in short, a lack of character. However, a scholar who possesses an incorruptible sense for truth and a firm character, who with one stroke hits the nail on the head and gets straight to the root of an evil, who irresistibly pushes things to the point of crisis; that is, decision—such a person no longer passes for a scholar. God forbid! He is a "Herostratus!" Quick! To the gallows with him, or at least into the pillory! But better into the pillory, for according to the publicized principles of contemporary Christian state law, death on the gallows is obviously and indisputably an act of killing; however, to die in the pillory—the civil form of killing—is a highly political and Christian death for reasons of insidiousness and hypocrisy. To be sure, it is killing, but a killing that only has the semblance of killing. Semblance and nothing but semblance is the essence of the present age in all matters that are somewhat ticklish.

No wonder, therefore, that this age of pretentious, illusory, and boastful Christianity has been so much scandalized by being confronted with the essence of Christianity. Christianity has become so degenerate and has been so much put out of practice that even its official representatives, the theologians, no longer know what it is. One only has to compare, if one would be convinced by one's own eyes, the charges brought against me by theologians concerning belief, miracle, providence, and futility of the world with the historical evidence I produce in my work; to wit, in this second edition which has now been significantly enlarged so as to include corroborative references, to realize that these charges are directed not so much against me, as against Christianity itself, that their indignation over my work is only an indignation over the true content of the Christian religion, a content, however, which has become alienated from the meaning of this religion. No, it is not surprising that in an age that has—apparently out of boredom—resuscitated with affected ardor the worn-out and now so petty opposition between Protestantism and Catholicism—an opposition which until recently even the tailor and the tinker had become oblivious of. No, it is not surprising that in an age that is not ashamed to pursue the dispute over mixed marriage as a serious and momentous matter, a work which proves on the basis of historical documents that not only the marriage between believers and unbelievers, but marriage as such is against true Christianity, that a true Christian—and obviously it is not the duty of Christian governments, Christian pastors, and Christian teachers to see to it that we are all true Christians—knows no other begetting than that in the Holy Ghost, that he is more concerned with populating the heaven rather than the earth, should be an infuriating anachronism in an age like the present one. No, it is not surprising at all.

However, precisely because it was not surprising, the whole storm about and against my work has not disconcerted me in the least. On the contrary, it has led me to subject my work in all calmness to a rigorous historical and philosophical scrutiny, thus purging it as far as possible of its formal shortcomings and enriching it by taking into account new developments, by introducing further illuminating factors, and by incorporating additional historical evidence that is conclusive and irrefutable. Now that the ratiocinative course of my analysis has been reinforced and punctuated—mostly at each step of the argument—by corroborative historical references, it is to be hoped that my readers, provided that they are *not stone-blind,* will realize and be led to the conviction—even if reluctantly—that my work represents an *authentic translation* of the Christian religion from the oriental language of images into straightforward, intelligible German. Indeed, my work does not wish to accomplish anything more than a faithfully sense-oriented translation or, to put it non-metaphorically, an *empirical* or *historico-philosophical analysis* of the Christian religion designed to resolve its enigmas. The general principles I have premised in the Introduction are in no way *a priori* or mere products of a personal speculation. Rather, they have emerged out of an analysis of religion; they are, like all basic ideas of my work, cognitive forms or categorical fixations of actual expressions of human essence—and, indeed, of man's religious essence—and facilitate a comprehension of these expressions. The ideas contained in my work are only conclusions or *inferences* from premises which in their turn are not just *ideas* but, rather, *objective* facts—either *present* or *historical*—facts which, because of their *bulky existence in folio,* could not have found room in my head. I completely and unconditionally reject *absolute, immaterial, self-complacent* speculation—that speculation which generates its material *out of itself.* I am worlds apart from those philosophers who pluck out their eyes to be able to see better; I, for my part, need the senses, above all the eyes, to think; I base my thoughts on *materials* that are given to us only through the activity of the senses; I do not produce the object out of the thought but, rather, the thought *out of the object,* for *that* alone is an object that exists *apart from the brain.* I am an idealist only in the sphere of *practical* philosophy, which means that I do not take the limits of the present to be the limits of mankind or the future. Rather, I unflinchingly believe that many things—yes, many things—that are today looked upon by shortsighted and pusillanimous practical men as mere fantasies, as ideas that can never be realized, as veritable chimeras, will have acquired full reality tomorrow; that is, in the next century—a century from the point of view of the individual is just a day from the point of view of mankind. In short, I am an idealist only in the sense that I believe in the idea of the historical future and in the triumph of truth and virtue; that is, the idea has only a *political* and *moral* significance for me. However, in the field of strictly theoretical philosophy, I subscribe—in direct contrast to the philosophy of Hegel, which holds exactly the opposite view—to *realism* or materialism in the mentioned sense. The maxim of all hitherto existing speculative philosophy, "All that is mine I carry with me," the old *omnia mea mecum porto,* I unfortunately cannot apply to myself. There are so many things *outside myself* that I can carry neither in my pocket nor in my head, and yet I must look upon them as belonging to me; that is, belonging to me not as an ordinary human being—with him we are not concerned in the present context—but as a philosopher. I am nothing more than an *explorer of nature equipped with mind.* However, an explorer of nature would be helpless without *instruments,* without *material means.* It is in this capacity—that is, as an explorer of nature equipped with mind—that I have written the present work which, consequently, contains nothing else than the principle of a new philosophy which has proved its truth practically, i.e., *in concreto,* to the extent that it has been developed from and successfully carried out in the presentation of a special object, but an object that has a universal significance: namely, religion. This new philosophy is *essentially* distinguished from all previous philosophy in so far as it corresponds to the *true, real,* and *whole* being of man. For that very reason, it is, of course, opposed to all superhuman, i.e., anti-human and anti-natural, religion and speculation which have corrupted and crippled man. It does not regard, as I have already said elsewhere, the goose quill as the only adequate organ for the revelation of truth, but also the *eye* and the *ear,* the *hand* and the *foot;* it does not equate the idea of a thing with the thing itself; it does not reduce real existence to mere existence on paper flowing from the writing pen. Rather, it keeps the two apart and precisely by doing so arrives at the *thing itself;* that is, not at the thing as it forms the object of abstract reason, but as it constitutes the object of the *real* and *whole man.* What it therefore cognizes as the *true* thing is the *real* and the *whole* thing itself. It is a philosophy that does not rest on an intellect *taken for itself,* on an absolute, nameless intellect, belonging one knows not to whom, but on the intellect of man with the qualification that it is not perverted by speculation and Christianity; and

it speaks the language of *man,* rather than a language that
is *incapable of naming real being;* that posits the *essence*
of philosophy, so far as both its subject matter and language are concerned, in the *negation of philosophy.* In
other words, it declares the true philosophy to be only that
which has been translated *in succum et sanguinem,* which
has been turned into flesh and blood, which has become
one with man. Hence, its greatest triumph consists in the
fact that it does not appear to have the character of philosophy for all those dull and scholastically warped minds
that see the *essence* of philosophy in what is only a *semblance* of it.

The present work is therefore a specimen of the kind
of philosophy that has for its principle not the Substance
of Spinoza, not the Ego of Kant and Fichte, not the Absolute Identity of Schelling, not the Absolute Spirit of Hegel;
in short, no abstract, merely ideated or imaginary being,
but rather the most *real* of all beings, the true *Ens
realissimum—man.* In other words, its principle is the most
positive and real, and it generates thought from the *opposite* of thought; namely, *matter, being,* and the *senses.*
Its relationship to its object is sensuous—that is, passive—
and receptive before it determines it conceptually. My
work, although it is on the one hand the true upshot of all
hitherto existing philosophy or philosophy turned into flesh
and blood, is so little to be categorized as speculation that
it is, in point of fact, the very opposite, indeed, the dissolution of all speculation. Speculation makes religion say only
what it has *itself* thought and expressed far better than
religion; speculation determines religion without itself being determined by it, for it does not step out of itself. As
for me, I let religion *itself speak;* I only listen to it and
function as its interpreter rather than its prompter. My
only objective has been to "uncover existence," to discover
rather than invent; my only endeavor has been to *see*
correctly. It is not I but religion that worships man, although it—or rather theology—denies this. It is not my
humble self, but religion itself that says: God is man, man
is God; it is not I but religion that denies *the God* who is

not man but only an *ens rationis,* since it makes God become man and then turns this humanized God, who can feel and think like man, into the object of its worship and veneration. I have only betrayed the secret of the Christian religion, only extricated it from theology's *web of lies and delusions*—and I am certainly guilty of commiting this sacrilege. If my work is therefore negative, irreligious, and atheistic, one must bear in mind that atheism—at least as understood in the context of their work—is the secret of religion itself; that religion itself, not indeed on the surface, but at bottom, not in its self-estimation, but in its heart, its true essence believes in nothing else than in the truth and divinity of the being of man. Contrariwise, let one *prove that the historical as well as rational arguments* advanced in my work are *fallacious.* Let these arguments be refuted, but pray, not by juristic defamations, or theological jeremiads, by hackneyed speculative verbiage, or some similar miserable trash, but by reasons, and indeed by reasons which have not already been thoroughly refuted by me.

To be sure, my work is negative, repudiatory; but, all said and done, only in relation to that which is *unhuman* in religion, not in relation to the human essence of religion. It consequently falls into two parts, one of which is mainly *affirmative* and the other, including the Appendix, mostly but not wholly, negative. In both parts, it is, however, the same thing that is demonstrated, albeit in different or even contradictory ways. The first part reduces religion to what constitutes its *truth* and *essence,* whereas the second part treats them in a way so as to reveal their *contradictions;* the first *develops* the theme, the second is *polemical,* which is why the former is understandably more calm, while the latter, more vigorous. While developing the theme you move slowly, but while contesting you advance swiftly, for development is at peace with itself at each stage, but a contest only at the final stage. Development is thoughtful, but a contest, resolute. Development requires *light,* but a contest, *fire.* Hence the circumstance that both parts are different even in form. I demonstrate in the first part that the *true sense* of theology is anthropology, that there is no difference between the predicates of the divine and the human essence, and consequently, also none between the divine and the human subject or essence, for whenever predicates are not just accidental attributes, as is certainly the case with theological predicates, but rather express the nature of the subject, there can be *no* distinction between predicate and subject, so that the predicate can be put in the place of the subject because of the *identity* of the two; in substantiation of this, the reader is referred to the *Analytic* of Aristotle or even to Porphyry's *Introduction.* Contrasted with this, I demonstrate in the second part that the *distinction* between theological and anthropological predicates dissolves itself into *nothingness* or *non-sense.* Here is a striking example. In the first part I prove that the Son of God in religion is God's Son in the same sense in which man is the son of man, and I see the *truth* and *essence* of religion in the fact that religion grasps and affirms as divine relation that which is at bottom only a human relation. In the second part, on the other hand, I demonstrate that the Son of God—of course, not directly in religion, but only in a reflection of religion upon itself —is not a son in the natural, human sense, but in a manner *entirely* contradictory to nature and reason, and therefore *nonsensical,* and I find in such a negation of human sense and understanding the untruth of and that which is negative in religion. The first part is thus the *direct,* the second the *indirect* proof that theology is anthropology. Hence, the second leads necessarily back to the first since it has no independent significance; its only aim is to show that the sense in which religion is taken in the first part *must* be the true one, *because any sense to the contrary is non-sense.* In short, I deal mainly with *religion* in the first part —I say mainly, for it was unavoidable not to include theology in it, just as it was equally unavoidable not to talk about religion in the second—whereas I deal with *theology* in the second, but not only with *common* theology as has been erroneously remarked here and there. Actually, I have, as far as possible, kept this trash away from me by confining myself everywhere to the most essential, rigorous, and necessary determinations of the object, as for example in the case of the Sacraments to only two of them —and, strictly speaking, there are only two—restricting myself, that is, to the determination that lends *general interest* to an object and *raises it above the limited sphere of theology;* I deal in the second part, therefore, not only with common theology, but also with speculative theology or philosophy, as will be revealed even upon a cursory glance. I say with theology and not with theologians, for everywhere I can define only that which is *prima causa,* which is the *original,* not the copy, *principles,* not persons, species, not individuals, *objects of history,* not objects of *chronique scandaleuse.*

If my work consisted only of the second part, one would be perfectly justified in accusing it of a negative tendency, and in characterizing its essential content as based on the proposition that religion is nothing, that it is an absurdity. However, I do not assert at all—that would have made the task so easy for me—that God is *nothing,* the Trinity is *nothing,* the Word of God is *nothing,* etc. What I demonstrate is that religion conceives the apparent, superficial essence of nature and mankind to be their true and inner essence; that it therefore conceives their true and esoteric essence as a separate and particular being, and that, consequently, what it defines or objectifies in its determinations of God or of the Word of God—at least in *those* determinations which are not negative in the mentioned sense—is only the true *essence* of the human word. The accusation that according to my work religion is nonsense, nothing, pure illusion would be justified only if it led to the conclusion that that into which I resolve religion, which I demonstrate to be its *true object* and *content;* namely, man or anthropology was similarly nonsense, nothing, pure illusion. But it would be grossly wrong if someone thought that I ascribed to anthropology only a subordinate meaning or no meaning at all or, say, a meaning that can be attached to it only so long as there exists a theology above and in contrast to it. My aim in reducing theology to anthropology is rather to raise anthropology to theology in just the same way as Christianity, by reducing God to man, elevating man into God, even if into a transcendent, fantastic God far removed from man. That is why I understandably take the word anthropology not in the sense of the Hegelian or the hitherto prevailing philosophy, but in an infinitely higher and more general sense.

Religion is the dream of the human mind. But even in dreams we do not find ourselves in nothingness or in heaven, but on earth—the realm of reality. The only difference is that we see real things not in the light of reality and necessity, but in the enthralling splendor of imagination and caprice. What I therefore do to religion—and to speculative philosophy and theology as well—is nothing else than to *open its eyes* or rather to turn *outward* its *inwardly directed* eyes; in other words, I only lead the object from its existence in the imagination back to its existence in reality.

But, naturally, for the present age, which prefers the picture to the thing pictured, the copy to the original, imagination to reality, or the appearance to the essence, this metamorphosis of the object, entailing as it does a shattering of illusions, is the same thing as its absolute destruction or wicked profanation; for *illusion* alone is *sacred* to this age, but *truth profane*. Indeed, sacredness grows in the eyes of this age in the same measure as truth declines and illusion increases, so that the *highest degree of illusion* is to it the highest degree of sacredness. Religion has disappeared and what has taken its place, even among Protestants, is the *appearance* of religion—the Church—in order at least that the faith may be imparted to the ignorant and indiscriminating masses. As if the Christian faith were still intact just because Christian churches exist today as they did a thousand years ago, just because the *external signs* of faith are as much in vogue today as in earlier times. That which no longer possesses any reality in faith (the faith of the modern world is faith only in appearance, is a faith that belies itself by *not* believing in what it professes to believe, and is, as has been sufficiently proved by myself and others, only an *undecided* and *im-*

becile unbelief) is still to appear as sacred. Hence, the
hypocritical religious indignation of the present age, the
age of hypocrisy and illusion, over my analysis of the
Sacraments in particular. But it cannot be expected of a
writer who does not covet the favor of the age, but rather
seeks the truth, that he should have, or create the impression of having, respect towards an empty appearance, especially as the object so appearing is the culminating point
of religion, the point at which religion becomes transformed into irreligion. So much in justification, rather than
in excuse, of my analysis of the Sacraments.

   With regard, moreover, to the real meaning of the
analysis of the Sacraments given, particularly, in the last
chapter, I remark only that I illustrate here the essential
content, the actual theme of my work, particularly with
regard to its practical significance, by making use of a
concrete example, that I here call upon the senses themselves to witness the truthfulness of the ideas contained
in my analysis and demonstrate *ad oculos,* indeed, *ad tac-
tum, ad gustum,* what I have taught *ad captum.* Just as
the water of Baptism, the wine and bread of the Last
Supper, taken in their natural power and significance, are
infinitely more than in a supernaturalistic and illusory significance the object of religion in the sense of my work—
namely, in an anthropological sense—it is an infinitely more
real and fruitful object of theory and practice than it is
in the sense of theology; for just as that which in water,
wine, and bread is or is to be communicated as something
distinct from these natural things, exists as such only in
conception and imagination, but not in truth and reality,
so in the object of religion, namely, the divine essence as
distinguished from the essence of nature and mankind—
should the determinations of the former, viz., intelligence,
love, etc., mean something different from what they mean
in relation to the latter—exists as such only in conception
and imagination, but not in truth and reality. This therefore is the moral of the fable that, in contradistinction to
theology and speculative philosophy, we should not make
the determinations and powers of reality, of real beings

and things, into arbitrary signs, into vehicles, symbols, and
predicates of a being that is distinguished from them, that
is transcendent, absolute, or, in other words, abstract.
Rather, we should take them in the sense that they have
in themselves, a sense that is identical with their quality;
that is, with that essential determination that makes them
what they are—only in this way do we come to have the
key to a *real theory and practice.* I do, as a matter of fact,
put in the place of the sterile baptismal water the real
water which possesses the quality of being pleasantly refreshing. One would exclaim: How "watery," how trivial!
Yes, indeed, trivial. But there was a time when marriage,
too, was a *very trivial truth* before Luther, possessed as he
was of a natural human sense, vindicated its truth in opposition to the threadbare sacredness of celibacy. It is true
that I regard water as a real thing, but the "unholy" spirit
of my work also uses it merely as a vehicle, image, example, or symbol; in the same way, the baptismal water,
the object of my analysis, also means both real and sym-
bolical water. The same holds true of bread and wine. Yet,
slanderers have drawn from this the ridiculous conclusion
that bathing, eating, and drinking are the *summa sum-
marum,* the positive upshot of my work. My reply is simply
this: If the whole content of religion is contained in the
Sacraments, and if, consequently, there are no religious
acts other than those performed in connection with Baptism and the Last Supper, then it is naturally true that the
whole content and the positive upshot of my work is bathing, eating, and drinking, since this work is nothing but a
faithful, rigorously object-oriented, historico-philosophical
analysis of religion, of the *self*-deception and the self-
consciousness of religion.

My analysis is *historico-philosophical* as against the
purely historical analyses of Christianity. The historian—
for example, Daumer—shows that the Last Supper is a
rite going back to the ancient cult of human sacrifice;
that once real human flesh and blood instead of wine and
bread were partaken. I, on the other hand, make only the
Christian significance, or the significance *sanctioned* within

the Christian position, that the object of my analysis and reduction in pursuance of the principle that *the significance* which a dogma or institution has in Christianity (naturally not in contemporary, but in ancient, true Christianity), no matter whether it prevails in other religions or not, is also the *true origin* of that dogma or institution *to the extent* that it is Christian. Or, again, the historian—for example, Lützelberger—shows that the narratives of the miracles of Christ resolve themselves into contradictions and incompatibilities, that they are later concoctions, that, consequently, Christ was never a miracle worker, never that which the Bible has made him out to be. For my part, I do not ask what the real, natural Christ was or may have been in distinction from the fictitious or supernaturalistic Christ; taking the Christ of religion for granted, I rather show that this superhuman being is nothing else than a product and object of the supernatural human mind. I do not ask whether this or that, whether a miracle *can* happen at all; I only show *what* a miracle is and, indeed, not *a priori,* but by referring to the *examples* of miracles narrated in the Bible as real events; in doing so, however, I answer the question as to the possibility, reality, or necessity of miracles in a way so as to liquidate the possibility of all such questions. So much concerning that which sets me apart from historians hostile to Christianity. But as regards my relation to Strauss and Bruno Bauer, with whom I am constantly bracketed, I would only like to point out that the difference separating our works is indicated already by the difference in the object of inquiry itself as is borne out by the title alone. The object of Bauer's criticism is the evangelical history, i.e., biblical Christianity, or rather biblical theology; for Strauss it is the Christian Dogma and the Life of Jesus (which, however, can be subsumed under the former), or, in other words, dogmatic Christianity, or rather dogmatic theology. In my case the object of criticism is Christianity in general; i.e., the Christian religion and, consequently, only Christian philosophy or theology. For that reason, I quote mainly and exclusively such men for whom Christianity

was not merely a theoretical or dogmatic object, for whom
it was not just theology, but also a religion. The main object of my inquiry is Christianity, is religion, as it is constituted in its *immediacy* by the *objectification of the essence of man.* I regard erudition and philosophy as only
the *means* by which the treasure hidden in man is to be
brought to light.

I must further emphasize that I neither intended nor
expected my work to reach the general public. It is true
that I have always regarded universal man, and not the
scholar or the abstract and particular professional philosopher, as the measure of the genuine mode of teaching
and writing; it is true that I have regarded man in general—
not this or that philosopher—as the criterion of truth, that
I have taken the highest virtue of the philosopher to consist in this, that both as a man and as an author he does
not advertise himself as a philosopher, that he is a philosopher not in form, but in substance, that he is a quiet
philosopher, not a loud, let alone a bragging one. In view
of these considerations, I have made the utmost clarity,
simplicity, and precision a law governing all my works
including the present one, so that they may be understood,
at least in terms of their main ideas, by every *educated*
and *thinking* man. And yet the fact remains that my work
can be appreciated and fully understood by the scholar
alone, and, of course, by that scholar *who loves truth,
whose judgment is sound,* and *who is above the opinions
and prejudices of both the learned and unlearned mob;*
for although a thoroughly independent creation, it is nevertheless a necessary outcome of history. I refer quite frequently to this or that historical phenomenon without ex-
plicitly mentioning it, because I thought it was superfluous
to do so. Clearly, such references are understandable to
the scholar alone. Thus, for example, in the very first
chapter where I discuss the consequences arising out of
the standpoint of feeling, I have in mind the philosophers
Jacobi and Schleiermacher. In the second chapter I allude,
from the very outset, mainly to Kantianism, Skepticism,
Theism, Materialism, Pantheism. In the chapter, "The

Standpoint of Religion," in which I discuss the contradiction between the religious or theological and the physical or natural-philosophical view of nature, I hark back to philosophy in the age of orthodoxy, above all to the *Cartesian* and Leibnizian philosophy where this contradiction shows itself in a particularly characteristic manner. Therefore, he who is unacquainted with the historical presuppositions and the historically constituted nature of the problems underlying my work, will miss the points whence my arguments and ideas proceed; no wonder my assertions often appear to him as unfounded, however firm the ground they stand on. There is no doubt that the theme of my work is of general human interest, or that its basic ideas will one day become the property of mankind, even if *not in the form* in which they have been expressed here or in which they can be expressed under present conditions, for at the present time it is only hollow and powerless illusions and prejudices contradicting the nature of man that stand in opposition to them. But I treated my subject in the first place as a matter of science, as an object of philosophy, for I could not treat it in any other way. Also, while wanting to rectify the aberrations of religion, theology, and speculation, I cannot but make use of their expressions. Indeed, it must even appear as if I were myself indulging in speculation and theological thinking—both are one and the same—although what I seek to do is to eliminate speculation; that is, to reduce theology to anthropology. As mentioned above, my work contains the principle—and a principle derived from *concrete facts*—of a new philosophy, of a philosophy that is for the sake of man rather than the schools. Indeed, it contains this principle, but only in so far as it *generates* it and, indeed, generates it out of the guts of religion. Hence, the new philosophy is secure—be it said in passing—against falling into the temptation to prove its agreement with religion by its agreement with Christian dogmas such as the old Catholic and modern Protestant scholasticism; born out of the essence of religion, it carries within itself the true essence of religion; it is philosophy *per se* and *qua* religion. However, a work that is genetical in the treatment of its subject, that undertakes to explain and demonstrate it, is precisely because of this formal quality not meant for the masses.

Finally, as supplementary reading to the present work with regard to many apparently unfounded assertions, I refer to my earlier works, especially to the following: *P. Bayle. A Contribution to the History of Philosophy and Mankind* and *Philosophy and Christianity*, where I have delineated with few but precise strokes the historical dissolution of Christianity, demonstrating that Christianity has long vanished not only from the reason but also from the life of mankind, that it is nothing more than a *fixed idea* which stands in a shrieking contradiction with our fire and life insurance companies, our railways and steam engines, our picture and sculpture galleries, our military and industrial schools, our theaters and natural history museums.

Bruckberg, 14th. February 1843

Fragments Concerning
the Characteristics of
My Philosophical Development*

1822

ANSBACH

He who abandons the desire for worldly things and sets his mind on that which is not mortal, is so firmly anchored that no gale or thunderstorm can shake him in the least. (Opitz.)

———

You should try to hide your virtues rather than your faults. (St. Bernhard.)

———

If you are praised, do not let this make you vain. Remember that in praising you one praises Him who works through you. If you perform a good deed, perform it not

---

* Only fragments! This means nothing as a whole, nothing in a completed form. Why? Partly because I have no time for and interest in my past and partly because relevant documents and notes are either lost or have wandered into other hands. Thus, for example, the immediately following excerpts are the only remnants from the most indifferent period of my life, namely, from my Gymnasium period which came to an end in 1822. Hence more influential moments are not represented in this collection of fragments; others are only faintly indicated. L. F.

for the sake of your own glory but for the glory of Him whom you owe the power to do good. Yours is only the ability to sin; whatever good you perform comes from God. (St. Augustine.)

1824

HEIDELBERG

Dear Father,

My wish for this Easter is to be able to transfer to the University of Berlin which I think is the most suitable place for my further theological and general education. You would surely remember from my earlier letters that Daub is the only man here who is completely to my liking. However, I have already taken his main seminars. In the last term I attended, in addition to the course in theological morality, his brilliant seminar on the origin of evil. In this term I attended his lectures on dogmatics, which is the very center of his whole spiritual being, the quintessence, as it were, of his mind. What is now left for me to do in this place after I have lost Daub, who was the only focal point of my life here? For Paulus, as I have already written to you, is unbearable in his exegesis and no less so in his church history. Even in a context like this, he cannot help dishing up his own wisdom and subjective opinions, and deriving his glorious ideas out of inglorious psychological motives. If I go to a lecture on church history, then I would rather have church history than the opinions and hypotheses of this or that gentleman who happens to be talking about it. One only has to present the facts—whether actions or ideas—objectively as they result from their own logic and as they determine each other necessarily and irrespective of whether they promise life or death, in order to see how history explains itself through itself and shows what is true and what is untrue. It does not need any commentary. In order to realize the greatness and sublime-ness of the Cathedral of Cologne, one really does not need the help of a modern architectural adviser.

Besides, the only philosopher we have here is Erhard, but he is a philosopher only in name, not in reality. He does, indeed, frequently have good and beautiful ideas, but, forlorn in his company like orphans, they grin at each other like dogs and cats instead of burning to-gether in one flame of love and losing themselves in one fundamental idea.

How advantageous would it therefore be for me—after having absorbed the best from the great Daub, absorbed not only through the ears but also through the mind and the soul—to continue my career in Berlin where unlike here, there stands not just one single tree of knowledge from which to pick the fruits of knowledge and science but a whole garden full of blossoming and fruit-bearing trees; where every science, indeed almost every single part of a science, is represented by famous and distinguished men; where I can hear the living word of the spirit not only *ex cathedra* but also from the pulpit of a Schleier-macher who is known to be the greatest clerical preacher of our time. Where else could I study exegesis and church history better than at the place where the great Schleier-macher teaches the former and the well-known and es-teemed Neander, the latter? Such seminars are extremely necessary for theologians, and I have long since craved for them. Philosophy in Berlin is truly in altogether dif-ferent hands than is the case here. Apart from the fact that I wholeheartedly desire to be thoroughly initiated into the study of philosophy, it is also made compulsory by the Government of Bavaria to attend philosophical sem-inars, and if this has to be done, then it is certainly better to attend genuine and not just so-called philosophical sem-inars so that one does not waste one's time on an empty word.

BERLIN

Dear Father,

It is only four weeks since I started on my courses, but they have already been infinitely useful. What was still obscure and incomprehensible while I was studying under Daub, I have now understood clearly and grasped in its necessity through the few lectures of Hegel which I have attended so far; what only smoldered in me like tinder, I see now burst into bright flames. Do not think for a moment that I am deceiving myself. It is indeed quite natural that someone inspired by a drive for knowledge, and coming to Hegel after he has been trained in thinking by a man like Daub, experiences the powerful influence of the richness and profundity of his ideas. Also, Hegel is not so unclear in his lectures as in his writings; he is rather clear and easy to understand, for he makes allowance for his students' capacity to grasp. But the marvelous thing about him is that he sticks to the heart of the matter even when he is not engaged in developing the concept of a thing strictly philosophically, but is dealing only with ordinary views.

1825

Dear Brother,

There is so much I would like to write to you about, but there is so little time and inclination to do so. Just this much: I have changed over from theology to philosophy. No salvation without philosophy! A man can satisfy others only if he can satisfy himself, and he can accomplish something only if he has the confidence to accomplish it. My longing for philosophy, however, guarantees my aptitude

for it. Since my stay in Berlin I have already made infinitely greater progress than ever before. Nowhere else
does one go ahead faster than in thought! Once delivered
of its limits, thought is like a current that irresistibly carries us away ever faster. To want me to go back to theology
now would be like forcing an immortal spirit back into
its dead and foresaken shell or like converting a butterfly
back into a cocoon.

1826

I have gone through the whole of Hegel. With the exception of Aesthetics I have heard all his lectures, and
those on Logic even twice. But Hegel's Logic is as it were,
the *corpus iuris,* the *pandects* of philosophy; it contains
the whole of philosophy according to its principles of
thought—both ancient and modern. Besides, it is the presentation of his method. But, of course, the most important
thing is to acquire a mastery not only of the contents but
also of the method of a philosophy.

1827–1828

DOUBTS

How is thought related to being, and the Logic to nature? Is the transition from the Logic to nature legitimate?
Wherein lies the necessity or the ground for this transition? Although in the Logic we see simple determinations,
such as being, nothing, other, finite, infinite, essence, and
appearance, go over into and supersede each other; in
themselves they are abstract, one-sided, and negative determinations. But how can the idea, in its capacity as the
totality encompassing all these determinations, be put in
the same category with its finite determinations? The necessity of the logical progression lies in the negativity of

the logical determinations themselves. But what constitutes the negative in the absolute and perfect idea? That it exists only in the element of thought? But whence do you derive the knowledge that there exists yet another element? From the *Logic?* Not at all, for, out of itself, the *Logic* knows only about itself and only about thought. In other words, that which is other than Logic is derived not from the Logic; that is, logically, but in a non-logical way. That means that the Logic goes over into nature only because the thinking subject finds—outside the Logic—nature or something immediately existing, and is compelled to acknowledge it due to its immediate, that is, its natural, giveness. If nature did not exist, the Logic, this immaculate virgin, would never be able to produce it out of itself.

How is philosophy related to religion? Hegel is particularly keen to make philosophy agree with religion, especially with the teachings of the Christian religion. At the same time, he conceives religion only as a stage in the development of the spirit. The existing religions, however, contain innumerable things that are repulsive to and at odds with the truth; but, should religion then not be conceived in a more general way and the agreement of philosophy with it be sought in the acknowledgement and justification only of certain of its teachings? Is there no other form of agreement?

In what way is Hegel's philosophy related to the present and the future? Is it not the world of the past in the form of the world of thought? Is it more than mankind's recollection of what it was but is no more?

1828

"DE RATIONE UNA, UNIVERSALI, INFINITA"

What is common to all men is that they think. Thinking is not only what some possess but others lack; it belongs to the essence of man. It is, therefore, something shared by and common to all. Reason constitutes the humanity of man; it is their species in so far as they are thinking beings. But what here is the nature of the relationship between the species and the individual, essence and existence, and reason and the thinking subject? Is this relationship of the same kind as that between the general and the individual, as for example, the relationship between nose as such and particular noses? Every nose is individual and particular, but the essence of a nose is not particularity; it does not lie in the fact that it is short or long, pointed or snub; in short, not in the fact that it is this particular nose but only in the fact that it is a nose.

Apart from its particular quality and singularity, this particular nose is not different from another; essence is self-identical in all. But there is no such thing as *the* nose —it is an abstraction. There are only different noses; the self-identical being is here only an idea, a thought. The question now is whether every man also has an individual and particular reason just as he has an individual and particular nose? Is reason, too, an abstraction? No! In so far as I think, that is, in so far as I am a thinking subject, the universal as universal and reason directly as reason are present and active in me. It is necessary that essence and existence are inseparably one here, that I, as one who thinks, do not in the act of thinking relate myself as an individual to reason as my essence in a way in which I, as a sensuous individual, relate myself to the species. In thought, I am *pure essence;* in thought, the difference between universality and particularity is abolished. Existing within the individual, reason at the same time exists *in itself.* Were it not so, it would no longer be reason and would fall into the category of sensuous being. It is not possible to abstract a general concept from reason that could be determined as species. Reason is inseparable from itself; it is its own species; it is pure self-identity; its essence is its existence, and its existence is its essence. What Plotinus says of the soul—"the soul as such and the essence of the soul cannot be distinguished, for the soul is pure form" —or what theologians say of God is true of reason. The essence of reason is not sensuous, because reason does not exist in the form of sensuousness, but rather in itself; that is, in the form of supersensuous essentiality and universality. Reason exists only in identity with itself, and its relation to existence is its relation to itself. In thought, as the act in which reason realizes itself, or as one who thinks, I am not this or that particular individual but rather no one at all; I am not *a* particular man but man as such, that is, not apart, different and separate from others—for I can be so only as a sensuous being—but I am *one with all*, that is, all men, precisely because reason as its own unity or as absolute identity constitutes the unity of all, for its existence, like its essence, is unity. The sensuous appearance of the infinite unity and universality of reason is language. Language does not make thought universal; it only shows or realizes what thought is in itself; namely, not my thought but that of all, at least as a possibility.

1829–1832

FROM THE LECTURES ON "LOGIC AND METAPHYSICS" AT ERLANGEN

Gentlemen, I am going to talk to you about Logic, but not in a way in which it is usually taught, although for the sake of completeness, I will be acquainting you historically with this as well. I will be presenting the theory of thought as theory of knowledge or as metaphysics. In other words, I will be talking about Logic as it was understood and presented by Hegel, although not in his words but only in his spirit; that is, not like a philologist but like a philosopher. But at the same time I will treat Logic not like Hegel, that is, not in the sense of the absolute, highest, and ultimate philosophy but only in the sense of the *organon* of philosophy. However, the organon of philosophy must itself be or generate philosophy, and the organon of knowledge must itself be or generate knowledge. Logic, in the sense of metaphysics, is a necessary result of the history of philosophy so far. The most adequate introduction to Logic is, therefore, a presentation of the history of philosophy.

1830

"THOUGHTS ON DEATH AND IMMORTALITY"

What is important now, above all, is to abolish the old dichotomy between the here and the beyond, so that mankind may concentrate on the world and the present with the whole of its heart and soul; for only this undivided concentration on the real world will again produce new life, great men, and great sentiments and deeds. Instead of postulating immortal individuals, the business of the "new religion" is rather to postulate men who are mentally and physically healthy; health has more value for them than immortality.

Only for the most wretched is the world wretched, and only for those who are empty is it empty. The heart, or at least the healthy heart, finds complete fulfillment here. A "new religion," if it were again to set a future or a beyond as a goal for man, would be just as wrong as Christianity. The new religion cannot be the religion of thought and deed that lives in the eternal present; it can only be that of feeling and fantasy, for only fantasy is the organ of the future. It cannot be a step forward, but only a step backward, for already Protestantism, in its own way, has reconciled religion with the real world.

The carriage of world history is small; just as one cannot get into it if one is not on time, so one cannot find a place in it unless one discards the utensils belonging to the old historical household and retains only that which is most necessary and essential. To those who (dragging their utensils along with them) emigrated with Bias out of

Priene, Bias must certainly have appeared very "abstract and negative." However, there is no other way for philosophy to emigrate out of Christianity than as of Bias out of Priene. He who does not agree with this—that is, he who wishes to abandon positive Christianity but at the same time keep intact the ideas of the Christian "beyond," even if with certain modifications—is better advised to stay completely within Christianity.

1834

"HUMOROUS AND PHILOSOPHICAL APHORISMS"

Hand in hand with my abstract scientific works—provided the spirit permits—there should appear at the same time writings that should impress upon mankind the love of philosophy and that—born as they are out of life—should have a bearing on life. What I have in mind in this connection is a peculiar genre. A partly unsuccessful attempt is provided by this writing.

1834–1836

DIARIES

Religion is the first love, the love of the youth—the love that believes that its object would be desecrated through *knowledge*. Philosophy, on the other hand, is conjugal love, the love of the man who possesses and enjoys its object, but thereby, naturally, also destroys all the charms and illusions that are linked with the mystery mongering of the first love.

To believe in Christ means not to be distracted from believing in man and his essential goodness in spite of the faults of one particular man and the sad experiences we have with single human individuals. Christ, as a human individual, was man as such. Belief in Christ is belief in man.

The faults of man exist in order for him to recognize and develop his virtues in opposition and contradistinction to them.

The faults of men are only the stranded projects of virtue; they are only virtue's pangs of conscience which it creates out of too severe demands.

The secret of virtue is habit.

You blame me for my faults? You wretched grumbler! If you took away my faults, you would also take away my virtues.

The faults of men are only their virtues incognito. Behind the mask of this particular fault, there is a virtue.

The well-known statement—"better is the enemy of good"—is particularly true of our religious and moral theories of perfection. We are supposed to become more perfect, but this means in truth that we become ever more imperfect. Man's imperfection indispensably belongs to his perfection. What you regard as deficiency is, seen from the point of view of nature, perfection. In virtue, it is man who expresses himself; in fault, it is nature.

Fault is the reaction of nature against the stiff rule of morality.

The faults of men are often better than their virtues.

Let me tell you this: The greatest fault in your life was

that you never did anything wrong, that you never committed a sin.

There are certain natures which only "sin" can redeem
and make free.

Guilt and sin are simply inseparable from man; they are
so interwoven with the concept of life that any beings
that we conceive as independent of them are beings only
of our imagination. Although not so in the Bible, the tree
of life is in reality the tree of the knowledge of good and
evil.

Do not grieve over your faults! Faults are *unhappy* virtues—virtues that lack only the opportunity to show themselves as such.

Talk as much as you like about the vanity of man;
human nature, however, shows also phenomena that are
nobler and contradict this—for example, the fact that we
look upon the other person as better and more perfect
than us, at least in moments when we see his good qualities
in full light. In such situations we are so moved and
shocked that we appear to ourselves as nothing. It seems
to us as if the other person has devoured all that is good
without leaving us anything except the feeling of our own
shortcomings.

Of nothing are we more unreliable judges than of our
own faults. Hence we can free ourselves from the reproaches of conscience, which result from mistakes we
have committed, only by confessing them to our friends.
We make a mountain out of that which to them is only
a molehill.

Reason exists in life in the form of real man; the "You"
is the reason of the "I." Truth speaks to us from the other

person and not from our own self, which is imprisoned in itself. The love of the other person tells you what you are; only to the eyes and hands of the lover is the true being of the beloved revealed. To *know* man is to *love* him.

Whereas with the ancient philosophers love was an illegitimate child begotten with the concubine of nature, with modern philosophers it is the legitimate daughter of their philosophy. Woman has been accepted into the community of the spirit; she is the living compendium of modern philosophy.

Did you say duty demanded renunciation? How stupid! Duty commands enjoyment. We must give ourselves to pleasure. Renunciation is only a sad exception to the rule, occurring only when dictated by necessity. In such a case, it is, of course, good and wise to make a virtue out of necessity.

Follow boldly your instincts and inclinations and follow all of them! Then you will not fall victim to any of them.

No living being is destined for happiness; but all are destined for life precisely because they live. Love, however, is the life of life.

You ask whether I will be happy with you? I do not know; all I know is that I am now unhappy without you. But how foolish it is to let a present and tangible evil exist for fear of only a possible and uncertain evil!

What you have once begun you must also complete, no matter whether its completion leads you to happiness or unhappiness, to paradise or hell. Happiness is luxury, but completion is necessity.

Prevent a tree from expressing itself in leaves, flowers,

and fruit and it will wither away. Prevent love from expressing itself, and it will be choked by its own vitality.

You can believe without having to prove your belief by acting, for belief is something that you have only for yourself. But you cannot love without confessing, expressing, and practicing your love, for love is something that you have not for yourself but for the other.

Go on denying what you deny *pro forma* or out of consideration for others, and in the end you will deny in reality and before yourself what you denied only apparently and only before others in the beginning.

Man is nothing without an object. It is better to embrace with love even the most idle and unworthy object than to shut oneself up unlovingly in one's own self. However, only the object of true love first develops and manifests the true essence of man.

Believe, indeed you must, but then believe that true love also exists among men, that the human heart, too, is capable of an infinite and all-forgiving love, and that human love, too, can have the attributes of divine love.

There is only one evil—egoism; there is only one good—love.

Love, but truly! All other virtues will automatically come to you.

What is love? The unity of thought and being. Being is woman, thought is man.

Who would be so inhuman as not to feel the urge to see again the beloved ones who are dead? But is it a proof of the reality of the world hereafter? Is it not rather the expression of a love that is already fulfilled and satisfied here? Is it not, therefore, an indirect evidence of the fact that all *that matters to us* is given *here?*

To say that I love you for ever means that my love for you ends only with the end of my consciousness.

Eternal is that whose end is my own end.

Love alone can solve the mystery of immortality for you.

The comforting function of the idea of immortality is as little a proof of its truth as the painfulness of its opposite idea is a proof of its falsity. Moreover, the idea of our finitude is painful only as long as we are not accustomed to and familiar with it.

Is it not a terrible weakness on our part to be most painfully affected if those we love are taken away from us? Not at all! Weakness is, rather, to refuse to accept the pains of love and the pains of life. That is why I am not alarmed to have borne you, oh ye tortures of love and ardent desire, and firmly believe that I am essentially a philosopher; for a philosopher must not only *know*, but must also and above all experience things.

Belief in immortality is, in the case of a woman, a feminine belief, but in the case of a man, a womanly belief.

To grasp every person in a way that is in keeping with his nature, and hence, to teach him philosophy in a way that is suitable for him as a particular person—this is the method which I follow both in my life and writing. The true philosopher is a physician, but one who does not let his patients know that he is the physician in that he treats them according to *their nature*, that is, cures them through themselves.

He who enlightens a man even on things that are nearest to him, kindles in him a general light; for it is precisely a quality of light also to illuminate distant objects.

The true and human method of teaching, at least in sensitive matters, consists only in the enunciation of premises; the conclusions should be left to the understanding of the reader or the listener.

How is thought related to knowledge? Thought is the premise, knowledge the conclusion; thought is the ground, knowledge the result.

It is better to expect of oneself too little rather than too much.

De gustibus non est disputandum. The happiness of one person consists in appearing more than he is; that of another in being more than he appears.

One should never directly make the future the object of one's thought and care. The *rational* enjoyment of the present should be the only rational care for the future.

The greatest mistake committed by parents is that they pre-empt through their reason the natural development of their children, that they wish to *construct a priori* the life of their children.

Do not make a decision before the time is ripe to make up your mind. Decisions at the wrong time are products of your capricious nature, which because engaged in conjectures leads to erroneous conclusions. However, decisions made under the pressure of necessity are the products of your necessary and, at least in a relative sense, infallible nature.

Away with lamentations over the brevity of life! It is a

trick of the deity to make an inroad into our mind and heart in order to tap the best of our sap for the benefit of others. The best of our sap? No! Only that part that is already at the point of turning sour and threatens to turn into poison if not immediately provided with an outlet. The shorter our life, and the less time there is at our disposal, the more time we really have; for the lack of time doubles our powers, makes us concentrate only on what is necessary and essential, and gives us presence of mind, initiative, tact, and determination. There is, therefore, no excuse worse than that of lack of time. What is generally termed as the lack of time is actually the lack of inclination, strength, and adroitness to break one's familiar routine.

"Man overcomes everything." But only if overcoming is a *necessity* for him; if he must, man can do anything. Oh holy necessity, I would rather be unfree if I only had the blessing of your compelling force!

Why does time pass more quickly in our riper years than in our youth? In youth, we live within the ambivalence between inclination and prescription. We must go to school, and we must sit and sweat there against our will. We long for the time when school is over. What we long for cannot be too soon in coming; our desire wanders across the limits of the present into far-away regions. We are not where we would like to be; the barrier of time lies in-between, so time becomes unbearably long for us. In riper years, on the other hand, all Sundays, holidays, all *dies academici,* and similar epoch-making moments disappear from our lives; one thought follows on the heels of another, and one deed is immediately succeeded by another. And even if we pause to attend to business to which we are not inclined, the fact remains that we think of the hour of rest only when it strikes, because we have no time to think about time. It therefore almost always comes too early for us—if not according to our desire, certainly ac-

cording to our reckoning, whereas in our youth it always
comes too late.

Time is the source of poetry. A glimpse into the past is
an incision in the heart that opens the poetic vein. Past
time is always beautiful time; it shines in the moonlight of
memory; it is idealized because it is now only an object of
imagination. The oldest history is everywhere poetry, and
the first songs of a race sing only of times and people that
are no more.

In space, the part is smaller than the whole; in time, on
the other hand, it is, at least subjectively, larger because
here the part alone is real, whereas the whole is only an
object of imagination. A second in reality is a longer
unit of time; it lasts longer than a decade of imagination.

It is strange—although easy to explain—that precisely
those who contribute the least to the progress of mankind
and who are even hostile to it, find themselves in their
religious and intellectual development still on the level of
centuries long past. Those who show the least sign of an
instinct for perfection in this life—I mean priests and theologians—are also those who emphasize most the gratification of this instinct as the reason for the necessity of another life.

What is the cause of the present struggle? What is the
reason for our indignation against those who require of us
to stick to the past—to the Bible in religion and to historical
right in politics? Mankind now demands the remuneration
for its labor; it will not have thought, strived, struggled,
and suffered for nothing; it wants to enjoy what it has
earned. The admonishers were not exactly able to obviate
labor; indeed, they favored it. And yet, they want to deprive us now of our remuneration.

The most interesting thing about writing is not that one becomes known to the world, but rather that through writing one comes to know the world—even if not from its best side.

One writes for others, not for oneself. I, at least, cannot write anything just for myself. Whatever I write must be directly addressed either to a definite person or to mankind. That is why I write as clearly and lucidly as possible. I do not want to be a nuisance to other people.

You call Schelling "one who is reborn!" I have nothing against this. But make sure that in the history of his development, Schelling has not suffered the fate of *Lepas anatifera;* that is, that his eyes are not left stuck in his old skin. (Burmeister, *Natural History of Rankenfusser,* 1834.)

Pietistic God behaves just like the surgeon in the *Diable Boiteux* who, in his desire to procure customers, inflicted injuries on people so as to have them for treatment.

1835

"LECTURES ON THE HISTORY OF MODERN PHILOSOPHY"

In order to usher in a new epoch, mankind must mercilessly break with the past; it must take for granted that whatever has happened so far is of no value. Only by doing so can it acquire the power and desire to create new things. Any link with the given would only paralyze its power to act. From time to time it must, therefore, throw away the child with the bath; it must be unjust and partial. Justice is an act of criticism; but criticism only follows upon, and does not itself become, the deed.

From the Catholic side, the modern era is designated as the original sin. However, it was the modern era that, like any other era, brought a new principle to light (for the old and the existing always claim to be sacrosanct and inviolable). As the original sin, the modern era is, however, beneficial "in its consequences through the gracious decree of God," but beneficial in itself because of its necessity. And Eve, who robbed man of the paradise of Catholic innocence and seduced him to pick the forbidden fruit from the tree of knowledge, was none other than sensuousness or matter. The modern era distinguishes itself from the Middle Ages only by the fact that it raised matter, nature, and the world to a divine reality or truth, that it grasped and determined the Divine and Absolute Being not as distinct from the world, nor as transcendent and heavenly, but as real and identical with the world. Monotheism is the essence of the Middle Ages; pantheism is the essence of the modern era and its philosophy. We owe all the great discoveries and achievements of the modern era in arts and science only to the pantheistic view of the world. For how can it be possible for man to be enthusiastic about the world if the world is an entity different and excluded from God—an ungodly entity? All enthusiasm is indeed deification.

1836–1841

BRUCKBERG

Once Berlin—and now this village! What an absurdity! But perhaps not quite so after all, my dear friend. Look, here at nature's own source, I am finally washing out the sand that the official philosophy of Berlin had thrown not only into my pineal gland—that's where it belongs—but, alas, also into my eyes. What logic is, that I learned at a German University; but what optics is—the art of seeing— that I learned first in a German village.

The philosopher—at least as I understand him—must be a friend of nature; he must know her not only from books but also from a face-to-face acquaintance. For a long time I craved for a personal acquaintance with her; how happy I am to be at last able to satisfy this desire! Although nature here is limited and poor, is what Leibniz said not perfectly true: *"On donne mal des limites . . . à la richesse et beauté de la nature, lorsqu'on . . . ne reconnoit pas l'infini en tout et l'exacte expression du plus grand dans le plus petit?"*

Nature everywhere links the most beautiful and the most profound to that which is ordinary in the human sense. A man therefore thinks in harmony with nature and follows her method if he links the highest objects of thought with the most common needs and phenomena of nature. Even in the intestines of animals, he finds spiritual food and material for speculation.

All abstract sciences mutilate man; it is natural science alone that restores him *in integrum* and demands the whole man—man with all his powers and senses.

The ancient peoples understood nothing without a sensuous sign that, in their opinion, confirmed their undertaking. A deep meaning lies at the core of this pagan superstition. We must, at least in all critical actions, consult not only the *ego* but also the *alter ego* or the external world. We can be sure of the success of an action only if it is justified; it is justified, however, only when the inner and the outer, will and fate, inclination and external necessity coincide. Hence, that was my last application for professorship (1836), but as could be anticipated, with no success. Surely, this is an omen that is easy to interpret! A new period now begins in my life; now I am entitled to pursue what I feel is my vocation. My innermost will has now been turned into an external necessity; now I can pay homage to my own genius and devote myself limitlessly, freely, and recklessly to the development of my own self.

Body and soul must always be together. What one denies mentally one must also deny bodily; otherwise life is a contradiction, an untruth. Would not your being at a university involve you in a contradiction with your essence; that is, would it not be an obvious lie? Is your philosophy compatible with theology? But is not philosophy, as taught at our universities, ex officio a devotee of theology?

Leave me in peace! Only as long as I am *nothing*, am I *something*.

The spirit must now emancipate itself from the state as it once emancipated itself from the Church. You can now achieve the immortality of the spirit only at the cost of a citizen's death.

1841–1845

"THE ESSENCE OF CHRISTIANITY"

My dear fellow, let me tell you that if ever someone was called upon and entitled to pass a judgment on religion, then that person was I, for I have not only studied religion in books but I have also become acquainted with it through life, indeed, not only through the life of others who demonstrated to me the causes and effects of religion from its good as well as its bad side, but also through my own life. Religion was already an object of praxis for me before it became an object of theory.

What one has only in one's head becomes a fixed idea, and one never gets rid of it. What one truly identifies with oneself, that is, what one transforms into flesh and blood, however, passes away and is preserved only according to its substance, for blood always changes and renews itself and does not tolerate fixity. In this sense, even today, there exist "devil's-fingers," ammonities, and innumerable monsters in the heads of scholars long after they have disappeared from life, becoming the flesh and blood of other and more noble animal races.

"All men are equal before God." Yes indeed! In religion, as is proved by history, no distinction is made between civilized and primitive peoples, between the wise and the foolish, between the cultured and the vulgar. Hence, beware not to uncover the secrets of religion if you do not want to be exposed to insults by both the common and the distinguished, the learned and the unlearned rabble.

Oh, these sharp-witted critics! They want to judge the character of my writings and are ignorant even of their formal qualities! They do not realize that I use the homoeopathic method in the treatment of my patients, that I express the principles that guide me not in words but in actions; that is, only in the application of those principles. They are unaware that I quite often talk negatively about what is positive, that I express myself generally in an inauthentic, enigmatic, ironical way; my greatest triumph, to the chagrin of all philosophical pedantists and learned philistines, is to clothe the earnestness of necessity in the play of chance, and to rarify the stuff out of which folios are made into the fragrance of an epigram.

How is my earlier standpoint, that is, the standpoint of *Philosophy and Christianity* related to the *Essence of Christianity?* In the former, I took Christianity only in the sense in which it is taken by itself; in the latter I take it also in my sense; that is, in the sense of anthropology. The Christ who means exclusively the divinity of Christ the man has a different sense from the Christ who means the divinity of man in general—the divinity of every man. To anyone who fails to realize this distinction, my book must remain an irreconcilable contradiction.

———

Is the *Essence of Faith According to Luther* for or against Luther? It is just as much for as against Luther. But is it not a contradiction? Certainly, but a contradiction that is necessary and lies in the nature of the object.

———

Which attitude or which religion is the religion of love? That wherein man can satisfy his soul through his love for man, wherein the riddle of his life is solved, and wherein he finds the final aim of his existence fulfilled. This final aim—love—is something that the Christian seeks in faith; that is, outside love.

———

"You shall love the Lord your God, with all your heart, soul, mind, and strength. That is the noblest commandment. Equally, you shall love your neighbor as yourself." But how can the second commandment be equal to the first, if the first claims the whole of my mind and strength. What is left of my heart for man if I am required to love God with the whole of it?

———

"How can he, who does not love his brother whom he sees, love God whom he does not see?" Thus asks the Bible. I, on the other hand, ask: How can he, who loves his brother whom he sees, love God whom he does *not see?* How can both the love for a sensuous and "finite" being and the love for a nonsensuous and "infinite" being exist in one and the same heart?

———

Only a real being, that is, only that which is an object of the senses, can also be an object of real love. To lay down one's heart for a being that exists only in faith and fantasy is to sacrifice real love to imaginary love.

———

Christianity is the Middle Ages of mankind. That means that we are still living in medieval barbarism. However, the birth pangs of a new era have begun of late.

"What good can come from Nazareth?" Thus think always the pundits and the know-alls. However the good, the new, comes always from a quarter *whence it is least expected*, and it is always *different* from what one had expected it to be.

The new is always received with contempt, for it takes shape in secret. Its obscurity is also its protecting spirit. Imperceptibly, it turns into a force. Were it to attract attention from the very outset, the old would mobilize all its powers to nip it in the bud.

Governments behave, to the fortune of mankind, in the same way as physicians, to the misfortune of mankind. As long as an evil—and every deep-reaching innovation is an evil for governments—is *in statu nascendi,* it escapes their attention; but when they notice it, it is already beyond cure.

What is the surest sign that a religion no longer possesses inner vitality? The answer is: When the princes of the world have to stretch their arms to put it back on its feet.

The true qualities of a man show themselves only when it is time for them to be shown; i.e., put into action. If someone played the role of a German emperor while being a student, he would certainly play the role of a student while being a German emperor.

"Initially, Luther did not intend to go as far as he later did." This is precisely the course things should take. He who sets out to achieve at the beginning what can only be an unintended and involuntary consequence of an ensuing process, misses his goal.

Those alone are truly historical deeds that are not preceded, but only succeeded by consciousness and whose meaning and purpose become perceptible only after they have already been done.

"This is as far as you are allowed to go and not one step further!" What a foolish caution! Let us simply go, for you can be sure that we will not always be moving on, but will also be stopping. Your function is only to ensure movement, but it is for life or history to put limits on it.

Nothing is more absurd than to acknowledge the necessity of the Reformation, and yet to found the right to bring it about on civil or canonical law. "I would be prepared to countenance his teaching," said one Cardinal of Luther, "but it is simply preposterous for someone at the center to be converted to a view from the corner." But, my dear Lord Cardinal, only Popes go forth from the Collegium of Cardinals, not reformists. A Reformation never adheres to propriety of form, but occurs always in an original, extraordinary, or illegitimate way. He who has the spirit and courage to be a reformist is necessarily a usurper; all Reformation is an act of violence committed by the spirit.

The intellect writes history, but passion makes it. The new is therefore always unjust to the old. The writer of history has the time—and it is his business—to see to it that justice is done to the old, but not the maker of history. The "pure" and impartial intellect, the historical conscience, awakens after the deed has long been committed. One can think without being unjust to or hurting anyone, for to think, nothing more is needed than the head; but one cannot act without acting with one's whole body; that is, without hitting and hurting in all directions, even against one's will.

History does not give you the knowledge of the present; it shows you only that a particular phenomenon is similar to another that has occurred in the past; it does not show you its distinctive character, individuality, or originality; the present can be grasped only directly through itself. In order to understand the present, you must belong not to the past but to the present, not to the dead but to the living.

"To believe is a necessity for mankind." Yes indeed. But to believe in what you believe is surely not a necessity. Even we, the unbelieving, believe, but we believe in exactly the opposite of what you, the believers, believe.

The condition of mankind is always determined only by itself; it derives its theoretical and practical principles always and only out of itself. How can you therefore imagine to possess something "positive, lasting, and unchangeable" in the Bible? Of course, the letter of the Bible is unchangeable; but its meaning is as changeable as the mind of mankind. Each era reads only itself out of the Bible; each era has its own, self-made Bible.

"The new teaching is true, but not practical, not for the people." In talking like this, you only prove that you are ambivalent about the new teaching, that it is only a theoretical and unpopular truth for you, and that it has not yet taken hold of the whole of your being. That which is a concern of your being also instills the certainty in you that one day—of course, in its own way—it will also become the concern of the people.

"Bother humanity! Germanity is our watchword. German we are and German we want to be." I have nothing against this, but why then does your patriotism zealously

combat only the consequences of Christianity; i.e., humanity and not Christianity itself? Christianity, however, does
not teach that God and the German are one, but only that
God and man are one.

In practice, men are on the whole so much the opposite
of what they are in theory that it would be better to raise
human hate rather than human love to an article of doctrine and faith. Whereas now men love one another in
religion—i.e., in theory—but hate one another in practice,
they would then perhaps hate one another in theory, but
love one another in life.

The sensuous deed is the essence of paganism, but the
"spirit," the abstract word, is the essence of Christianity.
The word of God has ultimately no other meaning than
the divinity of the word, just as the holy script(-ure) has
no other meaning than the holiness of the script. This
"essence of Christianity," however, has been grasped and
realized only by the "deeply Christian" Germans. That is
why the Germans are, and have, everything in word but
nothing in deed; everything in thought, but nothing in the
senses; everything in the spirit, but nothing in flesh; in
short, everything on paper, but nothing in reality.

1843–1844

"PRINCIPLES OF PHILOSOPHY"

God was my first thought, reason the second, and man
the third and the last. The subject of the deity is reason, but
the subject of reason is man.

"The fear of God is the *beginning* of wisdom—but not
its *end*."

"Objective spirit!" What is it? My spirit as it exists for

others, as it exists in my works. But is this objective spirit also not subjective spirit? Is it not mine; i.e., the spirit of this particular man that I am? Do I not know a man from his works? Do I not read Goethe when I read the writings of Goethe?

———

Where does man come from? First ask: "What is man?" Once his essence is clear to you, you will also know his origin. What? Thus asks a man; Whence? Thus asks a child.

———

"Man cannot be derived from nature." True! But man, as he directly emerged from nature, was only a natural being, not man. Man is a product of man, culture, and history. There are even plants and animals that have changed so much under human care that they are no longer to be found in nature. Would you then take recourse to a *deus ex machina* in order to account for their origin?

———

Where do the gaps and limits in our knowledge of nature come from? They come from the fact that knowledge is neither the ground nor the goal of nature.

———

"Science does not resolve the mystery of life." That may be true. But what follows from this? That you take refuge in faith? That would be falling out of the frying pan into the fire. What really follows is that you turn to life, to praxis. Doubts that theory cannot resolve are resolved by praxis.

———

"How can man result from nature or the spirit from matter?" First give me an answer to this question: How can matter result from the spirit? If you can't find an answer—at least a rational answer—to this question, you will realize that only the opposite question goes in the right direction.

———

"Man is the highest being of nature; I must regard as basic, and proceed from, the being of man if I wish to understand the origin and development of nature." Quite right. Precisely in man, however, "understanding does not come before years"; in him, matter precedes the spirit, unconsciousness precedes consciousness, purposelessness precedes purpose, sensuousness precedes reason, and passion precedes will.

———

"You presuppose man without much ceremony." How can you accuse me of doing this? Unfortunately, it was only through the negation of man that I arrived at man; I posit man after having realized and shown that the being which is presupposed in contradistinction to nature as the condition of man's existence, has its own source and condition of existence in man. The way I posit man is therefore no less assertive; it is mediated through the "negation of negation."

———

Do you know when you philosophize by yourself and without making any presuppositions? You do so at the time when you take the empirical as given prior to philosophy and intuition prior to thought, and given not in an imaginary and illusory way as in speculative philosophy, but rather as *in actual truth and practice*.

———

He who consciously and intentionally presupposes nothing, tends unconsciously to presuppose as true precisely what he is first required to prove as true. Only a man has a truly genetical thought whose final position stands in direct contradiction to his *conscious* beginning.

———

"The first must also be the last." Quite right. But precisely because of that you must—if you begin with intuition truly and not just *pro forma*—ultimately come back to intuition.

———

Wherein, therefore, lies my method? In reducing all that is supernatural to nature by way of man, and in reducing all that is superhuman to man by way of nature, but always only on the basis of experiential, historical, and empirical facts and examples.

What do I take as my principle? Ego and alter ego; "egoism" and "communism"; for both are as inseparable as *head and heart*. Without egoism, *you* have *no head;* without communism, you have *no heart*.

Your first duty is to make *yourself* happy. If you are happy, you will also make others happy. A happy man can only have happy people around him.

If you outright condemn "egoism," that is self-love, then you must, in the interest of consistency, also condemn the love for others. To love means to wish and do good to others and, hence, to recognize as legitimate the self-love of others. But why should you deny in your own case what you accept in the case of others?

To make philosophy the concern of mankind is the attempt with which I began. But whoever starts this way necessarily comes in the end to the position where he makes man the concern of philosophy, where he supersedes philosophy itself; for philosophy becomes the concern of mankind only by ceasing to be philosophy.

Once I held thinking to be the purpose of life, but now I hold life to be the purpose of thinking.

True philosophy does not consist in making books, but in making man.

No religion!—that is my religion; *No* philosophy!—that is my philosophy.

————————

What am I? Is that your question? Wait till I am no more.

————————

Index

Radical Thinkers ▼

André Gorz
Capitalism, Socialism, Ecology
Critique of Economic Reason

Max Horkheimer
Critique of Instrumental Reason

Fredric Jameson
Brecht and Method
The Cultural Turn
Late Marxism
A Singular Modernity

Karl Korsch
Marxism and Philosophy

Ernesto Laclau
Contingency, Hegemony,
  Universality
Emancipation(s)
Politics and Ideology in
  Marxist Theory

Henri Lefebvre
Introduction to Modernity

Georg Lukács
Lenin

Herbert Marcuse
A Study on Authority

Franco Moretti
Signs Taken for Wonders

Chantal Mouffe
The Democratic Paradox
The Return of the Political

Antonio Negri
The Political Descartes

Peter Osborne
The Politics of Time

Jacques Rancière
On the Shores of Politics

Wilhelm Reich
Sex-Pol

Gillian Rose
Hegel Contra Sociology

Jacqueline Rose
Sexuality in the Field of Vision

Kristin Ross
The Emergence of Social Space

Jean-Paul Sartre
Between Existentialism and Marxism
War Diaries

Edward W. Soja
Postmodern Geographies

Sebastiano Timpanaro
Freudian Slip

Göran Therborn
What Does the Ruling Class Do
  When It Rules?

Paul Virilio
The Information Bomb
Open Sky
Strategy of Deception
War and Cinema

V. N. Voloshinov
Freudianism

Immanuel Wallerstein
Race, Nation, Class

Raymond Williams
Culture and Materialism
Politics of Modernism

Slavoj Žižek
Contingency, Hegemony,
  Universality
For They Know Not What They Do
The Indivisible Remainder
The Metastases of Enjoyment
Welcome to the Desert of the Real

Alenka Zupančič
Ethics of the Real

Made in the USA
Columbia, SC
17 May 2020